Introduction to Semantics

An Essential Guide to the Composition
of Meaning

by
Thomas Ede Zimmermann
Wolfgang Sternefeld

De Gruyter Mouton

ISBN 978-3-11-030800-6
e-ISBN 978-3-11-031437-3

Library of Congress Cataloging-in-Publication Data
A CIP catalog record for this book has been applied for at the Library of Congress.

Bibliographic information published by the Deutsche Nationalbibliothek
The Deutsche Nationalbibliothek lists this publication in the Deutsche Nationalbibliografie;
detailed bibliographic data are available in the Internet at http://dnb.dnb.de.

© 2013 Walter de Gruyter GmbH, Berlin/Boston

Cover image: Pianotypesetter © Josh Shayne
Printing: Hubert & Co. GmbH & Co. KG, Göttingen
♾ Printed on acid-free paper
Printed in Germany
www.degruyter.com

MIX
Papier aus verantwor-
tungsvollen Quellen
FSC® C016439

Preface

This is an introductory textbook on linguistic semantics, the study of meaning in language. It does not require any prior experience with linguistics and should be accessible to anyone with some high-school background in grammar. Nor do readers need any previous knowledge of logic or set theory. We mention this because in this respect our text differs from at least some of the more traditional introductions. While relatively self-contained, this book does require some curiosity and inquisitiveness on the part of the reader, and at times the stamina it takes to master new formal techniques and notation. Numerous exercises scattered throughout the book will turn out to be particularly helpful in this respect; so readers are urged to take their time with them and not give up too easily! Only if you are fully convinced that you have found the solution (or that the exercise is unsolvable) should you take a peek at the appendix. The reward will be a thorough understanding of a part of human cognition whose very existence, nature, and complexity you are likely to not even have noticed before. So bear with us and be prepared for a formidable intellectual experience.

Textbooks rarely cover a whole field and this one is no exception. Limitations of time, space, and competence have required us to be selective, and at times a bit superficial. But then, from the reader's point of view, a textbook is only a first step that ought to be followed by a more extensive exploration of the field. To encourage this, we have included a number of references to the literature as well as some URLs that we hope to be stable enough to survive the next few years. And sometimes we have simply inserted a ☞ to indicate that readers should consult their favorite internet resources to learn more about a specific topic. Speaking of global notational conventions, we should also mention that throughout the text, we use English and German examples, typographically distinguishing the two object languages by *italics* for English vs. a sans-serif typeface for German. Finally, exercises, sections, and chapters marked with an asterisk are technically more involved digressions that may be skipped on a first and hasty reading.

The book has developed in three stages over a period of more than 10 years. At the beginning there were some 50 pages of German lecture notes written in the second half of 2000. The first author (TEZ) had provided these notes as online material accompanying a first-year undergraduate introductory linguistics course at Goethe University Frankfurt, where they have been used by various members of the teaching staff for the same purpose ever since; for copyright reasons, they are no longer publicly accessible. A few years later the second author (WS) came across these notes and adapted them for use in introductory semantics classes at the University of Tübingen. Since the courses were part of an international BA program, he translated the text into English, at the same time modifying, shortening, and extending various passages while keeping some of the German examples to allow for some variation in the data and the phenomena described. Most importantly, some logic background was added and the parts on the syntax-semantics interface increased in sophistication. When we finally decided to turn the class notes into a self-contained semantics textbook, more topics were added, including a chapter on presuppositions and one on compositional variable binding.

Given this long history and the many hands the various predecessors of this text have passed through, we are indebted to more people than we can list by name. First and foremost, there are several generations of Frankfurt and Tübingen students who have used our teaching material, and correctly complained about difficult or clumsy passages, which we then tried to avoid in later versions. Next come the colleagues who have been using the material in class and have given us their feedback and encouragement. We only mention Cécile Meier (Frankfurt) and Sam Featherston (Tübingen), who over the years have gathered more experience with the underlying material than either of us. Then there are those students and collaborators that took pains to read the pre-final version of the manuscript, pointing out a host of errors, omissions, and redundancies: Jan Köpping, Jacob Schmidkunz, and David Lahm. Finally, Kirsten Brock used her expertise to scrutinize what we thought would be the final version to actually produce it. Many thanks to all of you—and our apologies to those not explicitly mentioned. Of course, we take full responsibility for (m)any remaining errors.

Frankfurt and Tübingen, the Ides of March 2013

TEZ & WS

PS: The authors are listed in reverse alphabetical order (in case the reader hasn't noticed).

Contents

Chapter 1
Literal Meaning

The subject of **semantics** is the systematic study of the **meaning** of linguistic expressions like morphemes, words, phrases, sentences, or even texts. Before we can start with the investigation of their meaning, we will have to narrow down the subject matter of interest. The reason for this is that not everything that can be said about our understanding of linguistic expressions is relevant for a *theory of meaning*. Rather, we will only be interested in that aspect of "meaning" of a linguistic item that is associated with it by virtue of certain **linguistic conventions** of a specific type—this is what we will be calling the **literal meaning** of an expression.

1. Hidden Sense

Humans understand utterances automatically, immediately, effortlessly, and without explicitly thinking about meaning or about what they are doing when understanding language. Rarely are we forced to consciously reflect on meaning in a systematic way; sometimes such a situation arises when we are concerned with the "interpretation" of literary texts, e.g., **poems** or **lyrics**. Here is an example:

(1)

Heavy peony scent	*Schwerer Päonienduft*
From afar	*Von fern*
Le Ta	*Le Ta*
Spouse and child	*Gatte und Kind*
Abandoned	*Verlassen*
As the swan calls	*Wenn der Schwan ruft*
Ink drawn by a master hand	*Tusche von Meisterhand*
In snow	*Im Schnee*
Maiden	*Mädchen*
Of your birth	*Deiner Geburt*
Reminiscent	*Erinnern*
Script in the sand	*Schriftzeichen im Sand*

We clearly have to *interpret* the above lines in order to make sense of them (and we implicitly assume that *some* sense *can* be made of all this). Indeed, an obvious question these lines raise is: what do they mean?

The term "interpretation", [1] understood in this way, means that we unearth some **hidden meaning** that is not at all obvious to anyone confronted with (1). Given that *Le Ta* has no obvious meaning (and is not even an expression we could find in any dictionary), how are we to interpret it? Is it a proper name? After all, this seems plausible. But what about the other terms that do have a clear meaning? What about the connections between these words? How does all this make sense, and, if it does, what are the hidden meanings of these words that seem to contribute to an additional sense yet to be discovered? This is the kind of question literary criticism is concerned with.

The above poem is taken from Döhmer (1978), p. 9; in the same volume we also find the following contribution to an "interpretation" of the poem (p. 10):

The redundancy-purged denseness of the Middle Chinese bi-stanza Ritornello (I Shing Min) with the classical A XXXX A rhyme scheme endows this archetypal mythotope preeminently with its lyricalness *par excellence*.[2]	*In der redundanzfeindlichen Dichte des mittelchinesischen Doppelstrophen-Ritornells (I Shing Min) mit dem klassischen Reimschema A XXXX A gewinnt jenes archetypische Mythotop katexochen seine Lyrizität par excellence.*

Whether this quote improves our understanding of the poem is doubtful: this commentary is at least as difficult to grasp as the poem itself. At any rate, there is no need to bother about these questions too much here: both the poem and its interpretation are spoofs! The author's intention is precisely to create some feeling of hidden meaning, although he is only mimicking a certain style that pretends to be deep and meaningful.[3]

Fortunately, in semantics we are not interested in hidden meaning, but only in the obvious, primary meaning which is what the poem **literally** says. But even this is not easy to determine in the case at hand. One problem is

---

1   As the reader may have noticed we do not adhere to the (American) punctuation rule according to which commas and periods always go inside quotation marks—even if this goes against the content expressed. See Pullum (1984) for more on this preference of logic over aesthetics.

2   Thanks to Janina Radó for the translation into English.

3   One of the most famous real-life examples of a poem crying out for additional sense creation is *The Red Wheelbarrow* by William Carlos Williams (1923). You'll find thousands of internet pages in search of a hidden meaning (☞ The Red Wheelbarrow).

identifying the sentences or phrases in (1)—what should we make of incomplete sentences and incomplete phrases? Can we be sure that (2) is a complete sentence?

(2)
Of your birth	*Deiner Geburt*
Reminiscent	*Erinnern*
Script in the sand	*Schriftzeichen im Sand*

And if so, can this be interpreted as an old-fashioned way of saying the same as a plain and unpretentious, but undoubtedly grammatical sentence like (3)?

(3) Characters in the sand recall your *Schriftzeichen im Sand erinnern*
birth *an deine Geburt*

If this interpretation of (2) is correct, everyone can understand its literal meaning, namely that there are signs in the sand that are reminiscent of your birth. And that's it. Nonetheless, many details may still remain unclear: What does *your* refer to (the reader of the poem)? How does this sentence relate to the meaning of the entire poem (and to the intentions of the author)? Are the signs scratched into the sand or are they mere shadows? All this does not belong to the literal meaning of the sentence.

The general point to be illustrated here is that lyrics or poems seem to bear some surplus meaning not contained in the literal meaning of the words. This extra sense is the topic of literary studies, which goes in search of meaning behind the scenes. This may be interesting enough, but it is not what we do in semantics. Semanticists are primarily concerned with aspects of the literal meaning of words, phrases, and sentences: there are some signs or characters, there is some sand, there is an addressee referred to by "your", etc. Although literal meaning can be quite unhelpful in the context of poetry, this does not bother us in semantics. In semantics, we aim low and are content with dealing with the obvious only.

Now, compared with the discovery of *hidden* meaning, the description of *literal* meaning seems to be a thoroughly boring enterprise that does not deserve any scientific consideration. Given that *anyone can understand literal meaning in an effortless way*, why should scientists care about (literal) meaning? Is it worth the effort to study something that is grasped by anyone without the least difficulty?

The answer is that, although understanding utterances proceeds automatically and subconsciously, we still have no **explanation** for why and how this is possible at all. To mention an analogy from human perception: When hearing a noise we can often identify the direction of its source. However, how this can be achieved by the human organism is quite far from trivial and was not understood until recently (for more information, cf. ☞ spatial hearing). This kind of ignorance also holds for almost any aspect of human cognition: we have no idea how exactly the mind or brain works, and only recently have aspects of the working of human perception been explained by reference to certain neurophysiological mechanisms.

Consequently, there is something to be *explained* if we want to understand why and how humans can succeed in understanding phrases and sentences— in particular, sentences *they might never have heard before.* This is one of the central topics in linguistic theorizing. In fact, those of you who have had an elementary introduction to linguistics might recall that in syntax, one of the basic issues was "recursiveness", namely the fact that there is no upper limit to the length of grammatical sentences, although any dictionary of a particular language contains only a finite number of words. To put it another way:

(4)   *Fundamental research question in syntax:*
       How is it that we can, at least in principle, decide for arbitrarily long sentences (which we might never have heard before) whether or not they are syntactically well-formed?

Now, in semantics, we may ask the parallel question:

(5)   *Fundamental research question in semantics:*
       Given our restriction on literal meaning, how come that we can understand arbitrarily long sentences we have never encountered before, and, in particular, how come that we can tell whether or not they make sense (i.e., are semantically well-formed)?

This text goes some way towards answering this question.

2.   Irony and Implicature

Before we can embark on such an endeavor, let us explain more precisely our understanding of literal meaning. Imagine our colleague Fritz leaving the dining hall (aka the *Mensa*) of Tübingen University and meeting his friend Uwe, who asks about the quality of the meal. Fritz says:

(6) The steak was as always tender   *Das Steak war wie immer zart und*
and juicy   *saftig*

Now, according to the literal meaning, the quality of the food should have been excellent. But this is not the intended message; rather, Fritz wants to convey that the steak was as it always is, namely *neither* tender *nor* juicy. And Uwe, his friend, easily understands the message conveyed by (6). How can this be?

As a prerequisite for such an understanding it is absolutely necessary for Uwe to first understand the literal meaning. Knowing his friend and the usual quality of the food in the *Mensa* very well and having no evidence for a sudden lapse of taste on Fritz's part, he also knows that the literal meaning cannot possibly be the intended meaning. Besides, Uwe might detect a mischievous expression on Fritz's face. He therefore legitimately concludes that the utterance is meant in an **ironic** manner (☞ irony). And this implies that the conveyed meaning is exactly the **opposite** of the literal meaning. In order for this to work properly it is necessary for the literal meaning to come first: only on the basis of an understanding of the literal meaning is it possible to understand the utterance as saying the opposite of the literal meaning.

NB: In classical rhetoric, irony is always defined as expressing the opposite of the literal meaning. In ordinary language, however, the term *irony* is used in a much broader sense. Suppose Fritz continues his description of the meal by saying:

(7) And the dessert was not   *Auch der Nachtisch war nicht giftig*
poisonous either

Although this utterance can be called ironic, the term *irony* in its traditional narrow sense is not adequate in this case, because Fritz does not want to say the exact opposite of (7), namely, that the dessert was poisonous. Nor does he want to convey the literal meaning, namely that the quality of the dessert was such that one was not in danger of being poisoned. Rather, what he wants to say is something like:

(8) The quality of the dessert cannot be categorized as much better than not poisonous

Which implies that it was very bad.

In linguistics, this rhetorical effect is called an ☞ **implicature**. An implicature is something that goes beyond the literal meaning without contradicting it. The above implicature is of a special sort; it is called a *scalar implicature* because the conveyed meaning involves a scale of grades, in this case a scale that characterizes the edibility of food, ranging from deathly to three Michelin stars. "Not poisonous" seems to rank somewhere in the lowest range of the scale.

What we see from these examples is that the literal meaning often does not suffice to really understand an utterance; it must be augmented in some way or another. How this is done is explained in **pragmatics**, which is concerned with systematic aspects of the use of linguistic forms.

Within semantics we stick to the literal meaning, which is, as we have seen, a prerequisite for a full and correct understanding of an utterance.

3.   The Way You Say It

We have seen above that the intended effects of an utterance may go far beyond its literal meaning:

—   Numerous texts (in particular literary ones) exhibit a hidden meaning that reveals itself only to an educated person.

—   Rhetorical effects like irony, exaggeration, or scalar implicatures can reverse, augment, or modify the literal meaning.

—   A certain choice of words or a stylistic register can express the speaker's attitude, over and above the literal content of the word.

As an example for the last point, suppose that the manager of the *Studentenwerk*—the company that runs the *Mensa*—is interviewed by a journalist from a students' magazine, *The Campus Courier*. The junior editor was supposed to ask something like:

(9)   Are you really planning to raise   *Planen Sie tatsächlich eine An-*
the meal prices?   *hebung der Essenspreise?*

Now, what the journalist actually utters is this:

(10)   Are you serious about demanding   *Willst Du allen Ernstes für den*
even more dough for your grub?   *Fraß noch mehr Zaster*
verlangen?

There are of course several features of (10) that render this utterance inappropriate (can you describe them?). But thinking about the literal meaning of

(10) will reveal that by and large its relevant content is in fact the same as that of (9).

That is, both questions "mean" more or less the same. But in what sense of more or less? This again is a topic that is dealt with in pragmatics. It's not just what you say, it's the way you say it that is relevant for pragmatics. From the viewpoint of linguistic semantics we may say that the literal meaning of both sentences is almost identical, and that small differences can be neglected. Nonetheless the expressions used in (9) and (10) have different **connotations**. Although we may refer to the same kind of thing with two different expressions (e.g., the same person referred to with the personal pronoun *du* (Engl. *you*) and its polite alternate *Sie* (Engl. *you* again)), the connotations of these expressions may differ (cf. ☞ *connotation (usage)*). This part of the meaning can be more or less subjective; we thus do not expect speakers to share the connotations they may (or may not) associate with the words in (11):

(11)   toilet, lavatory, WC, loo, the facilities, bathroom, rest rooms, the dunny, latrine, the privy, the smallest room in the house, ...

EXERCISE 1:

   Another case of non-literal meaning is exemplified by so-called metaphors. Browse the internet for examples and for definitions of the term *metaphor*. What is the difference between metaphoric and ironic use of expressions? Discuss which of the following expression are likely to have idiomatic, metaphoric, or ironic uses. (The German reader might consider the examples in (13)):

   (12)   (a) kick the bucket, (b) you took a fine time to leave me, Lucille, (c) Joe and Sue are bread and butter together, (d) that's a fine thing to say, (e) my girlfriend is a tough cookie, (f) it's raining cats and dogs

   (13)   (a) *das hast du ja schön hingekriegt*, (b) *er hielt seine schützende Hand über das Projekt*, (c) *das war ein Schlag ins Wasser*, (d) *das war für die Katz*, (e) *ich mach das immer so!* (f) *ich glaub, ich steh im Wald*

4. Difficult Sentences

We have said that in general, grasping of the literal meaning proceeds automatically, unconsciously, and effortlessly, similar to other acoustic, visual, or
sensual perception—but unlike the understanding of hidden sense. However,
although this seems to be the case most of the time, occasionally one does
come across sentences that are somewhat difficult to decipher, even if one
confines oneself to the literal meaning of the words they contain. Consider,
for example, run-on sentences like:

(14)   The woman, whose sister, whose son, whose girlfriend studies in
        France, emigrated to Australia, resides in Italy, lives next door

An equivalent German translation is given in (15):

(15)   *Die Frau, deren Schwester, deren Sohn, dessen Freundin in Frankreich
        studiert, nach Australien ausgewandert ist, in Italien lebt, wohnt ne-
        benan*

In both languages these sentences are extremely hard to process. After a
while, having parsed their syntactic structure, one may discover that (15)
means the same as (16), which is much easier to understand and is not much
longer than (15), so the problem is not length! Rather, it is the construction
type that makes the sentence incomprehensible (without a tedious linguistic
analysis).

(16)   *Die in Italien lebende Schwester der   Frau   nebenan hat einen*
        The in Italy   living   sister   of-the woman next-door has a
        Sohn, dessen Freundin in Frankreich studiert und der   selbst   nach
        son   whose girlfrind in France   studies and who himself to
        Australien ausgewandert ist
        Australia emigrated   has[4]

Upon further reflection, however, one might argue that the problem with understanding (14)/(15) might not be due to semantics; rather, the complexity of
the difficult sentences already arises with the *syntactic* parsing of (14)/(15),
leading to a kind of recursive self-embedding structure that is difficult to an-

---

4   It seems to be more difficult to find an English paraphrase for (14) that is both easy
     to understand and not considerably longer than (14). Try it yourself! That's why we
     preferred a German example.

alyze syntactically and that is avoided in (16). On the other hand, syntax and semantics normally go hand in hand, so that the memory overload that may cause the problem in (14)/(15) might not only involve syntax, but probably semantics as well. *A priori*, it is therefore not clear whether the difficulty should be located in one domain or the other. However, Kluender (1998) makes a point in favor of additional semantic complexity by considering the self-embedding structure in (17):

(17)   a.   The woman, the man, the host knew, brought, left early
         b.   The woman, someone I knew brought, left early

In (17-b), we have replaced *the man* with *someone*, and *the host* with *I*. Intuitively, (17-b) is much easier to understand than (17-a), although the replacement of these elements does not effect the relevant syntactic structure. Rather, the difference seems to be related to the semantic nature of the cascaded subjects. Gibson (2000), for example, reports that center embeddings are considered less complex with first and second person pronouns in the most embedded subject position, compared to definite nouns and proper names in the same position. This implies that semantics does play a role in calculating the complexity of center embeddings, although of course syntax and prosody may still influence the comprehensibility of the construction.

Apart from constructional complexities as exemplified above, there might be additional reasons that make it difficult to grasp the literal meaning of a sentence. The following sentence is often (though probably inaccurately) attributed to the American classicist Moses Hadas, who is supposed to have started a book review with it:

(18)   This book fills a much-needed gap

That a book fills a gap is normally understood as something positive, and it is this positive expectation that drives our interpretation of the sentence. Moreover, the expression *much needed* is normally understood as something positive as well, except that—in this particular case—*much needed* is not attributed to the book but to a gap, that is, to the non-existence of the book. So the literal meaning of the sentence is that *we do not need the book but the gap*! In fact, the subsequent review is said to be totally devastating.

An even more complex case of semantic processing difficulty is exemplified by:

(19)   No head injury is too trivial to   *Keine Kopfverletzung ist zu trivial*
          ignore   *um ignoriert zu werden*

The example works in both languages, the only difference in structure being that the infinitive at the end must be expressed by using a passive voice in German.

At first hearing, this sentence seems to say that we shouldn't trifle with brain injuries. But in reality, analyzing the literal meaning, we may discover that the proposition made is very cynical, namely that any brain injury should be ignored! In order to see this, compare (19) with:

(20)   No beverage is too cold to drink   *Kein Getränk ist zu kalt, um*
                                                            getrunken zu werden

Now, a beverage that is too cold to drink is one that should not be drunk, and accordingly, (20) says that

(21)   Any beverage—as cold as it may be—can be drunk

But now, by analogy, (19) means the same as:

(22)   Any head injury—as harmless as it may be—can be ignored

The message that should be conveyed by the original sentence seems to be that even harmless injuries have to be taken particularly seriously and should not be ignored. But thinking about it and taking into account the analogy between (21) and (22), you will discover that this is just the opposite of its literal meaning!

In an internet post on this example,[5] linguistics blogger Mark Liberman adds to this a naturally occurring example he found (uttered by a certain Mr. Duffy):

(23)   I challenge anyone to refute that the company is not the most efficient
          producer in North America

Mark Liberman asks:

> Is this a case where the force of the sentence is logically the same with or without the extra not? Or did Mr. Duffy just get confused?

> I would certainly lean towards the latter explanation. But it's quite well-known that it is hard not to be confused. The coolest case I know is [(19)].

---

5   Cf. also ☞ http://languagelog.ldc.upenn.edu/nll/?p=3244 for a discussion of more examples.

I believe it was brought into the literature by Wason and Reich:

Wason, P. C., and Reich, S. S., 'A Verbal Illusion,' Quarterly Journal of Experimental Psychology 31 (1979): 591-97.

It was supposedly found on the wall of a London hospital. Actually, a Google search suggests that the ultimate source of the quote is Hippocrates (460–377 BC). By the way, a number of the Google hits seem to come from sites run by injury lawyers. Also, by the way, the full quote appears to be "No head injury is too severe to despair of, nor too trivial to ignore", which is even more mind-boggling, at least for my poor little brain.

So what we have learned in this section is that our normal, unconscious understanding of such sentences might go wrong in various ways, the result being that we are mistaken about the (literal) meaning of a sentence.

As a methodological side effect, these considerations also suggest that the literal meaning can be detected and analyzed in a systematic way without recourse to mere intuition (which, as we have seen, can be misleading); there is something systematic in the way meaning is built up that needs to be analyzed and explained. This is what semanticists do. They try to build up meaning in a systematic fashion so that the exact content reveals itself in a way that is predicted by a semantic theory, not by intuition alone.[6]

---

6   Perhaps the beginner should not be too optimistic in expecting to be able to rigorously analyze these difficult sentences (by the end of the course). Due to the particularities of the constructions involved, the examples quoted above are extremely difficult to deal with even for a trained semanticist.

Chapter 2
Lexical Semantics

Sentences, as long and complicated as they may be, always consist of (structured sequences of) single words. Therefore it seems natural to start off an investigation of literal meaning with the study of **word meaning** (as opposed to the meaning of phrases or sentences). Using linguistic terminology, the entirety of words of a specific language is called a **lexicon**, therefore the investigation of word meaning is often called ☞ **lexical semantics**. This is the topic of the current chapter.

1. What's in a Word?

Before we can look at the meanings of words, we need to make clear what we mean by *words*. To begin with, the words semanticists are interested in are *types* rather than *tokens*. To see the difference, you may convince yourself (maybe using a word processor) that the preceding paragraph contains 78 words. In that case what you have counted are word tokens. At the same time you may have noticed that some words appear more than once in that paragraph, which is why you counted them more than once; in fact, six out of the 78 words in that paragraph are occurrences of the definite article. If you like paradoxical formulations, you may say that one word, *the*, makes up six words in the paragraph, or even that six of those words are but one word. If you strive for clarity instead, you should prefer to say that six word tokens in that paragraph belong to, or are of, one and the same word type. Since semantics is about the conventional meaning of words (and linguistic expressions in general), it is about word types (and expression types in general) rather than tokens, for the meanings of words (and expressions in general) are conventional in that they are stable across different utterances. This is why from now on, when we talk about words, we will always mean **word types**.

The type–token distinction, which goes back to the American philosopher Charles Sanders Peirce [1839–1914],[1] applies not only to words but to arbitrary linguistic units like sounds, syllables, and sentences, and may even

---

1   Incidentally, Peirce (whose surname is pronounced like the noun *purse*) also counts as one of the founding fathers of modern logic. Cf. footnote 13 in Chapter 10.

carry over to other entities like events. However, straightforward though it may seem, it is not always easy to apply—not even in the case of words. As a case in point, the said paragraph contains three indefinite articles, but should those count as tokens of the same word (type)? After all, they do differ in spelling and pronunciation. Yet if we made a difference between two purported words *a* and *an*, why not distinguish between singular and plural *the* as two distinct words?[2] From a German point of view, this particular distinction may not even appear too far-fetched. In fact, speakers of German and English also tend to have different intuitions about whether a string of two words like *text marker* is to be analyzed as one word or as two. Speakers of German recognize the notion of text markers as a compound, written *Textmarker*, as compounds in German are written without a blank between the two expressions, qualifying them as a single word. This is normally not the case in English, which seems a potential reason for why speakers of English have less firm intuitions about words.[3]

Another issue related to the question of wordhood is this: is a single sequence of phonemes the realization of one or two words? Consider the following examples:

(1)   a.   *light* = *not heavy* vs. *illumination*
      b.   *rose* = a flower vs. past tense of *rise*
      c.   *left* = opposite of *right* vs. past tense of *leave*

Now, if a word consists only of a sequence of phonemes, the one word *left*, for example, would have two different uses, as indicated by the different meaning descriptions. But speaking of word types, this is absurd! Although the pronunciation is identical, the different meanings constitute clear evidence for two different words (which, as it happens, also belong to two different syntactic categories: *left* is either an adjective or a verb, *rose* is a noun or a verb, and *light* is an adjective or a noun).

But now consider the following examples:

---

2   Note that otherwise conceptually helpful structuralist subtleties like allomorphy or null morphemes are of no avail here; for they do not resolve the question of what should count as a *word (type)*.

3   However, recent discussion of German orthography has revealed that there may very well be borderline cases even in German (e.g., German-speaking readers may ask themselves: are *fallen+lassen, Rad+fahren,* or *liegen+bleiben* one word or two?).

(2)   a.   German: *Bank₁* (plural = *Banken*) = bank₂
              Bank₂ (plural = *Bänke*) = bench
       b.   German: *Schloss₁* = castle
              Schloss₂ = lock
       c.   English: *bank₁* = edge [of a river]
              bank₂ = financial institution

The words in (2-a) and the words in (2-b) do not differ in syntactic category, but they do differ in meaning. For each of them you will find two lexical entries in your dictionary, and therefore we feel entitled to conclude that these are two different words. For (2-a) this becomes apparent by looking at the different plural forms of *Bank*. As illustrated in (2-b), however, it may happen that we do not find any grammatical difference between two words at all, except in meaning. Thus, the two words *Schloss₁* and *Schloss₂* have the same syntactic category, the same gender (neutral), and the same inflection, though different meanings. In this case one often says that *the* word *Schloss* has two meanings. Saying this implies there is only one word, whereas above we insisted that *Schloss* represents not one word, but two. This is of course purely a matter of terminology. If we understand the term "word" as including meaning, then we have two words; if by "word" we understand only its form (with the exclusion of meaning), there is only one word. Unfortunately, the difference is usually neglected in everyday speech.

In this text we prefer to include meaning, so that a difference in meaning suffices for there to be two words with one form. Quite generally, we take (linguistic) *expressions* as consisting of forms together with meanings. The phenomenon that one form may carry more than one meaning is known as **ambiguity**. Thus different expressions with the same form are said to be **ambiguous**; and if they are single words, linguists also speak of **lexical ambiguity**. The expressions that make up an ambiguous form are called its *readings*. Thus, for instance, the German form *Bank* has (at least) two readings, corresponding to the unambiguous (disambiguated) words *Bank₁* and *Bank₂*. In this connection *forms* are usually taken to be sounds rather than letters. Hence the English phoneme sequence /lɛd/ is ambiguous between a noun denoting a metal and spelled *lead*, and the past tense of the verb spelled the same way (but pronounced /lid/); that spelling itself, however, does not count as an ambiguity.[4]

2. Homonymy and Polysemy

As we have seen above, if lexically ambiguous expressions with the same spelling need to be distinguished in a linguistic text, this may be done by way of subscripts. Of course, in normal speech this disambiguation by indices is out of the question. But then there is rarely any need for it. Various factors seem to be responsible for this. For one thing, lexically ambiguous forms have little chance of being confused with one another if the forms are of different syntactic categories; disambiguation is accomplished by the syntactic environment. Furthermore, sometimes particular readings may be rare or remote so that they do not come to speakers' minds all too easily. And in any case, the context of use will usually pick out the intended reading. In fact, it seems that most ambiguities go by unnoticed and without disrupting communication. Still, the use of ambiguous expressions like (3) may occasionally lead to misunderstanding:

(3)   Give me the glasses!

Imagine a particular situation with two wine glasses and a pair of spectacles on a table. Then it might still be unclear whether *glasses* is the plural of (*wine*) *glass*, or whether we mean (eye)glasses, i.e., spectacles. If the ambiguity has not been resolved, I will not know which to bring; but fortunately the circumstances more often than not allow for **disambiguation**. Still, ambiguity as such does not only arise when the context of use is insufficient to decide between different meanings. One can easily imagine that there is never any kind of misunderstanding in the use of $Bank_1$ and $Bank_2$, so that in every single utterance of one of them it is clear (and unambiguously determined by the context!) which meaning is intended. Even then we would still say that the sequence written as *Bank* is lexically ambiguous.

How can we be sure that wine glasses and eyeglasses are referred to by different words? One criterion could be gained from translating the sentence (3) into German; we would then have to decide between two terms: *Gläser*

---

4   Different words with the same spelling but possibly different pronunciations are sometimes called **homographs**. As a rich source for (mostly) lexical ambiguity in German we recommend Gernhardt and Zehrer (2007).

and *Brille*, the latter being the term for eyeglasses. Therefore we feel justified in concluding that there is an ambiguity. However, without translations, we would be less sure. And indeed, there are archaic dialects of German that would permit the same sort of purported ambiguity, so that *Gläser* could mean drinking glasses but could also mean eyeglasses. Can we still say that there is a real ambiguity involved here? After all, as spectacles are also made out of glass, one might say that the term *Gläser* is not ambiguous, rather it is underspecified with respect to the *kind* of glasses that is intended. It would just express a more general meaning as a cover term for all sorts of glasses.

And indeed, there are many cases where different meanings are somehow related to each other, or are very similar, so that there seems to be some vagueness involved here. Therefore linguists have strived to develop criteria that ideally should decide whether two terms are ambiguous. We will only discuss one of them here.

(4)   At the end of the day we were sorry to see that John had destroyed his glasses and Bill too had destroyed his glasses

This sentence seems to be okay even in the case where *glasses* may have the two different interpretations:

(5)   At the end of the day we we were sorry to see that John had destroyed his glasses$_1$ and Bill too had destroyed his glasses$_2$

But now, we may ask whether we can conclude from (5) that

(6)   At the end of the day we we were sorry to see that John and Bill had destroyed their glasses

Can (6) be used to express the same as (5)? This hardly seems possible, and the reason for this inability seems to be that *glasses* can only express one of the meanings, without being able to serve as a plural expression that covers both types of glasses.[5] In the case at hand, then, all signs point to ambiguity—despite the fact that there is an obvious connection between the

---

5   Similarly, (i) does not seem to allow an interpretation synonymous to (ii):

(i)   John destroyed his glasses$_1$ and Bill did too

(ii)   John destroyed his glasses$_1$ and Bill too destroyed his glasses$_2$

The lack of this interpretation can be used as a test for the ambiguity of *glasses*. Unfortunately, most ambiguity tests are unreliable; cf. Sadock and Zwicky (1975) for further discussion.

readings. Traditionally such cases of lexical ambiguity are subsumed under the notion of **polysemy** and distinguished from seemingly arbitrarily ambiguous forms like English *bank* or German *Schloss*, which are called **homonyms**. Both polysemy and homonymy require identical pronunciation, but whereas in homonymous pairs the different meanings are not related to one another, polysemous pairs require a close semantic relationship between the meanings of the words, ideally of the sort exemplified in (7):

(7)   a.   He still goes to school (*school* = the institution)
      b.   School is on strike today (*school* = all pupils, teachers, etc.)
      c.   Our school is classified as a historical monument (*school* = the building)
      d.   Schools should be identifiable as such from the outside (*school* = the building, but because of the additional *as such* at the same time also the institution)

These differences in meaning appear quite systematic, and it may well be that they are not listed in your dictionary; if being distinguished in a dictionary is a valid criterion, the differences we observe in (7) do not give rise to different words. Nonetheless, thinking of what the term expresses and of what kinds of things we refer to with the expression in these sentences, it is quite obvious that some distinction in meaning is undeniable. Such systematic differences, arising as variants of one core meaning (= the institution), have a special name: the phenomenon is called ☞ **regular polysemy**.[6]

The difference between homonymy, regular polysemy, and irregular polysemy, then, amounts to this. Homonymies and irregular polysemies like *bank* and *glasses*, respectively, are isolated phenomena, the difference being that the two readings of the latter word are felt to be obviously related; regular polysemy is something systematic that can be observed with a whole range of expressions, like *Schule/school*, *Krankenhaus/hospital*, *Kirche/church*, etc.).

Here are some more examples where the semantic relation between the two meanings is of the more opaque sort:

---

6   In fact, it may well turn out that regular polysemy is not a special case of lexical ambiguity at all but rather something akin to structural ambiguity, the topic of our next chapter; cf. Lang and Maienborn (2011) for an approach.

(8)   a.   bright: *shining* or *intelligent*
       b.   to glare: *to shine intensely* or *to stare angrily*
       c.   a deposit: *minerals in the earth*, or *money in the bank*, or *a pledge*, or ...

For the linguistic layman this kind of relationship between words seems to be the most interesting aspect of semantics, giving rise to endless debates and historical speculations about the nature of the similarity.[7] In any case, the borderline between polysemy and homonymy seems rather blurry if the criterion is whether typical speakers see a connection between the readings. We refer the interested reader to the pertinent literature for more on these largely unresolved matters of lexical ambiguity.

3.   Sense Relations

It is often implied in the literature that semantic theories should account for certain kinds of intuitive judgments of native speakers of a particular language. These judgments and the corresponding intuitions can be of several sorts. One is the evaluation of **semantic** (as opposed to *syntactic*) **well-formedness**, another is the language user's ability to assess certain systematic aspects of the meanings of words when they are compared to each other. Starting with the first, the reader will agree that the following sentences are strange (and thus marked with a hash sign):

(9)   a.   #The cook is singing a spice
       b.   #The fork doubts it

The meaning of (9-a) is unclear because only songs or texts can be sung. Somehow the verb and the object do not fit together. In (9-b) there is a mismatch between the verb and the subject. The reason for the awkwardness of these (syntactically well-formed) sentences is that they violate certain semantic well-formedness conditions that come with the verbs. These conditions are called **selectional restrictions** of the verb: *to doubt* requires the subject to be human, and the object of *to sing* has to be something like a song. Native

---

7   As it turns out, many ambiguities evolved from polysemies; for instance, the German example *Schloss* (lock/castle) started off with a single basic meaning corresponding to *lock*; the other reading is believed to have evolved from the typical location of castles as locking the way out of valleys.

speakers who have learned the meaning of the verbs are clearly able to activate intuitions of this sort, i.e., intuitions about selectional restrictions. All selectional restrictions are part of the meaning of particular lexical items.

Another semantic skill of speakers (and hearers) is their ability to make claims about the meaning of two words in comparison. This is exemplified in (10):[8]

(10)   a.   *Groundhog* means the same as *woodchuck*.
         b.   *Professor* and *bachelor* differ in meaning.
         c.   *Precipitation* is a more general term than *drizzle* .
         d.   *Dog* and *cat* are incompatible with each other.

These sentences are statements about so-called **sense relations**. (10-a) states that two words have the same meaning, i.e., they are *synonymous*. The sense relation expressed is **synonymy**. Synonymy of simple words makes different sentences express the same meaning:

(11)   a.   Rosemary is stubborn
         b.   Rosemary is obstinate

It's not only words that can be synonymous, but sentences can be too, viz., if, and only if, they have the same meaning. If two sentences have the same meaning, they are also said to be *paraphrases* of each other.

Synonymy between simple lexical items seems to be rare in natural language. It is sometimes said that "true synonyms", i.e., those whose connotations do not differ too much, are extremely rare (in German grammar writing, the phenomenon has been dubbed "*Synonymenflucht*", which means escape from synonymy). This has been explained by an economy principle to the effect that language does not contain redundant material in the lexicon.

However, given the host of synonym pairs in (certain) closed categories, this claim needs some qualification; *almost, nearly* in English and *obschon, obzwar, obgleich* (= *although*) in German are cases in point. Also, we observe that many new terms have been coined that were initially intended to replace old ones with the same meaning: compare *airline host* vs. *flight attendant, toilet cleaner* vs. *hygiene manager, garbage dump* vs. *recycling center*, etc. This has been called semantic environmental pollution (*semanti-*

---

8   In cases like (10-d) readers may have doubts as to whether the purported sense relation is actually a matter of linguistic competence rather than, say, basic biological knowledge. We will briefly return to this question in Chapter 8, Section 4.

sche Umweltverschmutzung). Note that most of these terms are compounds. It therefore remains true that there are hardly any two synonymous *simplex* (uncompounded) content words, and that fully synonymous content words with identical connotations are a rare species.

Example (10-b) states a *non-identity of meaning*; this can also be called a sense relation, albeit normally a very uninformative one. Example (10-c) is more interesting. It says that one notion includes the other, or, in other words, it logically implies the other. The more general including term is called a ☞ **hypernym** or sometimes **hyperonym** (*Oberbegriff*), the more special included term is called a ☞ **hyponym** (*Unterbegriff*). If a term A is a hyperonym of B, then B is a hyponym of A. The relation of inclusion is called **hyponymy**. The reverse relation of being included is called ☞ **hyperonymy**.

Finally, considering (10-d), assume that the utterance is not meant to report something about the behavior of cats and dogs; rather, one wants to say that the notions exclude each other. That is, if something is a cat it cannot be a dog, and vice versa. Similarly, what is white cannot be red. The relevant sense relation is **incompatibility**. The attentive reader should note that this relation is stronger than a simple difference in meaning. For example, *bachelor* and *professor* are not incompatible, but of course differ in meaning, as was just noted.

Apart from these typical relations there are a number of other relations between words, like the one illustrated in (12):

(12)   a.   John **kills** Bill
        b.   Bill **dies**

Here one would say that *kill* means something like (or is almost synonymous with) *cause to die*. Thus, dying is a sort of causal consequence of killing; hence the semantic relation is *causation*.

4.   Semantic Networks

As a result of identifying more and more sense relations, linguists have proposed that all sense relations that hold between words should be organized in a kind of ☞ **semantic network**. Networks consist of nodes labeled with lexical items and connected by semantic relations. These relations may contain all sorts of relevant information about the meaning of a lexical item; the most primitive networks represent sense relations only. Here is an example from an electronic data base called GermanNet:

(13)

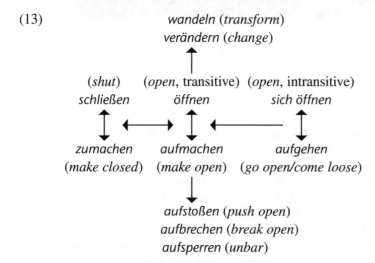

It is the task of lexical semantics to describe the network of a given language.

EXERCISE 2:

> Discuss which sense relations (hyponymy, synonymy, etc., including causation) are represented by the arrows in (13).

One of the potentially interesting things about networks is that they may have gaps. This is illustrated in a (fake) letter written to the editors of the *Duden*, reprinted and translated on the following page.[9]

Duden is a publisher of German language reference works which has attained in the popular perception the status of being authoritative in questions of German usage and orthography in the same way as the *Academie Française* is in France. While it has no official recognition as the defining authority, the near-universal belief that it does indeed occupy that position means that it does in practice define linguistic correctness in German. As far as we know though, the letter was never sent to them.

---

9   The hoax letter was first published in the journal *Pardon*, Vol. 11, 1975. Its true author was Robert Gernhardt (cf. Gernhardt et al. (1979), p. 313).

Schreiben, die bleiben   Höhepunkte abendländischer Briefkultur, ausgewählt von Kaplan Kläppstuhl, Folge 27.

An die Dudenredaktion, Abt. Neue Worte.

Betr. Anregung

Sehr geehrte Herren !

Mir ist aufgefallen, daß die deutsche
Sprache ein   Wort zuwenig hat.   Wenn man nicht
mehr " hungrig " ist, ist man "satt " .
Was ist man jedoch, wenn man nicht mehr "durstig"
ist ? Na ? Naa ? Na bitte ! Dann "hat man seinen
Durst gestillt" oder "man ist nicht mehr durstig"
und was dergleichen unschöne Satzbandwürmer
mehr sind . Ein k n a p p e s einsilbiges
Wort für besagten Zustand fehlt jedoch,
ich würde vorschlagen, dafür die Bezeichnung
" schmöll " einzuführen und in Ihre Lexika auf –
zunehmen .

Mit vorzüglicher Hoachtung

Werner Schmöll

To the data editors of the *Duden* publishers, dept. new words

re: suggestion

Dear Sirs,

I have noticed that the German language lacks a word. If you are no longer hungry, you are full. But what are you if you are no longer thirsty? Eh? Then you have 'sated your thirst' or you are 'no longer thirsty' or some similarly inelegant circumlocution. But we have no short monosyllabic word for this condition. I would suggest that you introduce the term 'schmöll' and include it in your reference works.

Yours faithfully,
Werner Schmöll

The remarkable thing is not the fact that we do not have words for particular (kinds of) things. This is quite normal. For instance, we do not have a word for blond girls that were born on April 1st. Although we could of course invent a notion like first-april-blonde, this is not a single word but an *ad hoc* compound. The problem is rather that *thirsty* lacks an **antonym**, a word that is incompatible and expresses the opposite. Thus, the opposite of *black* is *white*, the opposite of *slow* is *fast*, etc. This relation is another sense relation (cf. ☞ antonym, ☞ opposite (semantics)).[10]

Any economical description of a semantic network will take advantage of the fact that we can reduce some sense relations to others. A particularly useful method for doing so is to describe sense relations between words by analyzing synonymous paraphrases. For example, what is the sense relation between *brother* and *sister*? One way of approaching the problem is by using the synonymous expressions *male sibling* and *female sibling*. Since *male* and *female* are incompatible, we can immediately infer that *brother* and *sister* are too.

This implies a definition of *sister* as *female sibling*, and we might now go on and describe (or define) *siblings* as people having the same parents. Continuing in this fashion one might try to find more and more primitive basic notions (and relations) that can be used to express (or define) large parts of the dictionary, which in turn helps us to find semantic relations between individual lexical items. For example, the part–whole relation is an important one holding between all sorts of things; this further sense relation is called **meronymy**. For example, *toe* is a meronym of *foot*, since a toe is part of a foot.

Going on this way we will eventually arrive at lexical items that cannot be decomposed any further. The atomic primitives we arrive at at the end of such a procedure have been called **semantic markers** or **semantic primitives**. According to what was said above, one may expect *male, sibling, part of*, or *toe* to be such primitives. In general, though, it is not clear where this strategy will lead; should, for example, *clean* be defined in terms of *dirt* or vice versa? At the end of the day, all sorts of relations between items in such a web of semantic markers can be said to express sense relations.

---

10 One might ask whether we really need an antonym to *thirsty*. After all, you can booze till you drop. On the other hand, we do have the notion "*abgefüllt*" (filled) in German, though it has a broader meaning than *schmöll* (e.g., bottles can be *abgefüllt*, but they cannot be *schmöll*). The German-speaking readers should consult Wikipedia's ☞ *sitt*.

Sense relations hold not only between single words but also between complex expressions:

(14)   mare
        female horse
        horse of femail gender

(15)   black male showhorse
        black stallion
        mammal

It is clear that any complete semantic theory must give an account of these relations. However, this cannot be achieved by simply describing the meaning of words alone. What we need in addition is a way to describe *combinations* of meaning that make up a phrase and ultimately a sentence.

As it has turned out in the history of the discipline, it is not possible to develop a method of doing so by simply manipulating semantic primitives like markers. Rather, one might instead pursue the opposite strategy, starting with a comparison between the meanings of entire sentences and then finding out more about the meanings of their parts and how they combine. This way of approaching the problem of word meaning has turned out to be much more successful. The method is called **compositional semantics**, and it is this kind of semantics we will be concerned with in this book.[11]

---

11   Proponents of a compositional theory have criticized "markerese" semantics for not being a semantics at all, because it does not deal with the relations between symbols and the world of non-symbols—that is, with purportedly "genuinely semantic" relations (cf. the criticism in Lewis (1972))—a matter to which we return at the beginning of Chapter 4.

Chapter 3
Structural Ambiguity

1. Some Elementary Examples

We have seen that the same sequence of sounds or letters can express different meanings: words can be ambiguous. But ambiguity is not only found in words—as a phenomenon to be recorded in a dictionary. A sequence of words may well express two different meanings without containing any ambiguous words. Such ambiguities often result from different ways of arranging a string of words in syntactic structure. As it turns out, **structural** ambiguities of this kind are particularly revealing when it comes to analyzing the meaning of sentences. Let us look at an example:[1]

(1)   John told the girl that Bill liked the story

We will say that this sentence can have two different **readings**, meaning that it can be understood in two different ways. In one reading, a girl is being told (by John) that Bill liked the story. In this reading, the direct object of the verb *tell* is the *that*-clause. But there also is another reading: in this reading, a certain girl that is liked by Bill is told a story (by John). In the second reading, the direct object of *tell* is the noun phrase *the story* and the *that*-clause is a relative clause that modifies the expression *the girl*.

The different readings arise from different syntactic relations between the parts (or "constituents") of the sentence. We will represent these relations using boxes that indicate which parts of speech belong together according to the relevant syntactic analysis of the sentence. For example, the first reading of (1) can be associated with the boxes in (2):[2]

(2)   John | told the girl | that Bill liked the story |

---

1   Most sample sentences in this section are discussed in Frazier and Clifton (1996).

2   A word on the representation of constituent structure by boxes is in order. Here and elsewhere we will only represent those aspects of a construction that are relevant to our immediate concerns. This is why we don't have a box around *the girl* in (2). This also allows us to be neutral about syntactic details like a "flat" (ternary) structure as in (i-a)

Example (2) contrasts with the structure in (3) which represents the second reading:

(3)   John | told | the girl | that Bill liked | the story

The main point we want to make is that the syntactic structure, i.e., the particular way in which its words are combined to form a sentence, influences the meaning of the sentence. Of course, syntactic structure will also influence other properties of an utterance, e.g., intonation. Reading (2) aloud, you will observe that the reading associated with (2) is likely to come with a pause after the word *girl*, whereas the structure in (3) requires a pause after *liked*. This way, intonation may help to disambiguate a sentence.

Here is another famous example:

(4)   John saw the man with the binoculars

This sentence allows the two readings in (5):

(5)   a.   John used binoculars to observe a man
      b.   John observed a man who had binoculars with him

Again, the ambiguity goes hand in hand with different syntactic structures:

(6)   John | saw | the man | with the binoculars

In this structure, the prepositional phrase *with the binoculars* pertains to the act of seeing (the man); this corresponds to the paraphrase in (5-a). In the alternative reading, the prepositional phrase modifies *the man*, which can be represented by putting *the man* and *with the binoculars* in the same box.

(7)   John | saw | the man | with the binoculars

---

or the more articulated structure in (i-b):

(i)   a.   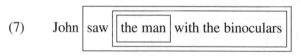 told | the girl | a story

      b.   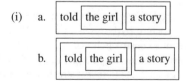 told | the girl | a story

Unfortunately, this time intonation is of little help in disambiguation, but nonetheless it is true that some sort of disambiguation is performed almost automatically whenever a reader or listener encounters ambiguous sentences.

When hearing a sentence, we will most often think it is unambiguous. As in the case of words, there are many reasons for this, one of them being that one reading may be pragmatically more salient than the other. Consider the following sentence:

(8)   The tourists didn't know the museum of the city they visited last year

A natural interpretation, surely the more prominent one, is induced by the following structure:

(9)   The tourists didn't know | the museum of | the city they visited last year |

The sentence does not claim that the tourists visited the museum last year; in fact, such an interpretation would be quite implausible unless we assume some sort of collective amnesia. But now consider *The tourists recognized the museum of the city that they visited last year*. This sentence more easily allows a different boxing, the one shown in (10),

(10)   The tourists recognized | | the museum of the city | they visited last year |

and another reading of the boxed constituent, namely one that implies that the tourists did visit the museum last year. The differences in interpretation occur because we naturally intend to interpret the boxed constituent in a way that is as plausible, relevant, and true as possible in a given situation or context of utterance, so that an alternative reading that makes the utterance implausible, irrelevant, or false is not taken into consideration.

Another reason for preferring one interpretation over another is that some syntactic structures are inherently more complex to process than others. For example, a sentence like (11)

(11)   The tourists admired the museum of the city that they visited last year

seems relatively neutral with respect to possible interpretations, yet there seems to be a bias towards assuming a structure like the one in (9) with the relative clause attached to the rightmost noun. This structure is claimed to be inherently easier to process than the one in (10), where the relative clause attaches to the more remote noun *museum*. This hypothesis has led to a vast amount of psycholinguistic investigation; cf. Frazier and Clifton (1996) for further reading.

The above discussion may suggest that we become aware of ambiguities by *syntactic* analysis. This could well be true in the cases considered so far, but it is not the rule. Although syntax and semantics seem to go in tandem, our intuitions are primarily about meaning, and it is these intuitions that guide our way to syntax. In order to establish ambiguities we do not primarily look at syntactic structure but instead try to find different readings by using **paraphrases** that are unambiguous and clearly differ in meaning. Such paraphrases have already been used in our discussion of (4) (*John saw the man with binoculars*) when explaining the two meanings in (5).

For example, looking back at the paraphrases in (5), we have to ask ourselves whether any situation described by (5-a) can also be reported by using (4) (restricting ourselves to the literal meaning of the sentences). Our intuition about the meaning of the sentences should tell us that this is indeed the case, and the same will hold for (5-b). This way we convince ourselves that (4) can indeed be interpreted either as (5-a) or as (5-b).

In order to test whether paraphrases really have different meanings, we rely on a principle that has been dubbed "**the most certain principle**" in semantics (cf. Cresswell (1982)):

(12)   If a (declarative) sentence S_1 is true and another sentence S_2 is false in the same circumstances, then S_1 and S_2 differ in meaning.

Proposition (12) is an axiom in our theory of meaning; we'll come back to this connection between meaning and truth (and falsity) on many other occasions.

Applying this principle to the case at hand, it is easy to imagine a situation with only John having binoculars, so one of the paraphrases is true and the other is false; likewise, when only the man has binoculars, the previously true sentence now turns false and the formerly false sentence becomes true. In such a case the method of paraphrases can be used as a watertight method for identifying ambiguities. We will rely on this method in other cases as well.

Summarizing so far, one might be tempted to say:

(13)   If a sentence may be both true and false in the same circumstances, it is ambiguous.

This slightly oversimplifies matters, though; the one pertinent question already discussed in the context of ambiguous words in the preceding chapter is this: is there only *one* sentence that is ambiguous, or do we have to assume *two* different sentences with different structures? Again this is a matter of terminology: if we abstract away from structure, we only have one sentence, if not, we have two. Above we decided that *bank*$_1$ and *bank*$_2$ are two different words. By analogy, an ambiguous "sentence" should rather be two sentences. But unfortunately, there is no commonly accepted term for what it is that is ambiguous (a "linear string of identical words having the category sentence"). So we reluctantly accept common usage, leaving (13) as it is, and continue to say that a sentence is ambiguous.

By definition, then, an ambiguity is **purely structural** if and only if the ambiguous sentence contains identical sequences of words, with no word-form being itself ambiguous. By contrast, ambiguities like

(14)   They can fish
   a.   They put fish in cans
   b.   They are able to fish

are lexical, because the same string of phonemes belongs to different syntactic categories; the sentence contains different words and different parts of speech. On top of this, of course, the two readings also differ in structure.

Relying thus on our previous discussion of ambiguity of word-forms we should critically assess our former examples from the perspective of clear unambiguity at the level of words and morphemes. Are these ambiguities really purely structural? For example, going back to (4), one may well ask whether the preposition *with* has the same meaning in both construals: Does it mean something like *belonging to* in one reading, and *using as an instrument* in the other? Or is there a very abstract common meaning that covers both occurrences of *with*?

A similar potentially problematic example involving prepositions is (15):

(15)   He put the block in the box on the table

Example (15) can be used to describe two different scenarios: (a) He put something on the table, namely the block in the box. (b) He put something in the box standing on the table, namely the block. This looks like a purely structural ambiguity:

(16) a. He | put | the block in the box | on the table

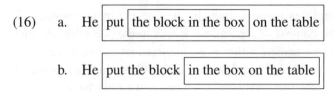

  b. He | put the block | in the box on the table

However, when translating these sentences into German, we observe that in (16-a) the preposition *in* comes with dative case marking of *the box* (cf. (17-a)), whereas in (16-b) *the box* has accusative case marking, and vice versa for the German translation of *on*: *auf* assigns accusative case in (17-a), whereas *auf* in (17-b) assigns a dative case marking:

(17) a. *Er tat den Block in der Box auf den Tisch* (= (16-a))
  b. *Er tat den Block in die Box auf dem Tisch* (= (16-b))

This correlates with a difference in meaning: accusative is used to express an additional directional "meaning" of *in* and *auf*, whereas dative case expresses a purely local meaning. The question then arises of whether there are four prepositions in_1 (= *in*), in_2 (= *into*), auf_1 (= *on*), and auf_2 (= *onto*) or only two. In the first case, the ambiguity would **not** be *purely structural*, while in the latter case, it would.

We believe that most semanticists today would agree that there should be only one core meaning for each preposition, but of course it remains to be explained how this meaning interacts with the semantics of the construction that contains the preposition. In particular, it is the interaction between the preposition and the verb *put* that seems to generate some surplus meaning that is not present when the preposition interacts with the noun *block*. This is of course a side effect of the syntactic structure, and as such—given that there is only one core meaning for each preposition—the ambiguity is purely structural.

Another case in point is the status of the word *that* in (1), repeated in (18). Nowadays, most syntacticians would agree that *that* is simply a subordinating functional element in clause-initial position.

(18) a. John | told | the girl | | that Bill liked the story

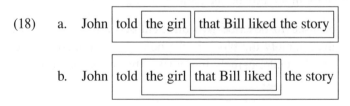

  b. John | told | the girl | that Bill liked | | the story

In particular, it is **not** assumed that, in contrast to in (18-a) where *that* is a so-called complementizer, *that* in (18-b) is a kind of relative pronoun. If this were the case, the ambiguity would not be purely structural. But if *that* is a complementizer in both clauses, as assumed in the literature, one source of potential lexical ambiguity has been ruled out.

A final remark about the role of syntax and the notion "structural" might be in order. Consider the following sentences:

(19)   a.   John ate the broccoli raw
       b.   John ate the broccoli naked

The most plausible reading of (19-a) attributes *raw* to the broccoli, whereas the predicate *naked* in (19-b) preferably applies to John. Does this imply that the sentences in (19) have different structures? This seems to depend on the underlying syntactic theory one is willing to assume. Following purely semantic intuitions we might propose the two structures in (20):

(20)   a.   John │ ate │ the broccoli raw │

       b.   │ John │ ate the broccoli │ naked │

Unfortunately, most syntacticians would not be too happy with either of these proposals; for reasons we cannot discuss here they would prefer a structure like (21):

(21)   John │ ate │ the broccoli │ wet │

Sentence (21) is ambiguous in that *wet* could either behave like *raw*, or it could be interpreted like *naked*—either John could be wet or the broccoli—but still the structure of (21) is assumed to be unambiguous. Hence, the ambiguity is neither lexical nor strictly structural, much as the referential ambiguity of the pronoun in (22):

(22)   *John aß den Broccoli. Er   war nass*
       John ate the broccoli. He/it was wet

Here, the gender system of German allows the pronoun (*er*) to refer either to John or to the broccoli, without there being any structural ambiguity involved. The ambiguity is thus due to different referential relations between the pronoun and its so-called antecedent. Likewise, it can be assumed that *wet* contains a hidden semantic argument relation (also called predication or subject relation) connecting *wet* with either *John* or *the broccoli*. But whether or not this relation is also encoded in the syntactic structure is theory dependent; most theories today would not express it as part of an enriched syntactic structure.

In conclusion, then, what counts as a structural ambiguity depends on how much structure we are willing to assume and how semantic relations are encoded in syntactic structure. In general, however, the term "structural ambiguity" is used in its broadest sense, so that all kinds of intra-sentential grammatical relations count as "structural", even if they are not reflected in constituent structure. According to this terminology, the relation between the predicate *wet* and its subject can be construed in two different ways, so that the ambiguity **is** "structural" in the broad sense of the term. In contrast, there is arguably no structural ambiguity in (22) because the ambiguity depends on the semantic relation between *er* and its antecedent, rather than on an intra-sentential relation between *wet* and its semantic argument.

EXERCISE 3:

> Discuss the semantic differences in your understanding of the *when*-clause in the following sentences:
>
> (23) a. Fred will realize that Mary left when the party started
> > b. Fred will realize that Mary left when the party starts

EXERCISE 4:

> Discuss potential structural ambiguities in (24) and draw different box structures for the two readings:
>
> (24) a. John realized that Mary left when the party started
> > b. John said the man died yesterday

EXERCISE 5:

> What are the different structures for (25) and how can the ambiguities be paraphrased?
>
> (25) a. a table made of wood (that was) from Galicia
> > b. the girl with the hat that looked funny
> > c. the girl and the boy in the park

The upshot of the foregoing discussion is a certain parallelism between syntax and semantics. In a sense, then, we have "explained" semantic ambiguity by reducing it to syntactic ambiguity. In many cases, the ambiguity is one of attaching a constituent either to a higher or to a lower box. In fact all the examples in the exercises above are of that type. The ambiguity is similar to the one in (26):

(26)   ten minus three times two

    a. $10 - (3 \times 2)$
    b. $(10 - 3) \times 2$

Formula (26-a) corresponds to low attachment of $\times 2$, and (26-b) corresponds to high attachment.[3]

In this section we discussed ambiguities as a preparatory training for the study of compositional meaning. We stressed that the composition is guided by the syntax, but we did not yet explain why the sentences have the meanings they have. It is thus insufficient to discover syntactic ambiguities; the real work that ultimately explains why the sentences have different meanings has not yet been done. This should become clear by looking at a simple example where syntactic ambiguity alone does not suffice to induce semantic ambiguity: arguably, $x + y - z$ is not semantically ambiguous between $(x + y) - z$ and $x + (y - z)$ because the result is always the same number. It is the particular semantic rules combining the boxes (the constituents in a syntactic structure) that ultimately do the job, but no such rules have been stated yet. This is precisely what we are going to do in Chapter 5.

---

3   The analogy with mathematics is not as far-fetched as it may seem: it can be shown (cf. Scheepers (2009)) that subjects who had to calculate one of the two formulae above solved the natural language completion tasks with examples like

(i)   The pensioner complained about the content of the fliers that...

in different ways. The completion task can be solved by attaching the relative clause beginning with *that* either high (referring to *the content*) or low (referring to *the fliers*). High relative clause attachment was more frequent after having solved (26-b) (and vice versa). The result shows that the mathematic equation had a priming effect on the perception of natural language structure.

2.   Scope and Syntactic Domains

In this section we will approach the important semantic concept of **scope** by first characterizing it in terms of more familiar syntactic relations between phrases. To this end we will once more look at ambiguities. As demonstrated above, semanticists often have basic intuitions about the semantic relations between particular words or phrases, and it is these relations that are relevant for ambiguities to arise. Let us discuss this further by looking at an example that will reveal an ambiguity of a new kind:

(27)   The doctor didn't leave because he was angry

A straightforward paraphrase is this:

(28)   The doctor stayed because he was angry

The alternative second paraphrase is more involved:

(29)   The doctor left and he was angry, but the latter was not the reason for the former

Or perhaps more conspicuously:

(30)   The doctor left for some reason, but not because he was angry

Observe that (28) and (29)/(30) make different, in fact, contradictory claims: in one, the doctor left, but according to the other, he didn't. Since only one of them can be true (in the same situation), it follows by (12) that the sentence is ambiguous.

Moreover, it is plausible that no lexical ambiguity is involved; on the other hand, ambiguity of structure may not immediately seem to be reasonable either. So: how, if at all, does this ambiguity correlate with different structures?

Intuitively, in one reading the *because*-clause states the reason for the doctor's staying. On the other reading, it denies a possible reason for the doctor's leaving. We say that in the first reading—call this the high attachment reading (for reasons that will become obvious in a minute)—the staying, i.e., the expression *didn't leave*, is in the *domain* of the *because*-clause. In the second reading—call this the low attachment reading—the domain of the *because*-clause does not comprise the negation; only the verb *leave* is in its domain.

Let us now focus on the role of negation in this example, analyzing the ambiguity from a different perspective: in the low attachment reading, the causal relation is denied, and we say that the *because*-clause is in the domain of *didn't*. This becomes particularly clear in paraphrase (30), where the negation *not* immediately precedes *because*. By contrast, in the high attachment reading, the domain of the negation is restricted to the verb *leave*.

These semantic considerations give us a clue to potentially different syntactic analyses, suggesting the following structures:[4]

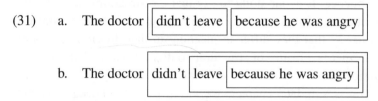

(31)   a.   The doctor │ didn't leave │ because he was angry

       b.   The doctor │ didn't │ leave │ because he was angry

These structures illustrate, as the reader may easily verify, that both the negation and the *because*-clause have different domains in (31-a) and (31-b). However, we still need to precisely *explain* or *define* the very notion of a domain. Such a definition is provided in (32):

(32) X is in the **syntactic domain** of Y if and only if X is not contained in Y but is contained in the smallest box that contains Y.[5]

Applying the definition to (31), the reader may confirm that the *because*-clause is in the syntactic domain of *didn't* and the verb alone is in the domain of the *because*-clause. By contrast, the box containing negation in (31-a) does not contain the *because*-box, thus the *because*-clause is not in the domain of the negation.[6]

The semantic counterpart to the syntactic notion of a domain is that of **scope**; hence the ambiguity under scrutiny can be characterized as a *scope ambiguity*. More specifically, one may say that, in the case at hand, the nega-

---

4   A viable alternative to (31-a) is (i) with the *because*-clause attached even higher to the main clause:

   (i)   │ The doctor didn't leave │ because he was angry │

   Both analyses satisfy the restriction that the negation is in the domain of the *because*-clause.

5   Readers with some background in syntax should notice the obvious similarity to the concept of c-command in Generative Syntax. Presupposing a customary definition of c-command, it follows that X is in the domain of Y if and only if Y c-commands X.

6   Returning to the structure proposed in foonote 4, the definition in (32) urges us to look at the *smallest* box containing negation; this box is shown in (i):

tion either has only *leave* in its scope, or it also takes scope over *because*,
in which case it is the causal connection that is negated. Likewise, the *be-cause*-clause either scopes over *leave* only, or it has scope over the negation
and the verb. The semantic notion of scope thus matches the syntactic notion
of a domain. In fact, one may wonder what the difference is. But there is
one: domains are a matter of syntactic configuration, while scope is a matter
of semantic influence. It is one thing to say that the structures in (32) differ
in that different expressions are in the respective domains of negation; it is
another thing to say that they differ in meaning in that different things are
negated. The former is a matter of structural configuration, the latter is some
kind of semantic effect, viz., the effect of being "influenced" by whatever the
negation *n't* expresses. In later chapters we will investigate in detail what precisely this semantic effect consists in—just what it means for something to
be negated. There we will also see what it takes to exert semantic influence
in general. For the time being, we will only collect additional evidence for
the intuition emerging from examples like (31): that there is a correlation between domain configuration and scope. In fact, one of the guiding principles
connecting semantic intuition with syntactic structure is (33):

(33)   *The Scope Principle*
       If α takes scope over β then β is in the syntactic domain of α.

Applying the principle to our mathematical example (26), multiplication in
(26-a) expressed by "$\times$" is in the scope of subtraction expressed by "$-$",
whereas $-$ is in the scope of $\times$ in (26-b). The ambiguity of (26) is resolved
by the use of brackets. Instead of brackets, we could have used boxes:[7]

(i)

But since the smallest box is contained in the one shown in (i) of footnote 4 and since
the larger box already excludes the *because*-clause, it is not really necessary to consider
the more fine-grained structure. We will henceforth ignore many structural details that
are irrelevant for the case in point.

7   Of course, we could also have used brackets in our linguistic examples, but boxes are
     much easier to read. Even more transparent are tree representations as they are used in
     Generative Grammar. In this book we don't want to commit ourselves to any syntactic
     theory and so we have even refrained from using trees, which play no role in other types
     of syntactic theories, e.g., HPSG.

(34)   a. $\boxed{10 - \boxed{3 \times 2}}$

      b. $\boxed{\boxed{10 - 3} \times 2}$

In (34-a), – has wide scope over ×, and × has narrow scope with respect to –, and the reverse holds in (34-b). The difference between wide and narrow scope reflects which opertations come first when calculating the meaning of an expression. Detecting a scope ambiguity therefore requires finding two different orderings in which certain elements of the same clause (particular words or phrases) can be considered when calculating the meaning of an expression. In many, but, as we will see, not in all cases, these different orderings go hand in hand with syntactic ambiguities.

Instead of attempting to give a definition of scope, let us further exemplify the notion by applying it to another standard situation that illustrates the intended range of applications. To see how the notion is put to work, take (25-c), repeated as:

(35)   the girl and the boy in the park

The syntactic ambiguity is one of attachment: assume that *in the park* is attached to *the boy*:

(36)   the girl and $\boxed{\text{the boy in the park}}$

The crucial ambiguity results from the relation between the term that expresses coordination (*and*) and what is coordinated. In (36), the conjunction *and* has wide scope over the predicate *in the park*, so that intuitively only the boy must be in the park. A more elaborate structure is (37):

(37) $\boxed{\boxed{\text{the girl}}\ \text{and}\ \boxed{\text{the boy in the park}}}$

Alternatively, *in the park* could syntactically attach to the conjoined noun phrase *the girl and the boy*, which means that *in the park* has wide scope over the conjunction *and*. This is shown in (38):

(38) $\boxed{\boxed{\boxed{\text{the girl}}\ \text{and}\ \boxed{\text{the boy}}}\ \boxed{\text{in the park}}}$

Under this construal, the boy and the girl must both be in the park. A paraphrase for this reading would be something like:

(39)   the girl and the boy who are in the park

Note that the intended reading could also be expressed by

(40)   the boy and the girl in the park

But (40) is not a perfect paraphrase (for any reading) because it is itself ambiguous. A perfect paraphrase would use the same critical expressions and be semantically and syntactically unambiguous.[8]

3.   Syntactic Domains and Reconstruction

In this section we will discuss a type of scope ambiguity which at first glance does not lend itself to an analysis in terms of syntactic ambiguity, but which, upon closer scrutiny, can nonetheless be explained in terms of ambiguous hidden structures. The point can perhaps best be illustrated by reference to the syntax of German; similar but more involved versions of the phenomenon also exist in English, which will be discussed at the end of the section.

Let us first discuss a pertinent example from the perspective of semantic ambiguity. Consider:

(41)   *Beide Studenten kamen nicht*
        both   students   came   not
        'Both students didn't come'

This sentence is ambiguous; it can either mean (42),

(42)   Reading *A*: neither of the two students came

or it can mean (43):

---

8   Of course, if *A* is a paraphrase of *B*, *A* and *B* should be synonymous. Unfortunately, like true love, true synonymy is hard to find. For example, the paraphrase we attempted in (39) seems to work fine because it uses the verb *be* with its plural morphology which unambiguously makes it clear that both the girl and the boy are in the park. Unfortunately, however, the finite verb also bears tense information (the present tense in (39)). However, this additional piece of meaning is not contained in the original expression. Strictly speaking, therefore, the paraphrase does not meet the criterion of synonymy. But this failure seems tolerable, because (39) is still a good approximation if no ideal paraphrase can be found.

(43)   Reading *B*: not both of the students came (one of them came)

The second reading requires support from intonation: a rise on *beide* and a fall on *nicht*. It is easy to verify that if *A* is true, *B* is false, and if *B* is true, then *A* must be false (in a given situation).

Let us first identify the crucial elements that induce the ambiguity. These seem to be the negation *nicht* and the determiner *beide*. Reading *A* is characterized by *beide Studenten* taking scope over *nicht*, whereas the reverse holds for reading *B*. In a standard syntactic structure like (44), however,

(44) | *beide Studenten* | *kamen nicht* |

the negation is in the syntactic domain of *beide Studenten*, but not vice versa, therefore we only get reading *A*; reading *B* is not what we immediately see in the structure. The only way to get the intended scope relations in syntax would be the boxing in (45):

(45) | *beide Studenten kamen* | *nicht* |

This structure, however, is otherwise unmotivated and incompatible with the syntax of German, as it seems to suggest that negation can be attached to an entire clause. But this prediction is not borne out, as can be seen from the ungrammaticality of (46):

(46)   **Beide Studenten sind gekommen nicht*
         both   students   have come   not

The correct way to say this would be:

(47)   *Beide Studenten sind* | *nicht gekommen* |

And (47) is still ambiguous the same way that (41) is. Hence, the structure (45) cannot explain the ambiguity. Therefore we find ourselves in a predicament as there seem to be no tangible options that could account for the existence of reading *B* in accordance with the Scope Principle (33).

However, a closer look at the syntax of German will reveal that this contradiction is only apparent. Let us examine more closely how the structure of (41) comes about. There are two leading assumptions that guide the analysis of German. One is that German is a so-called *SOV*-language. This means that the unmarked word order in German subordinated clauses is: subject (*S*) before object (*O*) before verb(s) (*V*). A typical case of *SOV* is subordinate clauses introduced by the subordinating expression *dass* (*that*):

(48)   *dass beide Studenten (S) ihren Professor (O) verehrt   hatten (Vs)*
       that both   students   their professor   worshipped had

The structure of (48) is (49):[9]

(49)

The second assumption concerns main clauses. In German, all such clauses have the finite verb (the verb that morphologically agrees with the subject) in second position, which is why German is also called a *V2*-language. In a *V2*-language, the first position preceding the verb can be oc-cupied by any of the major constituents (subject, objects, verbs or adverbs):

(50)   a.   *Beide Studenten (S) hatten ihren Professor verehrt*
       b.   *Ihren Professor (O) hatten beide Studenten verehrt*
       c.   *Verehrt (V) hatten beide Studenten ihren Professor*

All these constructions are well-formed main clauses in German.

The crucial link between the *SOV*-property and the *V2*-property is the as-sumption, entertained in the tradition of Generative Grammar (though not ex-clusively so), that the *V2*-property is the result of two movement operations: starting with an *SOV*-structure and the finite verb V_{fin} in the final position, *V2* is derived by moving V_{fin} into the second position (the upper arrow in

---

9   Note that a more fine-grained structural analysis could add more boxes, as illustrated in (i):

(i)   a.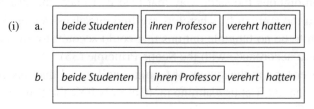

       b.

There is something to be said for both structures, but since the additional boxes are irrelevant for the argument, there is no need to decide between them here.

(51)) and another constituent (any of *S*, *O*, or *V*) into the first position (one of the lower arrows in (51)):

(51)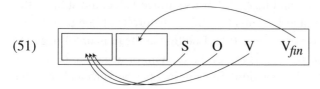

Applying this analysis to sentence (41), it is assumed that the subject *beide Studenten* has been moved into the first position (also called the pre-field position) by the abovementioned syntactic movement operation (traditionally called "topicalization"). In order to derive a syntactic ambiguity it will be crucial to ask: what is the structure *before* movement? In fact, there are two possibilities, as attested in subordinated clauses:

(52) a. *(dass) beide Studenten nicht kamen*
          (that) both students   not   came
      b. *(dass) nicht beide Studenten kamen*
          (that) not   both students   came

Both clauses are grammatical and differ in meaning: in (52-a), the negation is in the scope of *beide Studenten*, which corresponds to reading *A*, whereas *beide Studenten* in (52-b) is in the scope of negation. The structural ambiguity thus amounts to the two possibilities shown in (53) and (54):

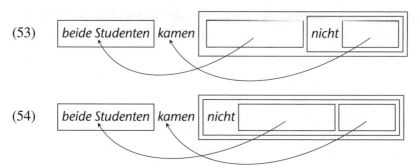

Given these structures we now see that we can indeed represent reading *B* if we are allowed to semantically interpret *beide Studenten* in the position occupied before movement. This way, we can save the Scope Principle, because by moving back the subject into the position of its original box, the subject is **reconstructed** into the syntactic domain of the negation to the effect that negation has scope over the subject, as desired.

If we don't reconstruct and take (41) at its surface value, the subject still has scope over negation and it seems that this structure could be used to explain reading *A*. But this is not quite true. Looking at the domain of negation in (53), it turns out that the verb is not in the domain of negation, because it has been moved into the *V2*-position! But intuitively, the verb and only the verb is negated in reading *A*. Here the solution is again reconstruction: the verb has to be interpreted semantically in the empty box it originated from. Hence, reconstruction is justified independently of the scope interaction between the subject and negation. In general, this kind of movement of a single word (so-called head movement) always requires reconstruction, whereas reconstruction of phrases is optional.

The above explanation can be generalized and applied to many more examples that allow for an ambiguity precisely because a certain movement has taken place. Let's take movement of an object into the first position as an example. Most speakers of German would agree that (55) has two readings.

(55)   *jeden Schüler$_{object}$ lobte   genau ein Lehrer$_{subject}$*
        every pupil   praised exactly one teacher

(56)   a.   Reading *A*: For every pupil there is exactly one teacher who
              praised him
        b.   Reading *B*: There is exactly one teacher who praised every pupil

In order to see how the meanings differ, consider first a situation with three teachers and six pupils. The relation of praising is represented by lines:

(57)   teachers   pupils

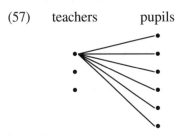

In such a situation both reading *A* and reading *B* are true: every pupil is praised, and there is only one teacher who is praising. In consequence, (57) does not suffice to disambiguate the situation. But now consider (58):

(58)   teachers   pupils

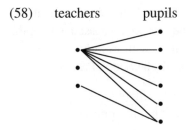

In this situation (56-b) is still true because the additional teacher does not praise every student (but only one), so there is still exactly one teacher who does. On the other hand, (56-a) is false because there is one student who is praised by more than one teacher.

Next, consider (59):

(59)   teachers   pupils

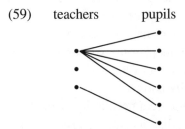

In this setting (56-b) is false because no teacher praises all of the pupils. In contrast, each pupil is praised by a teacher, and no one is praised by more than one teacher, hence (56-a) is true.

We have thus shown that the construction is ambiguous, and we can now relate the ambiguity to movement.

(60)   *jeden Schüler lobte* | *genau ein Lehrer* |

Reading *A* is the one where the subject is in the scope of the object. This reading corresponds to the (surface-)structure shown in (60). The second reading is the one where the object is in the scope of the subject. This reading can be derived from (60) by reconstruction, i.e., by moving the object back into the original position in the domain of the subject.

Summarizing so far, we have shown that certain ambiguities can be described as consequences of movement. We would expect that in a structure that does not involve movement, no ambiguity would arise. And in fact, subordinate sentences with *SOV*-structure as in (61), where no movement has taken place, do not exhibit any ambiguity of the sort we discussed above; the sentence is perceived as unambiguous in German, with *exactly one teacher* having wide scope over *every pupil* in accord with the Scope Principle:

(61)   *ich glaube, dass genau ein Lehrer   jeden Schüler lobte*
        I   believe that exactly one teacher every pupil   praised
        'I believe that exactly one teacher praised every pupil'

(62)   *...dass* | *genau ein Lehrer* | *jeden Schüler* | *lobte*

Note that this explanation crucially relies on a particular mechanism, namely movement, that is not part of everyone's syntactic toolbox. We therefore cannot stay completely neutral as concerns syntactic theorizing. Movement can be implemented in different ways, with Transformational Grammar as its most popular proponent. In what follows, we adopt some version of movement theory as the technically most simple account of the data, without presupposing that the simplest theory is necessarily correct.[10]

So far it seems that ambiguities of this kind are a peculiarity of the German language. In as far as German but not English has the *V2* property, this is correct. That English is not *V2* can easily be demonstrated by the ungrammaticality of the *V2*-constructions parallel to (50) (the star in (63) indicates ungrammaticality in the intended reading with *their professor* as the object and *both students* as the subject of *worship*):

(63)   a. *Both students had their professor worshipped
        b. *Their professor had worshipped both students
        c. *Worshipped had both students their professor

However, English still has the *V2*-property in *wh*-questions like

(64)   a. Who$_{subject}$ had worshipped his professor?
        b. Who$_{object}$ had both students worshipped?
        c. Why$_{adverb}$ did each student worship his professor?

---

10 Our motivation here is to keep the complexity of semantic machinery to a minimum in this text; in no way do we presuppose that movement accounts of ambiguities, as prevalent in Generative Grammar, are necessarily correct. But we acknowledge that alternative theories without movement are semantically much more complex and thus beyond the scope of this book.

We might then ask whether residual *V2* gives rise to the same kind of ambiguity, and in fact it does, although the data is somewhat more involved. Consider:

(65)   How many dogs did everyone feed?

There are at least two readings for (65), which can be paraphrased as follows:[11]

(66)   a.   For which number n are there n dogs such that everyone fed these n dogs?
        b.   For which number n does it hold that for everyone, there are n dogs she fed?

The subtle difference in meaning between (66-a) and (66-b) can best be explained by way of describing a situation in which two different answers to (65) could be given.

Suppose there are three persons a, b, and c and three dogs x, y, and z. Assume further that a fed x and y, b fed x and z, and c fed x and z.

(67)   persons   dogs
        a ⟩⟩⟩⟩ x
        b ⟩⟩⟩⟩ y
        c ⟩⟩⟩⟩ z

On one reading, then, the answer is "one" because x is the only dog fed by everyone. According to the other reading, the answer is "two", because everyone fed two dogs.

Let us pin down the difference in terms of scope. What are the crucial scope-inducing elements involved? By comparing the above paraphrases, we see that in one, namely (66-a), the expression *everyone* (a so-called quantifier) is in the scope of the numeral n (or the expression n *dogs* as part of

---

11   Some speakers may also hear a third reading, called the pair-list reading, which can be paraphrased as:

(i)   For which person x and which number n does it hold that x fed n dogs? Well, Fred fed 9 dogs, Mary 5, and John 2.

There is also a so-called "cumulative" reading which counts the totality of dogs being fed. Given the situation described in (i), the answer would be 16. These readings will be ignored in the discussion of (65).

the meaning of *how many dogs*), whereas the reverse holds in (66-b). More schematically, the situation can be presented as in (68):

(68)   a.   For which (number) *n*: everyone fed *n* dogs
        b.   For which (number) *n*: for *n* dogs: everyone fed (them)

(68-b) closely resembles the surface order of (65), whereas in (68-a), *n* dogs, and thereby crucially the numeral *n*, appears in the object position of *fed* and thus in the scope of *everyone*. This accounts for the semantic ambiguity and has been described in the literature as a case of partial reconstruction: it's not the entire *wh*-phrase *how many dogs* that reconstructs to the object position, but only a semantic part of it, with the question operator *how many* still resting at the top of the structure. Without being able to go into the details of a syntactic or semantic analysis, we thus see that reconstruction is also operative in English, though in a slightly different way, namely as partial reconstruction of the numeric expression *n dogs*.

EXERCISE 6*:

> [This one is for speakers of German. If you are not one, try to find an informant and elicit his or her judgments.]
> Try to account for the ambiguity of:

> (69) a.   *Genau 5 Bücher hat jeder   gelesen*
>   exactly 5 books has everyone read
>   b.   *Genau 5 Bücher hat keiner   gelesen*
>   exactly 5 books has nobody read

> Observe that *jeder* (*everyone*) and *keiner* (*nobody*) are the respective subjects. For each sentence, give two paraphrases and analyze the two readings of the respective sentence by describing two types of situations that make the paraphrases true and false.

4.   Logical Form

4.1.   The LF Scope Principle

We have seen in the previous subsections that syntactic movement contributes to the explanation of semantic ambiguity if it is assumed that semantic interpretation relates either to the landing site of movement or to the "take off" position. The latter choice was called reconstruction and was implemented by moving the expelled material back into the original position, where it can be interpreted in accord with the Scope Principle. The resulting structure, which possibly differs from the surface structure, is also called the **Logical Form (LF))** of a sentence. A subcase of structural ambiguity then arises if a sentence structure can be interpreted with respect to different Logical Forms. Examples already discussed above are the following:

(70)   *Beide Studenten kamen nicht*

a. LF_1: | *beide Studenten* | *nicht kamen* |

b. LF_2: | *nicht* | *beide Studenten kamen* |

(71)   *Jeden Schüler lobte genau ein Lehrer*

a. LF_1: | *jeden Schüler* | *genau ein Lehrer lobte* |

b. LF_2: | *genau ein Lehrer* | *jeden Schüler lobte* |

Recall that head movement (i.e., the movement of the verb into $V2$-position) is always reconstructed, therefore the LFs do not coincide with an input structure. Otherwise, however, LFs may correspond to what we see (the so-called surface structure), in particular when no movement takes place. The general idea is that each sentence has a Logical Form that disambiguates it by providing a syntactic representation of semantic scope in line with the Scope Principle. The level of LF is thus intended as an unambiguous syntactic representation in accordance with the following principle:

(72)   *The LF Scope Principle*
       At the level of LF, an element α has scope over β if and only if β is in the domain of α.

The LF Scope Principle differs from our previous Scope Principle only in that it takes into account the possibility of LF-movement, i.e., of movement that modifies the surface structure to the effect that the modified structure serves as the unambiguous input for semantic interpretation.

Given the possibility of reconstruction, we thus far have had no difficulty in providing LFs for the sentences discussed. In the case of an attachment ambiguity, the surface order itself is ambiguous, that is, the same linear structure is assigned two different surface structures and these structures may also count as the respective LFs. The second type of ambiguity was explained by reconstruction, as discussed above. However, there are a number of problematic cases in which neither reconstruction nor an attachment ambiguity seems to work; no obvious link can be found between scope and syntactic domains. The most prominent representatives of such a category will be discussed in the next two subsections. In both cases it has been argued in the literature that a new kind of LF-movement can solve the problem.

4.2.   Quantifier Raising

Sentence (73) has an unmarked (natural) and a marked (more far-fetched) reading, paraphrased in (74):

(73)   A student read every book

(74)   a.   For some student it holds that he read every book
        b.   For every book there is a (possibly different) student who read it

The marked reading paraphrased in (74-b) is not that easy to get (perhaps it helps to put some stress on *student*). The unmarked reading (74-a) is easy; it is also called the linear reading because the scope of the quantifying phrases *a student* and *every book* corresponds to the linear precedence relation of the phrases in (73) in the obvious way. In contrast, the marked reading is called the reverse reading, because, as the paraphrase reveals, the scope relation in the paraphrase (74-b) reverses the linear order of the quantifiers in the original sentence (73) in that the wide scope item follows the narrow scope item. It seems to be a peculiarity of the English language that some speakers seem to accept such a reading; the literal translation of (73) into German is unambiguously linear.[12]

Nonetheless, in some situations the reverse reading, despite being somewhat marked, may be the only one that makes sense. Consider the following example:

---

12   The reason for this seems to be that German word order rules allow the accusative object to be placed to the left of the nominative subject, which generates a linear correspondence between the surface order of quantifying expressions and the intended scope relations in semantic interpretation. It seems, then, that the possibility of expressing scope in a linear way to some extent blocks the additional possibility of reversed scope readings.

(75)   a table touched every wall   *ein Tisch berührte jede Wand*

The linear reading would require that there be (at least) one table that is in contact with all walls. Now, imagining a room with four walls, this situation (with the room being so small that the table is touching every wall) seems extremely unlikely; therefore, after some reflection, many linguists agree that the reverse reading (76) is a possible reading for (75).[13]

(76)   Each wall is touched by a table

Consider also:

(77)   A mirror borders every wall (to reflect the image of a finely honed athlete on each of their surfaces ...)

The problem for the now salient reverse reading is that there seems to be nothing in the syntactic structure that would point to a syntactic ambiguity; the structure seems to be unambiguously (78) for English and something like (79) (after reconstruction) for German:

(78)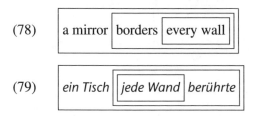

(79)

Likewise, the structure of (73), namely (80),

(80)   a student read every book

does not allow for syntactic or lexical ambiguity. This is a severe problem indeed, and it has led to a variety of very different solutions within different theoretical frameworks. In a theory that strictly correlates syntactic domains with scope, the problematic reading would require a structure like this:

---

13   As to speakers of German, opinions are mixed. Perhaps some speakers allow the reversed reading only to make sense of an otherwise nonsensical structure. The question then arises of whether this is a case of deliberately ignoring rules of grammar, or whether additional rules are activated. The situation in English is different; as explained in the previous footnote, English is much less restrictive than German.

(81)   a.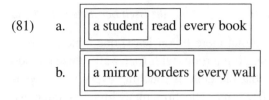

        b.

For reasons of syntactic analysis, though, such a structure is not an option for a language like English (nor for any other language).

A popular solution consists in deriving structures similar to (81) by brute force. Many linguists thus propose a syntactic movement operation that effectively generates a new structure (a new Logical Form) by applying a process that takes (80) as input and then moves the object into a new position in which *a student* is in the domain of *every book*. This movement rule is called **Quantifier Raising (QR)**. QR is an LF-movement rule, i.e., a rule that is invisible to phonetics but of course effects semantic interpretation. Depending on whether QR operates to the left or to the right, the resulting structures are (82) or (83):

(82)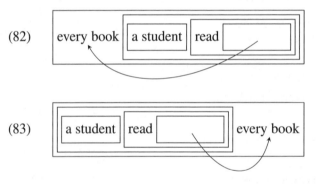

(83)

Both (82) and (83) can serve as LFs for the problematic marked reading of (73) in accordance with the LF Scope Principle.

At this point it should be mentioned that linear order is irrelevant at the level of LF. This is because crucial notions like scope and syntactic domain are not linear notions: they are purely hierarchical and all that matters is whether one box is contained in another. Notwithstanding, it has become common practice to assume that QR goes to the left, in accordance with conventions in mathematical logic and the fact that in the unmarked case, the scope-inducing element precedes the scope-dependent element in natural language. The problematic reading under discussion is an exception to the unmarked case, but the structure in (82) would rectify the imperfection by simply putting the object in front of the remainder of the sentence.

EXERCISE 7:

Explain the ambiguity in (84):

(84)   A student is robbed every day in Tübingen

Explain (informally) why the ambiguity is resolved in (85):

(85)   A student is robbed every day in Tübingen and he is fed up with it

4.3.   Opaque and Transparent Readings

The following sentence is ambiguous in both German and English:

(86)   Gertrude is looking for a book about   *Gertrude sucht ein Buch über*
        Iceland   *Island*

One might imagine two different situations that could truthfully be described by (86).

(87)   There is a certain book about Iceland (the one Gertrude's sister requested as a Christmas present) that Gertrude is looking for

The other situation would be:

(88)   Gertrude is trying to find a present for her sister and it should be a book on Iceland (but she has no particular book in mind)

This ambiguity seems to be related to the different ways the indefinite article *a (ein)* can be used. The reading of *a book* we paraphrased as *a certain book* is often called the **specific, referential, or transparent reading** of the indefinite phrase *a book*, whereas the reading in which the identity of the book does not matter is called the **unspecific, notional, or opaque reading**.

Following work by Quine (1956) and Montague (1973), semanticists have analyzed this difference as a difference in scope, accompanied by a difference in Logical Form. As usual we first have to identify the two elements whose scope converts in the LFs of an ambiguous sentence form. One of them is the indefinite phrase *a book (about Iceland)*. The only second element involved is the verb *look for*, or for that matter the verb *seek* as in Montague's example

John seeks a unicorn. In fact, only certain verbs allow the unspecific reading; there is no such ambiguity in *Gertrude found/read/destroyed a book*. Exceptional verbs like *seek, owe, look-for, resemble*, and *miss* that allow the unspecific reading are also called **opaque verbs** (they induce the opaque reading) whereas ordinary verbs and their readings are called **transparent**.

Suppose we paraphrase *seek* in *Gertrude is seeking a book* as *try to find*, as in the paraphrase (88):

(89)   Gertrude is trying to find a book

Example (89) exhibits the same kind of ambiguity as (86). Since *find* is a transparent verb, the only source of the ambiguity is the verb *try*.

(90)   Gertrude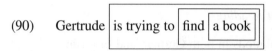

The example shows that the ambiguity is not merely a peculiarity of the relation between a verb like *seek* and its object. In fact, *a book* in (90) is the object of a transparent verb *find*. However, both in (90) and in (86), the indefinite *a book* is in the domain (and in the scope) of an opaque verb (*try, seek, owe*, etc.). In the specific, transparent reading, however, the indefinite should not be in the scope of that verb, and one way to resolve the conflict would be to move it out of the scope of the opaque verb. In the tradition of Montague it is therefore assumed that the transparent reading is the result of QR, as shown in (91):

(91)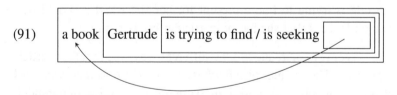

The object now having gained wide scope, the LF (91) only allows an interpretation along the lines of the paraphrase given in (87), whereas a structure without QR only allows the opaque reading.[14]

---

14   Note that this account of the ambiguity relies on a syntactic operation (QR) that also explained the scope ambiguities between quantifying expressions, as discussed in the previous subsection. However, this latter ambiguity seems to exist only in a minority of languages, whereas the ambiguity discussed here exists in most, if not all languages of the world. This begs the question of how to deal with languages that in general do not

EXERCISE 8:

> Identify the opaque verb in (92) and explain the ambiguity by different
> syntactic analyses and different paraphrases.

> (92)   My brother wants to marry a Norwegian

4.4. More Hidden Structure*

The following brain-teasing ambiguity requires a sophisticated logical analysis:

(93)   I know what I'm saying   *Ich weiss was ich sage*

The two readings can be paraphrased as in (94) or more formally as in (95):

(94)   a.   I only say what I know (to be true)
        b.   I am totally aware of what I am saying

(95)   a.   If I say that p then I know that p
        b.   If I say that p then I know that I say that p

(95-a) paraphrases the only-the-truth-teller whereas (95-b) is the total control
guy.

We may then ask how this ambiguity can systematically be derived and
whether or not it can be described as a structural ambiguity.

As it turns out, there are indeed two different syntactic constructions that
can help explain the ambiguity. We may distinguish between two types of
complements of *know*: one is an indirect question, the other is called a free
relative clause. Let us start with the latter by considering a typical example:

(96)   I will eat what(ever) you are cooking   *Ich esse was du kochst*

The constituent beginning with *what(ever)/was* is sometimes (misleadingly)
called a *concealed question*, but in fact our semantic intuition tells us that
(96) contains no question at all. Rather, the paraphrase in (97) reveals that the
construction involves a relative clause that modifies the object of *eat*.

(97)   I will eat everything that you are   *Ich werde alles (das) essen, was*
        cooking   *du kochst*

---

have QR but still allow transparent readings. We suspect that certain alternatives to QR
are more adequate to explain transparency, but cf. fn. 10, p. 44.

Therefore, *what you are cooking/was du kochst* is often analyzed as a relative clause which is attached to an empty head, as shown in (98):

(98)   I will eat | Ø | what you are cooking | *Ich esse* | Ø | *was du kochst*

The empty element is the element the relative clause is attached to; hence the relative clause is called *free*, i.e., it lacks a head noun. This is interpreted at the level of LF as something like:

(99)   For any x: if you cook x then I will eat x

For the purposes of our discussion, it is immaterial how this interpretation comes about (most semanticists seem to believe that the larger box containing the empty operator undergoes QR at LF). The point here is that, by analogy, we also get a free relative clause structure for (93), and a semantic interpretation that parallels (99):

(100)   a.   I know | Ø | what I am saying |

        b.   For any p: if I say that p then I know that p

Given that "I know that p" is equivalent to "I know that p is true", (100-b) can also be paraphrased as "When I say something, I know that it's true", and this is almost identical to what we proposed as a paraphrase in (94-a) above.

    Let us next turn to an alternative syntactic parse. This is much simpler; according to this analysis, the *what*-clause is plainly a complement (the object) of *know*. Let us illustrate this with a simpler example:

(101)   I know | who came to the party |

This complement is called an **indirect question**. Following Hintikka's semantic analysis of indirect questions (first proposed in Hintikka (1962)), (102) is a paraphrase for the meaning of (101):

(102)   If some individual x came to the party, then I know that x came to the party

Observe that in this analysis the complement of *know* is no longer an indirect question, but an ordinary *that*-clause. This reduction of questions to ordinary propositions is an important step in the analysis of questions, indirect or otherwise. In Chapter 8 we will see how to handle expressions like *knowing that* which take *that*-clauses as complements. Given this, it is easy to reduce the semantics of questions to that of *that*-clauses (surely including additional components like the conditional and the handling of the variable *x*, as illustrated in (102)). The relevant point here is that this can be done without involving any sort of QR.

By analogy, it now follows that (93) can be paraphrased as (103):

(103)   If *x* is something I am saying, then I know that I am saying *x*

If I have this reading in mind, I claim that I am aware of what I am saying, and this is precisely the paraphrase we offered above in (94-b).

We have thus shown that the two readings correspond to different syntactic analyses: since each construction brings along its own semantics, we get different interpretations, despite a superficial identity of expressions.[15]

5.   Summary

Semanticists love to analyze ambiguities, and beginners can profit enormously from this obsession. Why?

—   The study of ambiguities may give you a rough idea of what semanticists are concerned with and consequently, what semantics is about.
—   Ambiguities can be revealed only by disambiguation, which forces the student of semantics to consciously reflect on meaning and on how complex meanings emerge.
—   Ambiguities also provide a testing ground for theories: if we know that a certain construction should be ambiguous but the theory fails to predict this (e.g., if we only get opaque readings), it is in need of further elaboration or revision.

---

15   One of the requirements for an ambiguity to be purely structural was identity of lexical material in terms of identical meaning. For the above ambiguity to be purely structural, we must require that the expression *was/what* in the indirect question has the same meaning as in the free relative clause. Whether or not this holds is a matter of the semantic analysis of these types of constructions and it depends on how different theories handle these expressions. Unfortunately, most theories would assign different meanings, either to the pronouns *what/whatever*, or to some additional material like empty operators, which are not pronounced, but are parts of the syntactic analyses. Hence the ambiguity is not purely structural.

Ambiguities also tell us something about Logical Form and the relation between so-called overt syntax on the one hand (the surface syntax that forms the input to phonology) and covert syntax on the other (the structures called Logical Form, which serve as the input for semantics). However, not all semanticists accept Logical Forms that depart too much from the surface; hence the study of LF is not necessarily a silver bullet for the study of semantics.

As you might have experienced, it's not all that easy to describe an ambiguity, and it's even more difficult to detect its reason or source. Nonetheless, giving an account of such intuitions about ambiguity is precisely what a semantic theory is about: such a theory should be able to explain the fact that we can understand these sentences in different ways. Thereby, we hope to account for the more general ability of humans to understand sentences. Any theory (primarily and correctly) dealing with unambiguous cases should, to the extent that it is correct, also be capable of explaining the more complex ambiguous cases.

Moreover, disambiguations call for a precise language, a language that does not itself allow for ambiguities. It has become common practice to paraphrase sentences of natural language using notions of mathematical logic and set theory. These notions will be introduced in the chapters to come.

EXERCISE 9*:

>   Another example, known as Russell's ambiguity, is discussed in Russell (1905):
>
>>   I have heard of a touchy owner of a yacht to whom a guest, on first seeing it, remarked,
>>
>>   (104)   I thought your yacht was larger than it is
>>
>>   and the owner replied, 'No, my yacht is not larger than it is'. What the guest meant was, 'The size that I thought your yacht was is greater than the size your yacht is'; the meaning attributed to him is, 'I thought the size of your yacht was greater than the size of your yacht'.
>
>   In one reading, my belief is contradictory: it's impossible that your yacht is longer than it (in fact) is, and therefore it is highly implausible that I entertained a belief in such a contradiction. In the natural reading, however, no such contradiction arises. Try to analyze the ambiguity in terms of the respective scope of the *than*-clause and the verb *thought*.

EXERCISE 10*:

Consider the following example, inspired by Musan (1997):

(105)   20 years ago the professors were   *Vor 20 Jahren waren die Pro-*
         even younger   *fessoren noch jünger*

Sentence (105) can mean something very trivial, namely this:

(106)   For each professor it holds that 20 years ago he was younger than
         he is today

This is a self-evident truism, people simply get older, and because (106) is so obviously true, it is most probably not the intended meaning. Rather, one wants to say something like

(107)   The average age of a professor twenty years ago was lower than
         the average age of a professor nowadays

This assertion makes much more sense; it is not a self-evident truism (although probably wrong). Observe that in the trivial reading we compare each individual's age in time, whereas in the non-trivial reading we are comparing two entirely different groups of people, namely the professors today and the professors 20 years ago. Moreover, in this reading we are talking about the *average* age of professors, which brings in an additional aspect of meaning we cannot discuss here. Ignoring this detail, you should try to account for a purely structural aspect of the ambiguity by identifying relevant scope-bearing elements and the scope relations that induce the ambiguity.

COMMENT: Given that the paraphrases in (106) and (107) come close to different Logical Forms of (105), the example reveals that these paraphrases may contain semantic material not explicitly expressed by the original sentence, although it must implicitly be contained in the respective readings. Hence, the example suggests that the "distance" between a surface expression and its LF may be surprisingly big. It is a non-trivial task for the semanticist to bridge this gap in a systematic, non-*ad-hoc* way. For completing the exercise, this additional complexity must be ignored.

Chapter 4
Introducing Extensions

1. Frege's Principle

In the preceding chapter we argued that the source of many ambiguities can
be traced back to an ambiguity of syntactic structure. The general principle
that motivates such a move is that sentence meaning depends not only on
the meaning of individual words but also on syntactic structure, i.e., the way
these words are put together in syntax. For example, two unambiguous words
can be arranged in different orders AB or BA, as in (1):

(1)   a.   *Fritz   kommt*
             Fritz is-coming
        b.   *Kommt   Fritz*
             is-coming Fritz

Whereas the verb-second structure in (a) is normally interpreted as a declarative sentence, the verb-first structure in (b) is interpreted as a yes-no-question.
The two arrangements lead to different meanings, although the lexical material is the same (and no ambiguity is detectable).

   The strategy we will pursue in what follows is to take the meanings of
words and then combine them alongside and in tandem with syntactic structure. Such a procedure is called **compositional** and the principle behind it is
this: the meaning of a complex expression is fully determined by its structure
and the meanings of its constituents. Once we know what the parts mean and
how they are put together, we have no more leeway regarding the meaning
of the whole. This is the principle of compositionality, which can be traced
back to the German philosopher ☞ **Gottlob Frege** and has become a central
assumption in contemporary semantics:

(2)   *Frege's Principle of Compositionality*
        The meaning of a composite expression is a function of the meaning
        of its immediate constituents and the way these constituents are put
        together.   (cf. ☞ *Frege's Principle*))

It thus follows from (2) that not only do the meanings of the words determine
the meaning of the whole; it also holds that the meaning of a complex expres-

sion is computed locally and can only depend on the meaning of its **immediate** constituents (also called daughter nodes in Generative Grammar; these are the largest boxes contained in the box that contains the complex expression whose meaning is to be computed), together with the specific syntactic combination of constituents (e.g., modification of nouns by adjectives, predication, combinations of article and noun, or of adverb and verb, etc.). Hence syntactic structure is all the more important for any calculation of meaning. Each constituent must be assigned a meaning on the basis of the meaning of its immediate constituents. Immediate constituents may themselves be complex, having immediate constituents of their own. This way, the procedure matches the recursiveness of syntax: the semantic calculation must also be **recursive**. The recursiveness of semantics, then, explains why it is possible to understand sentences we might never have heard before.

2. A Farewell to Psychologism

Given Frege's Principle, it is necessary to have a clear concept of the meaning of a word. In Chapter 2 we approached this question by considering meaning-based *relations* between words, the so-called *sense relations*. Two words can be synonymous, incompatible or hyperonymic, etc. because their meanings stand in the corresponding relation of being identical, excluding each other, being more general, etc. In concentrating on meaning-based relations between words we managed to avoid developing a clear concept of the meaning of these words. While this so-called *structuralist* strategy may have its merits, it also has its limits. In particular, it does not easily lend itself to cross-linguistic comparison, and it does not generalize from certain expressions—notably "content" words like (most) nouns, verbs, and adjectives—to all expressions of a language, including conjunctions, determiners, and sentences.[1] Moreover, rather than shunning this admittedly troubling question, semantic theory should be based on some conception of what meanings are, and not just how they are related with each other. To this we now turn.

---

1 Like linguistic structuralism in general, the structuralist view on meaning goes back to the Swiss linguist Ferdinand de Saussure [1857–1913] and was elaborated in various directions during the first half of the 20th century, but without much success beyond the lexicon. It motivated the approach to (lexical) meaning in terms of semantic markers mentioned at the end of Chapter 2.

When learning a new word, we learn how to combine a certain pronunciation, its phonetics and phonology, with its meaning. Thereby, a previously meaningless sequence of sounds like *schmöll* becomes vivid, we associate with it the idea of someone who isn't thirsty any more. In this case, one might be tempted to say that the **meaning** of an expression is the idea or conception (*Vorstellung*) a speaker associates with its utterance.

A number of objections have been raised against such a "**psychologistic**" notion of meaning, particularly by the founding fathers of modern "logical" semantics (see the historical remarks at the end of this section):

—   **Subjectiveness**: Different speakers may associate different things with a single word at different occasions: such "meanings," however, cannot be objective, but will rather be influenced by personal experience, and one might wonder how these "subjective meanings" serve communication between different subjects.

—   **Limited Coverage**: We can have mental images of nouns like *horse* or *table*, but what on earth could be associated with words like *and, most, only, then, of, if, ...* ?

—   **Irrelevance**: Due to different personal experiences, speakers can have all sorts of associations without this having any influence on the meaning of an expression.

—   **Privacy**: The associations of an individual person are in principle inaccessible to other speakers. So, again, how can they be used for interpersonal communication?

In view of these considerations, many authors have concluded that we need a more objective notion of meaning.

Suppose you have just learned the meaning of *schmöll*. What you have acquired is not only associations, but also the facility to apply the expression in an appropriate way: you might refuse a glass of orange juice because you are *schmöll*. You say: "*Danke, ich bin schmöll*" ("Thanks, I'm *schmöll*"). Given that your communicative partner has somehow acquired the same meaning, this common behavior is based on the following assumptions:

—   Each partner has learned the meaning of an expression in a similar way, most frequently by **reference** to the kinds of things, events, properties, etc., that the expression is intended to **denote**: we refer to horses (or pictures of horses) when we make a child learn the word *horse*; we smile when we teach the word *smile*; we refrain from drinking when we are *schmöll*, etc.

— Each partner wants to convey information in a way that guarantees that the content of the message is identical for both the speaker and his audience; otherwise, misunderstandings would be the rule rather than the exception.

— Each partner is capable of extracting certain abstract meanings from the use of certain words like *and* which do *not* have a depictive meaning.

The first aspect of this notion of meaning captures the fact that by using words we can refer to things in the "outside world", i.e., in our environment; this is an objective feature of the word in relation to the world, called the **reference** or the referential meaning of an expression.

The second aspect of communication is that, while speaking, there is some flow of information that may change the mental state of the listener in a specific way, depending on what has been said (and of course how it has been said, but as we discussed before, this is not part of the literal meaning). In other words, an utterance is useful because it can change the **state of information** the listeners are in.

Simplifying somewhat, we may say that any description of the semantics of an expression involves two aspects: a referential one that enables us to refer to things by using linguistic expressions—this will be called the **extension** of an expression—and another aspect that deals with the information conveyed, which will be called the **intension** of an expression. In this chapter we deal only with extensions; we will come back to intensions in Chapter 8.

We end the section with a few historical remarks. In this text, we adhere to the tradition of logical semantics, which was originally designed (at the end of the 19th century) in an attempt to make the language of mathematics more precise. As it turned out, the methods developed there proved flexible enough to also be applied to the semantics of natural language.

The most important pioneers of logical semantics were the philosophers ☞ Gottlob Frege [1848–1925] and ☞ Bertrand Russell [1872–1970], who both investigated the foundations of mathematics at the end of the 19th century. Interestingly, both authors considered natural language too irregular to be rigorously analyzed with the logical methods they developed; their primary interest in this respect was the development of a language which, **unlike** natural language, should be devoid of vagueness and ambiguity.[2] Nonetheless, their influence on modern linguistics, and notably that of Frege's article *On Sense and Reference* (*Über Sinn und Bedeutung, 1892*) and Russell's *On Denoting* (1905), cannot be overestimated. However, the conceptual tools and methods of logical semantics were not applied to natural language fully and rigorously before the late 1960s, perhaps most significantly influenced by the work of the US logician Richard Montague [1930–71].

The distinction between *extension* and *intension* is similar to Frege's use of the terms *Bedeutung* and *Sinn*; it originates from the work of Rudolf Carnap (cf. Carnap (1947)). The term ☞ *intension* should not be confused with the homophone *intention*; there is no relation whatsoever between the terms.

3.   Extensions for Words and Phrases

3.1.   *Referential Expressions*

For some expressions of natural language it is fairly obvious that they refer to things or persons, for other expressions, a little bit of reflection is necessary to find an appropriate extension, and for a few there seems to be no reference at all. Let us look at some examples:

(3)   — Tübingen, Prof. Arnim v. Stechow (**proper names**)
   — the president of the US (**definite descriptions**)
   — table, horse, book (**nouns**)
   — bald, red, stupid (**adjectives**)
   — nobody, nothing, no dog (**negative quantifiers**)

Proper names and definite descriptions are the simplest cases. *Tübingen* and *Heidelberg* clearly name and thus refer to certain cities in Germany; and *the president of the US* uniquely describes and thus refers to a person, viz., Barack Obama (at the time of writing). Names and descriptions are thus clear cases of **referential** expressions. On the other hand, *nobody* and *nothing* do not seem to refer to anything at all, or if they do, it is a mystery as to what; the mystery will not be resolved before Chapter 6. Adjectives and nouns are somewhere in between: a noun like *table* does not refer to a particular table, but still a certain reference is recognizable. In what follows we will try to

---

2   To get a glimpse of what such a language looks like, readers should wait till the end of the very last chapter.

find suitable kinds of objects (sometimes of a very abstract nature) to serve as the objects of reference of different types of expressions of natural language. These objects will be called the **extensions** of the respective expressions.

It should be noted that we say that it is the proper name *Heidelberg* itself that refers to the city of Heidelberg. However, it has been objected that it is not the name but the language user that refers to Heidelberg when uttering the name. However, while we do not deny that reference is a pragmatic relation holding between persons (referrers) and things (referents), we can see no harm in using the same term for a semantic relation between (referring) expressions and things (extensions), as long as the two are not confused. In particular, we do not mean to prejudge the notoriously difficult issue of the interdependence of these two relations, which has played a major role in 20th century philosophy of language. For us, the equivocation is but a matter of convenience. The reader should note, though, that the near-synonym *extension* does not support the same kind of ambiguity; it is expressions, not speakers, that have *extensions*.

Let us now look at the above examples more closely. As already said, names and definite descriptions denote individuals. However, there is a difference between the two kinds of expressions. First of all, the relation between a name and its bearer is purely conventional: what the name refers to, i.e., what its extension is, only depends on certain communicative (i.e., linguistic) conventions as they are established in the course of, for example, a christening. With definite descriptions, matters are different. Although who happens to be the referent of *the president of the US* is partly a matter of linguistic convention—what precisely the definite article *the*, the noun *president*, and the partitive construction with *of*, etc. mean—it is only partly so; for a large part, it is up to the American voters to decide, and their decision does not bear on linguistic convention; after all, they decide who is going to *be* their president, not (just) who is going to be called *Mr President*. In fact, after at most two elections, the extension of the description *the president of the US* is going to change, but linguistic conventions will stay the same, and the description will keep its meaning. Quite generally, one may say that, over and above linguistic conventions, the extension of a definite description depends on (mostly) extra-linguistic facts, on situation and context. This situational dependence is a general trait of extensions, which will accompany us throughout the rest of this book. Names (and some other expressions), which are not affected by it, can be seen as limiting cases (of null dependence), to which we will return in Chapter 8.

As a second difference, unlike names, definite descriptions do not always have referents in the first place. This may be illustrated by an example made famous (in linguistics and philosophy) by Bertrand Russell, who brought it up at a time well after *La Grande Nation* had turned into a republic: **the present king of France**. The example shows that extra-linguistic facts may not only bear on who or what a description refers to; in some situations the expression may fail to have any referent at all. The point is that the lack of reference at that time is not the result of linguistic convention, but the result of the Franco-Prussian war.

This failure to refer to anything rarely happens with proper names. After all, we cannot give names to places, persons, or things and then discover that they do not exist. If anything like this ever happened, we would have to conclude that something went seriously wrong in the act of baptizing. As a case in point, some 19th century astronomers hypothesized a planet they called *Vulcan* in order to explain irregularities in the planetary path of Mercury; only later did they find out that no such planet exists. It would thus seem that the name *Vulcan* had been coined illegitimately, and—despite appearances— never had a referent.

For the next few chapters, we will pretend that all referential noun phrases—names, descriptions, and pronouns—refer to individuals, which may thus serve as their extensions. Hence we will ignore both empty descriptions like *the present king of France* and somewhat neurotic names like *Vulcan*, returning to empty descriptions in Chapter 9.

3.2.   Common Nouns

What both proper names and definite descriptions have in common, then, is their reference to **individuals** (*Individuen*). From now on, this term will be used as a technical term applying to anything linguistic expressions like names, descriptions, or pronouns refer to. In contrast, common nouns like *king* or *table* do **not** refer to individuals; they show what is sometimes called **multiple** or **divided reference** in that they potentially relate to more than one individual of a kind. Instead of saying that such terms have more than one extension, we take their extensions to be **sets** of individuals. Thus, for example, the extension of the noun *table* is the set of all tables.

Sets play an important role in semantics. The notion derives from mathematics, namely from set theory (as you might have guessed). A set is an abstract collection of things or distinct objects; it is completely determined by its **elements**, the members of the set. Thus, if we are speaking of the set of cities, each city is an element of this set, and this is all we can find in there: there are only cities in there.

In order to name a set, we can list its members; this is most often done using curly brackets. For example, the set of cities can be listed by specifying a list like

(4)   {Madrid, Venice, Berlin, Tübingen, Rome, . . . }

The order of elements here is immaterial. Now, to express that Berlin is a city, we formalize this by saying that Berlin is an **element** of the extension of *city*. This is written as

(5)   Berlin ∈ {Madrid, Venice, Berlin, Tübingen, Rome . . . }

Of course this only works for small sets. It is impossible for us to even give a complete list of German cities, but in principle, this could be done, and has been done; ☞ *Städteverzeichnis Deutschland.*

Note that the denotation of *city* depends on some sort of convention, namely that a place can only be called a city if it has got a certain legal title, its town charter (*Stadtrecht*). It also depends on the facts of the world whether or not a settlement has gotten that title. Moreover, things may change over time: what is a city now may not have been a city 100 years ago, or may lose its city status by becoming part of a larger city in the future. Thus, the extension of *city* depends on the facts in the world.

This we observed already with definite descriptions. The common feature of descriptions and common nouns is explained by the fact that descriptions contain common nouns as constituents. For instance, the description *the largest city in Germany* contains the common noun *city*, whose extension may vary. Consequently, the extension of the description can vary as well. Likewise, the extension of *king of France* is nowadays empty (i.e., there is no king of France) because the denotation of the (complex) noun *king of France* is the empty set. Note that the extensions of the expressions *king of France* and *king of Germany* are identical (at the time of writing)—both coincide with the empty set. Yet it is clear that the meaning is different; the extension only describes a limited aspect of the meaning.

It has been proposed that the extension of each common noun (at a given time) is a set. Assuming that these extensions depend on the facts, and given that our factual knowledge might be limited, it follows that we sometimes simply don't know the extension of a word. That is, we do not always know which elements exactly make up the extension of a given word like *table*. But in practice and in theory (and as far as linguistic theorizing is concerned) this lack of knowledge is less important than one might think. First, one should bear in mind that the actual extension of a word should not be confused with its meaning. Hence, not knowing its actual extension does not imply not knowing its meaning. The fact that we do not know all the details of the world we inhabit has nothing to do with our linguistic conventions and abilities. Second, not knowing the actual extension does not imply that we are unable to decide (on demand) whether a given entity is a table or not: of course we can apply the notion to things we have never seen before and whose existence we didn't know anything about. This implies that we are endowed with ways of determining the extension of a word without knowing it in advance.

Thirdly, in scientific inquiry we are often entitled to abstract away from certain insufficiencies. For example, the meaning of almost any noun is vague: there can always be borderline cases. Consequently, the extensions can be vague, too. Although it would be possible to capture this in a vague set theory (called the theory of "fuzzy sets"), we may well ignore this additional complication. This does not imply that vagueness is always unimportant: for example, we might be uncertain where to draw a line between *cup* and *mug* in English or between *Tasse* and *Becher* in German; and it is not even obvious which factors determine these distinctions. However, the semantic phenomena studied in this book are independent of these questions and will thus be ignored.

Apart from nouns, adjectives can be said to denote sets, too. These are the sets of things to which an adjective can be truthfully attributed. For example, *red* would denote the set of individuals x such that for each x in that set the sentence "x is red" would be true. And again, we find vagueness and borderline problems. Thus, for instance, color terms like *red* and *green* are notoriously vague: where exactly is the borderline between *red* and *green*? Again, for the purposes of this text, these difficulties can and will be ignored.

3.3.   *Functional Nouns*

As a rule, then, nouns like *sphere*, *professor*, or *city* have sets of individuals as their extensions. However, there are exceptions to this rule, and in this subsection we take a look at one important class of them, exemplified by the nouns *birthplace*, *mother*, and *surface*. These three nouns not only refer to multitudes of individuals, but at the same time relate these individuals to others. After all, birthplaces are not particular kinds of places; rather, a place is *somebody's* birthplace by being biographically related to that person in a certain way. Similarly, being a (human) mother does not mean being a special kind of person (which she still may be), but being related to other persons— her offspring—in a certain biological way. And surfaces are always surfaces *of objects*—spheres, tables, oceans, etc. —i.e., more or less precisely identifiable parts or regions of these objects. Thus saying that nouns like *birthplace*, *mother*, and *surface* refer to sets of individuals would miss their main trait, viz., that they refer to places *as* birthplaces of (usually) persons, to females *as* mothers of persons (or more generally, living beings), and to spatial regions *as* surfaces of objects. It thus seems that these "*as*-objects" should make up the extensions of such nouns, i.e., objects that are identified relative to certain other objects.

The simplest and most common way of representing objects v as depending on other objects a is by way of **(ordered) pairs** $\langle a, v \rangle$. As a case in point, while Liverpool is an element of the (current) extension of the noun *city*, it does not itself appear in the extension of *birthplace* but only as the birthplace of each of the four Beatles (as well as of many other persons, to be sure), i.e., as part of pairs $\langle a, \text{Liverpool} \rangle$, where $a \in \{\text{John, Paul, George, Ringo,} \dots\}$. Note that pairs $\langle a, v \rangle$ must not be confused with the corresponding sets: although the set $\{a, v\}$ is the same as $\{v, a\}$, the pair $\langle a, v \rangle$ is different from $\langle v, a \rangle$ (unless $a = v$).[3] To avoid confusion, the members of pairs are called *components* instead of *elements*.

Using ordered pairs the extensions of our three exceptional nouns come out like this:

(6)   *birthplace*: {⟨Adam, Paradise⟩, ⟨Eve, Paradise⟩, ⟨John Lennon, Liverpool⟩, ⟨Yoko Ono, Tokyo⟩, ... }

(7)   *mother*: {⟨Cain, Eve⟩, ⟨Abel, Eve⟩, ⟨Stella McCartney, Linda McCartney⟩, ⟨Sean Lennon, Yoko Ono⟩, ... }

(8)   *surface*: {⟨Mars, Mars' surface⟩, ⟨Earth, Earth's surface⟩, ⟨Table 2, surface of Table 2⟩, ⟨Table 3, surface of Table 3⟩, ... }

---

3   Still, somewhat surprisingly, ordered pairs can be constructed in terms of (unordered) sets. A very elegant reduction goes back to the Polish logician Kazimierz Kuratowski [1896–1980], who proposed that pairs $\langle a, v \rangle$ be identified with sets $\{\{a\}, \{a, v\}\}$.

The reader should note in passing that the extension in (8) mostly consists of pairs of unnamed and rather ill-defined objects. This is partly due to the abovementioned ubiquitous vagueness of language (which we choose to ignore), and partly to the fact that, while many things in the world do not have a name, they may still be referred to by description, i.e., using nouns (and other expressions); only when it comes to specifying the pertinent extensions would one have to create *ad hoc* names for them in the meta-language (= English, as it is used in writing about English or German, the object languages), as we have done in (8) for illustration (and which, if need be, we will continue to do).

Unlike the extensions of the nouns discussed before, the ones in (6)–(8) consist of pairs of individuals. This difference not only matches our intuitions about the referential function of these nouns. It will also turn out to be helpful when it comes to explaining the difference between the meanings of, say, *Paul's place* and *Paul's birthplace*. We will return to these matters in Chapter 5.

A closer look at the extensions in (6)–(8) reveals that they are not just random sets of ordered pairs. Given that everyone has one birthplace and one mother, and everything has (at most) one surface, the second component in each pair is determined by the first one, i.e., each of these extensions f satisfies the following condition:

(9)   If both $\langle a, v_1 \rangle \in f$ and $\langle a, v_2 \rangle \in f$, then $v_1 = v_2$.

Sets f that satisfy (9) are called **functions**, which is why nouns like *birthplace*, *mother*, and *surface* are called **functional nouns**. The terminology is reminiscent of mathematics; and indeed, for (almost) all intents and purposes, mathematical functions can be identified with sets of ordered pairs satisfying (9). Thus, for instance, as a set-theoretic object, the squaring function on natural numbers consists of the pairs $\langle 0, 0 \rangle, \langle 1, 1 \rangle, \langle 2, 4 \rangle, \langle 3, 9 \rangle$, etc.[4] Functions are not only of interest to us as extensions of functional nouns but will be em-

---

4   It is customary to define this function by the equation "$y = x^2$". However, as already pointed out by Frege (1904), this notation is inaccurate in that an equation is something that may be true or false (depending on what x and y are), which a function cannot be. To make up for this notional embarrassment, logicians have invented a special notation for defining functions, so-called *functional abstraction*, which is usually expressed by way of a so-called 'lambda operator', after the Greek letter λ (Lambda). In this notation, the squaring function is denoted by the term "$\lambda x . x^2$", which is not an equation but merely describes the function as consisting of all pairs $\langle x, x^2 \rangle$. Popular though they may be, particularly in the kind of semantic framework briefly sketched in Section 3 of Chapter 6,

ployed in quite different connections off and on throughout this text. Let us use the occasion, then, to introduce some standard terminology and notation that prove to be useful in dealing with functions.

Even though functions may be identified with sets of ordered pairs, this is not what they are conceived of when they are put to use. Rather, a function—whether in arithmetic, economics, or indeed semantics—is a representation of dependent objects. In the case of birthplaces, the object is a place that is represented as relative to, or depending on, a particular person. In this connection the object itself is called the **value** that the function assigns to the **argument**, i.e., that object that the value depends on. Thus the extension of *birthplace* assigns to each person—the argument—his or her birthplace as its (the function's) value. The totality of all values assigned by a function f—the set of all v occurring as the second component of some pair $\langle a, v \rangle \in f$—is called the **range** of f; and the set of all arguments is f's **domain**. Also, f is said to be a function from its domain **from** A to a set B if all elements of f are pairs $\langle a, v \rangle$, where $a \in A$ and $v \in B$; in other words, a function from A to B is a function whose domain is A and whose range is a subset of B. In this terminology, the function indicated in (6) has the set of persons as its domain, whereas the range consists of all places in which anybody has been born at all; so it is a function from the set of all persons to the set of all places.

Given a particular argument a of a function f (i.e., an element of f's domain), there is precisely one value that f assigns to a. This, of course, follows from the condition (9) on functions, reflecting that the value is presented as depending on the argument. In other words, a function f and its argument a together determine the value. This is why this value can be named by reference to the function and the argument alone, viz., as $f(x)$. Thus if f is the extension of *birthplace*, then $f(\text{Yoko Ono}) = \text{Tokyo}$, and $f(\text{Yoko Ono}) \neq f(\text{John Lennon}) = f(\text{Paul McCartney})$, etc.

Functional nouns are not the only ones whose extensions consist of ordered pairs. Indeed, a noun like *brother* also seems to refer to persons relative to other persons and should thus have famous pairs like $\langle$Ethan Coen, Joel Coen$\rangle$ in its extension. But the extension of *brother* can hardly be said to satisfy (9), for it contains the pairs $\langle$Deborah Coen, Ethan Coen$\rangle$ and $\langle$Deborah Coen, Joel Coen$\rangle$, but of course, Ethan $\neq$ Joel. Nouns like *brother* are called **relational nouns**, reflecting the fact that arbitrary sets of ordered pairs are

---

Lambdas are not really needed in the approach taken in this text, which is why we only briefly introduce them in the final section of the last chapter of this book.

called (two-place) **relations** in set theory. We will not go into relational nouns in this book, but relations and functions as such will play a crucial role in the next subsections.

Apart from relational ones, another class of nouns that we will ignore in the following is **substance words** or **mass nouns** like *milk*, so called because they refer not to individuals but to bits and parts of a substance. Maybe we could say that any bunch of molecules that makes up a quantity of milk is an element of the milk set. However, this method raises a number of questions we cannot discuss here, which is why we will ignore these kinds of expressions and turn to ones that are more readily handled in terms of sets.

3.4.   Verbs and Verb Phrases

Sets can also be used as extensions of verbs. For example, the verb *sleep* has as its extension the set of all sleepers (in a given situation). As a first approximation to its meaning (to which we will get in a minute), a sentence like (10) can then be construed as describing the extension of the subject, the individual John, as an element of that extension of the verb, the set of sleeping individuals.

(10)   John is sleeping

For transitive verbs, however, this simple-minded approach to extensions leads to difficulties. Take the verb *kiss* as an example. Intuitively, in a sentence like

(11)   John kisses Mary

two individuals are involved, connected by the relation of kissing. Hence the extension of the verb cannot just be a set of individuals: if it consisted of kissers, it would lack the "kissees"; if only the latter constituted its extensions, the kissers would be missing. However, given the previous section, there is a natural way out here if we again invoke ordered pairs and say that the verb in (11) makes (multiple) reference to both kissers and kissees, which come in pairs like ⟨Mary, John⟩. The ordering in the pair is, of course, crucial to distinguish it from ⟨John, Mary⟩, which is said to be in the extension of *kiss* according to (12):

(12)   Mary kisses John

We thus find that (11) says that the pair ⟨John, Mary⟩ is an element of the **relation** of kissing, whereas (12) expresses that the pair ⟨Mary, John⟩ is such an element. For this to make sense, we must assume that *kiss* denotes a relation, i.e., a set of ordered pairs. And this construction of verb extensions generalizes to cases where there is more than one object:

(13)   a.   *sleep*: the set of sleepers
      b.   *kiss*: a relation between kissers and kissees, i.e., the set of pairs ⟨x, y⟩ such that x kisses y
      c.   *donate*: a three-place relation, a set of triples

The notion of a triple should be obvious: whereas a pair is a list of two items, a triple is a list of three items. Even more generally, an *n*-tuple is a list of *n* items. (Hence pairs are 2-tuples, and triples are 3-tuples.)[5] We may thus summarize our descriptions of certain extensions in the following table.

(14)

type of expression	type of extension	example	extension of example
proper name	individual	*Paul*	Paul McCartney
definite description	individual	*die größte deutsche Stadt*[7]	Berlin
noun	set of individuals	*Tisch*	the set of tables
intransitive verb	set of individuals	*schlafen*	the set of sleepers
transitive verb	set of pairs of individuals	*essen*	the set of pairs ⟨eater, eaten⟩
ditransitive verb	set of triples of individuals	*schenken*	the set of triples ⟨donator, recipient, donation⟩

Recall that our list in (3) also contains the negative expressions *nobody*, *nothing*, and *no dog*, the extensions of which we have yet to determine; this task will only be tackled in Chapter 6.

---

5   Once ordered pairs have been reduced to sets, as indicated in footnote 3 p. 67, one may continue and define *n*-tuples in terms of pairs; for example, the triple ⟨a, b, c⟩ may be identified with the pair ⟨⟨a, b⟩, c⟩.

7   the largest German city

4.   Truth Values as Extensions of Sentences

Looking at the verbs in (13), one may detect an increasing complexity concerning the so-called **valency** of verbs: one-place verbs only need a subject; two-place verbs (called transitive) need a subject and an object; three-place verbs are called ditransitive: they require a subject, a direct object, and an indirect object. Corresponding to these types of predicates there are three-place tuples (triples), two-place tuples (pairs) and one-place tuples (individuals). The generalization here is that predicates can be represented by sets of n-place tuples. So there is a simple connection between the valency of a verb and the n-tuples in its extension: the higher the former, the longer the latter. We thus arrive at the following observation:

(15)   *Parallelism between valency and type of extension:*
        The extension of an n-place verb is always a set of n-tuples.

What is remarkable about this parallelism is the fact that it not only holds for lexical expressions, but it holds for complex expressions as well. For instance, *walk* is a one-place predicate, and so is *walk slowly*, therefore *walk slowly* will also denote a set of 1-tuples. *Slice* is two-place, and so is *slice slowly/carefully*, etc. Moreover, by adding an object to a two-place relation, e.g., adding *the salami* to *slice*, we get *slice the salami*, which itself only requires a subject. This implies that adding an object turns a two-place relation into a one-place predicate. Likewise:

(16)   give (three-place)
        give a book (two-place)
        give a book to the student (one-place)

(17)   I give a book to the student (zero-place)

The last step in (16) suggests that one-place predicates are one-place "relations"; this terminology might seem somewhat counterintuitive, since relations are normally conceived of as two-place. But there is nothing wrong with extending the terminology this way, and this is indeed standard practice in mathematics.

What might be even more puzzling is the step from (16) to (17); the qualification "zero-place" is in fact intended to suggest that the valency of a sentence is zero and that sentences are nothing but zero-place verbs or zero-place relations. This is quite remarkable, but still somewhat mysterious, unless we know how to deal with zero-place relations.

Speaking of sentences as zero-place verbs might be felt as undue terminological hardship. Perhaps a more intuitive conception is to replace the notion of an n-place verb with that of a sentence with n gaps. Thus, a transitive verb is a sentence with 2 gaps, an intransitive verb is a sentence with 1 gap, and a sentence is a sentence with no gaps. The connection would then be that a sentence with n gaps denotes a set of n-tuples.

Let us illustrate this in a table, taking (18) as a sample sentence:

(18)   *Der Papst zeigt dem Präsidenten den*   The Pope shows the Vatican
       Vatikan   Palace to the president

(19)

verb or verb phrase	valency	extension
zeigt	3	set of all triples $\langle a, b, c \rangle$ where a shows b to c
zeigt *dem Präsidenten*	2	set of all pairs $\langle a, b \rangle$ where a shows b to the president
zeigt *dem Präsidenten* *den Vatikan*	1	set of all 1-tuples $\langle a \rangle$ where a shows the Vatican Palace to the president

We might then continue in the following way:

(20)

sentence	valency	extension
Der Papst zeigt dem Präsidenten den Vatikan	0	set of all 0-tuples $\langle \rangle$ where the Pope shows the Vatican Palace to the president

To see what (20) amounts to, we first need to ask what a zero-tuple is. Why, obviously, it's a list of length zero! Mathematicians assume that such lists exist. Of course, there is only one such list, the empty list. For the sake of simplicity, we identify it with the empty set:

(21)   There is precisely one zero-tuple, viz., the empty set $\emptyset$.

As a consequence, the set of all zero-tuples contains the empty set $\emptyset$ as its one and only element; in other words (or symbols), $\{\emptyset\}$ is the set of all zero-tuples. Note that $\emptyset$ and $\{\emptyset\}$ are two distinct sets: the former has no elements, the latter has precisely one element (viz., the former). The difference will become important in a moment.

According to (20), the extension of (18) comes out as the set of all 0-tuples, where the Pope shows the Vatican Palace to the president. What set is this? That depends on the facts:

—   Suppose that the Pope does not show the Vatican to the president. Then the set would have to be empty; for if there were a 0-tuple where the Pope shows the Vatican to the president, then the latter would be the case—contrary to what we assumed. Hence, if (18) is false, the set determined in (20) is the empty set.

—   If, on the other hand, the Pope does show the Vatican to the president, the set in (20) would contain all 0-tuples there are, because it would be true (though awkward) to say of any such 0-tuple that it is a 0-tuple, where the Pope shows the president the Vatican. Hence, if (18) is true, the set determined in (20) is the set of all 0-tuples, i.e., a one-membered set or *singleton*, viz., $\{\emptyset\}$.

We thus conclude that (18) has one of two possible extensions depending on whether or not it is true: if it is, we get $\{\emptyset\}$; if not, we have $\emptyset$. Our next step is to note that this not only works for the particular sentence under discussion. It works for all sentences the same way! That is, if a sentence is true, its extension is $\{\emptyset\}$, and this holds for all true sentences. This means that all true sentences have the same extension, namely $\{\emptyset\}$. Likewise, all false sentences have the same extension, namely the empty set $\emptyset$. These two sets are also called **truth values**. In logic and semantics, they are also represented by the letters "T" and "F" or by the numbers "1" and "0":[8]

(22)   *Frege's Generalization* [9]
          The extension of a sentence S is its truth value, i.e., 1 if S is true and 0 if S is false.

---

8   Incidentally, the identification of 0 and 1 with $\emptyset$ and $\{\emptyset\}$, respectively, is in line with the standard set-theoretic construction of the natural numbers, the *von Neumann ordinals*, named after the Hungarian mathematician John von Neumann [1903–57].

9   The generalization, and the very term *truth value* (*Wahrheitswert*)—though not the identification of truth values with numbers—go back to Frege (1892). The set-theoretic argument used in this section is from Carnap (1947).

It should have become clear by now that, being its truth value, the extension of a sentence cannot be identified with its meaning; for otherwise all true sentences would be synonymous. But we already remarked above that there is more that contributes to the meaning of a sentence, namely the information it conveys, its intension. However, before going into intensions, let us see what we can do with simple extensions. The basic question we will address is this: can the extensions of phrases and sentences be determined on the basis of the extensions of words they contain, and if so, how?

EXERCISE 11:

Suppose that the extension of the verb *pass*, as in *Arthur passed Frederick the diary*, is the set of triples $\{\langle a, f, d \rangle, \langle f, d, d \rangle, \langle a, b, d \rangle\}$, where a is Arthur, b is Berta, f is Frederick, and d is the diary. Now assume that the first position in the triple represents the passer, the second the receiver, and the third whatever is passed. Determine the extension of

(23)   Frederick passed Berta the diary

5. Thematic Roles

The attentive reader might have felt a little bit uneasy in Section 4 when trying to understand the reduction of a three-place relation (set of triples) to a one-place relation (set of individuals, or 1-tuples). A potential problem may have been caused by the fact that triples always have a fixed order of components, the arguments of the verb, that must somehow be related to the syntactic encoding of these arguments as subjects, objects and indirect (or sometimes prepositional) objects. These grammatical relations are (hierarchically) ordered in syntax, and ideally this ordering should correspond to or be mirrored by the order of elements in the triples that represent the denotation of the verb in question. There are a number of facts that are relevant to this question, and in this section we will focus on the problem of whether the fixed order can be the same across different languages.

The first observation is this. The order of arguments of the English sentence *The Pope showed the Vatican to the president* corresponds to that in the triple $\langle a, b, c \rangle$:

(24)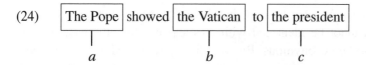

In contrast, the order of elements in German is different:

(25)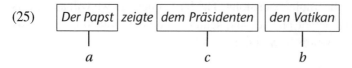

The question then arises as to whether or not the tuples should differ for German and English, although intuitively the meaning and *ipso facto* the extension of the verbs should be identical.

A possible answer could be provided by a closer look at the process that reduces the length of the tuples. Above in Section 4 we assumed that the first argument that is dropped from the three-place relation *zeigen* is c, which comes first in the structure shown in (26):

(26) | der Papst | zeigt | dem Präsidenten | den Vatikan |

But now recall that this structure is inconsistent with the otherwise well-motivated assumption that the German word order is derived from an underlying verb-end structure. So we better assume the order in (27):

(27)   *(dass) der Papst dem Präsidenten den Vatikan zeigt*

Above we argued that this is in fact the input to semantic interpretation. We would therefore have to assume a structuring as in (28), which crucially differs from that in (26):

(28)   *(dass)* | der Papst | dem Präsidenten | den Vatikan | zeigt |

Now the first argument that must be eliminated in order to get a two-place relation is not c, but the direct object b, contrary to our calculation in (19). This is illustrated in (29):

(29)

verb or verb phrase	valency	extension
zeigt	3	set of all triples $\langle a, c, b \rangle$ where a shows b to c
den Vatikan zeigt	2	set of all pairs $\langle a, c \rangle$ where a shows the Vatican to c
dem Präsidenten den Vatikan zeigt	1	set of all 1-tuples $\langle a \rangle$ where a shows the Vatican to the president

Keeping with the assumption that the syntactic structure indeed determines the order of elements in a semantic representation, and that the nominal arguments always correspond to the last (rightmost) components of the verbal extensions (as illustrated in (29)), we now arrive at the conclusion that the n-tuple for German is indeed $\langle a, c, b \rangle$, corresponding to the linear order in (25). Turning next to English, a potential structure for (24) is shown in (30):

(30)   the Pope ‖ shows | the Vatican ‖ to the president

But given (30), the order of elements in the triple for *show* is not the linear order $\langle a, b, c \rangle$ in (24), but rather the hierarchical order that is determined by the application of reduction rules in line with the right-to-left assumption stated above, namely $\langle a, c, b \rangle$. If so, the order of the triple is exactly the same as in German, and our problem is solved. Hence, the answer to our initial question is that the semantic representation is identical for both languages.

Unfortunately, however, linguists have argued that the structure in (30) is incorrect. The proof is based on data like (31):

(31)   a.   Mary gave every dog to its owner
        b.   John told nothing to anyone
        c.   Sue showed Max to himself

In each case it can be argued that the *to*-phrase is in the scope of the direct object. This, however, is inconsistent with the Scope Principle and the structure in (30). As the reader may verify the smallest box containing the direct object *the Vatican* contains only the verb, but it should contain the prepositional object as well. This and other observations and problems (the full argument

can be found in Larson (1988)) have led to a revision of major assumptions
about the structure of simple sentences and a refined architecture that allows
empty elements to be filled by movement, as illustrated in (32):

(32)   the Pope

This structure must be transformed by moving the verb into the empty position between subject and direct object; this transformation, being a case of
head movement, does not affect meaning. The important feature of (32) is that
the smallest box containing *the Vatican*, and by analogy *every dog*, *nothing*,
and *Max* in (31), also contains *the president*, *its owner*, *anyone*, and *himself*
respectively, in accordance with the Scope Principle.

If this is correct, it now follows that the extension hierarchically corresponding to (32) is again identical to the linear order of the syntactic arguments. Whereas we assumed that in German the order of elements in the triple
is $\langle a, c, b \rangle$, it must be $\langle a, b, c \rangle$ in English. We are thus no better off than before
and are thrown back to the question of whether the semantic representation
of the verb *show* in English is different from that of *zeigen* in German. If
one were to insist that a representation of meaning should be language independent, how can their obvious synonymy be accounted for, given that the
representations by extensions differ?

A number of answers can be found in the literature, the most radical being that underlying syntactic structures relevant for the semantic relations
under discussion (also called *argument structure*) should be universal, i.e.,
identical across languages, whereas syntactic surface structures can be adjusted by additional syntactic transformations that may apply in one language
but not necessarily in the other. This hypothesis has been ventured by Mark
Baker (1988) and has become known as the "Uniformity of Theta Assignment Hypothesis" (UTAH). We think that the transformations necessitated
by the UTAH ought to be motivated by independent, preferably syntactic,
regularities. If this cannot be guaranteed, the hypothesis becomes empirically
vacuous: without independent syntactic motivation such adjustment rules can
hardly be explanatory. Now, many linguists believe that the transformations
required to maintain the UTAH are really difficult to justify empirically; they
would prefer to stay on the safer side by adopting a weaker theory. We will
therefore dismiss this hypothesis; but before doing so, we must briefly turn to
the concept of "Theta Assignment", which plays a key role in this discussion.

Above we used expressions like *subject, direct object*, or *indirect object* in order to characterize the arguments of a verb. Unfortunately, these terms for grammatical relations are purely syntactic, and part of our problem results from the fact that these notions can also be language dependent. For example, it has been argued in Generative Grammar that *him* in

(33)   John gave him a book

is a direct object, based on the evidence that the direct object immediately follows the verb and is promoted to the subject position in passive constructions, as evidenced by (34):

(34)   He was given a book

In German, however, the analogous passive construction (35-a) is ungrammatical. Rather, the corresponding pronoun *ihm* would be considered an indirect object, which cannot become a subject but remains an indirect object in the passive construction (35-b):

(35)   a. *Er wurde ein Buch gegeben*
        b. *Ihm wurde ein Buch gegeben*

That *him* in (33) should really be considered a direct object is disputable, but whether correct or not, the data clearly show that grammatical relations behave in language-typical ways. However, they have semantic cognates, viz., notions like *agent, theme, goal, experiencer, source, patient, instrument, recipient*, and others, that describe the semantic contribution of an argument relative to a verb and seem to be identifiable across languages; they lend themselves as candidates for describing the extensions of verbs in a language-independent way.

In the case at hand, we would want to say that *him* in (33), *he* in (34), and *ihm* in (35-b) are goals; *the Pope* in previous examples is an agent and *the Vatican* a theme. Concerning the president—i.e., the extension of *the president*—s/he might be described as a goal. These notions have also been called **thematic roles** or **thematic relations** because they highlight the role that an argument plays in relation to the state or event described by a verb. Thematic roles are abbreviated as so-called theta-roles, written as θ-roles with θ being the letter of the Greek alphabet pronounced "theta".

Unfortunately, there is no agreement in the literature as to which and how many roles there are or what their theoretical status is. For example, if one favors a semantic theory that rephrases the verb *show* as "cause to make one see", then the Pope may as well play the thematic role of a causer, the president could be an experiencer, and the Vatican could be called a theme. Despite this disagreement, we endorse the common idea behind the concept of thematic roles, namely the identification of different participants of the event or situation described by a verb, without committing ourselves to a particular choice of roles.

The advantage of thematic roles is that they enable us to describe verb extensions in purely semantic terms, independently of syntax. And inasmuch as they are universal, ordering the (components of) n-tuples in the extensions of verbs becomes a matter of ordering these roles once and for all—which could be achieved by some convention (e.g., alphabetically, or by frequency, or by certain hierarchies to be justified by prominence relations between the theta-roles). Alternatively, one may replace the n-tuples by (two-place) relations between thematic roles (or their names) and role players. For example, the triples in the Pope-scenario could be replaced by relations of the form given in (36):

(36) $\{\langle agent, a \rangle, \langle experiencer, b \rangle, \langle theme, c \rangle\}$

Such a relation is not a triple; it is unordered and therefore independent of syntax. In fact, (36) is a *function* whose domain is a set of roles. Hence the triples in the extension of *show* may be replaced by functions with the domain { agent, experiencer, theme }, also called the θ-*grid* of the verb. Similarly, the extension of a transitive verb like *kiss* would consist of functions with the domain { agent, patient }, instead of pairs of individuals; the individuals would instead constitute the range of the functions. And an intransitive verb like *sleep* would not have (one-tuples of) individuals in its extension but functions with a very small domain consisting only of the agent role as its theta-grid. In general then, the n-tuples in the extensions of n-place verbs (or verbal constituents) according to (15) would be replaced by functions whose domains consist of n thematic roles. For lack of a standard term, let us call the resulting extensions *thematic*. The following schematic comparison shows how an ordinary verb extension according to (15) relates to a thematic one:

(37)   a.   Ordinary: $\{\langle x_1, \ldots, x_n \rangle, \langle y_1, \ldots, y_n \rangle, \ldots\}$
         b.   Thematic: $\{\{\langle \theta_1, x_1 \rangle, \ldots, \langle \theta_n, x_n \rangle\},$
                 $\{\langle \theta_1, y_1 \rangle, \ldots, \langle \theta_n, y_n \rangle\}, \ldots\}$

The ordinary extension (37-a) consists of various *n*-tuples, each of which just lists the relevant role players in some fixed order. The thematic extension in (37-b) replaces each of these lists by a function that assigns the players to their roles—and these roles are the same across the whole extension of the verb. Note that this replacement of *n*-tuples by functions does not make the verb extension itself functional: only the elements of the thematic extensions are functions; the extensions themselves remain (unordered) sets.

EXERCISE 12:

> Suppose that John and Mary kiss each other, Bill kisses Fred, and Paul kisses Mary, and no further kissings occur. Spell out the ordinary and the thematic extensions of *kiss* and *kiss Mary* for such a situation.

Thematic extensions thus replace the arbitrariness of order in the extensions of verbs by an unordered but at the same time principled identification of the individuals these verbs make reference to. As a result, then, the ordinary *n*-tuples are determined by syntactic structure, but the real semantic representation is not and is indeed language independent.

Once such a solution is adopted, an immediate question concerns the relation between θ-grids and syntactic structure. Above we assumed that this relation can be language specific, but nonetheless there seem to be some almost universal tendencies, for example, that the agent is universally realized by (or mapped to) the subject position. We also say that the subject is *assigned* the agent θ-role; this is an instance of θ-assignment, a notion that occurs in the "Uniformity of Theta Assignment Hypothesis". The general question of how this assignment is governed by regularities is the topic of the so-called **Linking Theory**, which concerns the connection between theta-grids and syntactic positions.

This is a vast topic of research we cannot do justice to here. Let us, for the sake of illustration, mention just one of the many questions that must be addressed in Linking Theory. Consider the sentences in (38):

(38)   a.   The children fear ghosts
       b.   Ghosts frighten the children

Arguably the phrase *the children* has the same thematic status as experiencer in both sentences, though it is assigned to different grammatical relations. This seems to suggest that the UTAH is too strong even language internally, given that identical theta-roles are not necessarily assigned to the same grammatical relation. On the other hand, the actual distribution might still follow from other general linking rules. Assume, for the sake of argument, that the thematic extensions contain the following sets:

(39)   a.   {..., {⟨theme, ghosts⟩, ⟨experiencer, the children⟩}, ... }
       b.   {..., {⟨causer, ghosts⟩, ⟨experiencer, the children⟩}, ... }

Now, if the causer is always assigned higher in the structure than the experiencer while the theme is always low in the structure, the distribution of the arguments in (38) follows from these general rules.

As mentioned above, however, the choice of θ-roles as well as linking rules is highly controversial and the literature on the topic is vast (cf., e.g., Grimshaw (1990), Reinhart (2003), or Wunderlich (2006)). Since we cannot do justice to the debate, we will largely ignore the issue by simply assuming ordinary n-tuple extensions as needed in the context of future discussions.[10]

---

10   As a final remark, we should mention that a different solution to the problem dismisses with n-tuples altogether. The interested reader should read up on a theory called ☞ *Neo-Davidsonian Event Semantics*. Though we believe that this is a viable alternative to the approach we are suggesting, for reasons of simplicity and exposition we adhere to the more traditional approach here.

Chapter 5
Composing Extensions

The *Principle of Compositionality* stated in Chapter 4 goes a long way toward explaining how speakers and hearers are able to use and understand expressions they have not come across before: starting with the smallest 'atoms' of syntactic structure, the words or morphemes provided by the lexicon, the meanings of ever more complex expressions can be determined by combining the meanings of their parts. Hence the language user only needs to learn and know the meanings of the lexical expressions and the ways in which they are combined.

The meanings thus determined in turn may serve to relate to the extra-linguistic world around us in ways not accessible by lexical meanings alone. Insects are cases in point. They rarely have names[1] and usually cannot be referred to by lexical expressions other than pronouns. However, even a nameless bug long gone and far away can be singled out by a definite description like *the creature that bit me on my left earlobe half a year ago.* And compositionality explains how this is possible: the lexical meanings of the parts combine into the meaning of the entire description, which in turn determines a certain animal (provided there is one that fits the description). Now, whatever this meaning is, it somehow encodes information that suffices to determine a particular nameless insect—reference to which thus becomes possible by a suitable composition of lexical meanings.

Although in general the extensions of complex expressions are determined by compositionally determining their meanings first, it turns out that, more often than not, there is a more direct way. It is a remarkable fact about language that in many (though not all) cases, the referent of an expression can be determined by combining the *extensions* of its parts in a compositional way. In this chapter we will look at a variety of such cases, some of which will also help us to find out what the extensions of particular expressions are in the first place. Only thereafter, in Chapters 7 and 8, will we look at the limitations of the composition of extensions and the nature of meaning in somewhat more general terms.

---

[1]   A. A. Milne's beetle Alexander (http://allpoetry.com/poem/8518989-Forgiven-by-A.A._Milne) may be an exception, but then again it may also be a piece of fiction ...

1.   Truth Tables

Identifying the extensions of (declarative) sentences as truth values has important—and somewhat surprising—consequences for the semantic analysis of complex sentences. For it turns out that, in certain cases, the extension of a complex sentence is entirely determined by the extensions of its immediate parts. (1) is a case in point:

(1) | Harry is reading | and | Mary is writing |

Under the (disputable) assumption that the conjunction (*and*) and the two boxed sentences form the immediate parts of (1), we may observe that the truth value of the entire sentence is fully determined by the truth values of these boxed parts: if either of them is false, then so is (1); otherwise, i.e., if both are true, (1) is as well. In a similar vein, we observe that the truth value of (2) also depends on the extensions of the boxed parts:

(2) | Harry is reading | or | Mary is writing |

In the case of (2), the whole sentence is true as long as one of the boxed sentences is; otherwise, i.e., if both are false, then so is (2). Hence the extensions of coordinated sentences like (1) and (2) depend on the extensions of the sentences coordinated in a way that is characteristic of the respective coordinator. These dependencies can be charted by means of so-called **truth tables**:

(3)

$[\![$ Harry is reading $]\!]_s$	$[\![$ Mary is writing $]\!]_s$	$[\![(1)]\!]_s$
1	1	1
1	0	0
0	1	0
0	0	0

(4)

$[\![$ Harry is reading $]\!]_s$	$[\![$ Mary is writing $]\!]_s$	$[\![(2)]\!]_s$
1	1	1
1	0	1
0	1	1
0	0	0

Tables (3) and (4) show the possible distributions of truth values of the sentences coordinated, and the effect they have on the truth value of (1) and (2), respectively. In both cases this effect may be thought of as the output of a certain operation acting on the inputs given by the constituent sentences. As the reader may immediately verify, the operation described in (3) (called **conjunction**) always outputs the minimum of the input values, whereas the one in (4) (called **disjunction**) uniformly yields their maximum.[2]

Using standard notation of formal logic, these operations may be indicated by the symbols '$\land$' for conjunction and '$\lor$' for disjunction. Hence the truth table in (3) can be written symbolically as '$p \land q$', where p and q are the truth values of its constituent sentences, and $p \land q$ is the value determined according to the table in (3); similarly '$p \lor q$' denotes the truth value determined as in (4).

Since truth values are the extensions of sentences, (3) and (4) show that the extensions of coordinations like (1) and (2) only depend on the extensions of the coordinated sentences and the coordinating operation. Let us denote the extension of an expression A by putting double brackets '$[\![\ ]\!]$' around A, as is standard in semantics. The extension of an expression depends on the situation s talked about when uttering A; so we add the index s to the closing bracket. Generalizing from the above examples to any declarative sentences A and B, we thus get:

(5) $\quad [\![\, A \text{ and } B \,]\!]_s = [\![\, A \,]\!]_s \land [\![\, B \,]\!]_s$

(6) $\quad [\![\, A \text{ or } B \,]\!]_s = [\![\, A \,]\!]_s \lor [\![\, B \,]\!]_s$

Equations (5) and (6) show in what way the extension of a sentence coordination depends on the extensions of the sentences coordinated and the choice of the coordinator. The latter, it would seem, contributes a specific combination of truth values. It is therefore natural and, indeed, customary to regard this contribution itself as the extension of the respective coordinator. In other words, the extension of *and* (in its use for coordinating declarative sentences)

---

2   Of course, this description turns on the identification of the truth values with the numbers 0 (= false) and 1 (= true), which we have treated as a matter of convention and convenience (although it could be motivated further). Incidentally, the combination described in (3) coincides with the (ordinary arithmetical) multiplication of truth values, again conceived of as numbers, and the one in (4) boils down to subtracting the product from the sum!

is the combination ∧ of truth values, as charted in (3). Similarly, the extension of *or* may be identified with the operation depicted in (4). We thus arrive at:

(7) $[\![\,\text{and}\,]\!]_s = \wedge$

(8) $[\![\,\text{or}\,]\!]_s = \vee$

Equations (7) and (8) allow us to compositionally derive the truth values of (1) and (2), respectively, directly from the extensions of their immediate parts, without first determining their meanings:

(9) $[\![\,(1)\,]\!]_s$
= $[\![\,\text{Harry is reading}\,]\!]_s \wedge [\![\,\text{Mary is writing}\,]\!]_s$ cf. (5)
= $[\![\,\text{Harry is reading}\,]\!]_s [\![\,\text{and}\,]\!]_s [\![\,\text{Mary is writing}\,]\!]_s$ by (7)

(10) $[\![\,(2)\,]\!]_s$
= $[\![\,\text{Harry is reading}\,]\!]_s \vee [\![\,\text{Mary is writing}\,]\!]_s$ cf. (6)
= $[\![\,\text{Harry is reading}\,]\!]_s [\![\,\text{or}\,]\!]_s [\![\,\text{Mary is writing}\,]\!]_s$ by (8)

It is easily seen that the third lines in (9) and (10) each derive from their predecessors by applying the equations (7) and (8), respectively. If they still look unfamiliar, this may be due to the fact that—just like '∧' and '∨'—the notations '$[\![\,\text{and}\,]\!]_s$' and '$[\![\,\text{or}\,]\!]_s$' both stand for arithmetical operations that can be applied to truth values. And it is precisely this application to the truth values of the sentences coordinated that delivers the truth value of the entire coordination. According to (9), then, the extension of (1) is obtained by applying the extension of one of its parts, viz., *and*, to the extensions of the other two parts, and similarly for (2). Hence in both (1) and (2) the extension of the entire expression is determined by the extensions of its (immediate) parts in the same way, i.e., by applying the extension of one of them to the extensions of the others. We will discuss the meaning of '∧' and '∨' more thoroughly in Section 5.

Truth tables also come in handy when it comes to interpreting *negation*, which can be expressed in a variety of ways:

(11)   a.   It's not true that Homer likes donuts
       b.   It's incorrect that Homer likes donuts
       c.   It's false that Homer likes donuts
       d.   That Homer likes donuts is false
       e.   Homer doesn't like donuts

In what follows we will refer to any of the above ways of negating a sentence
S as '*not* S'. Obviously, negation reverses the truth value of a sentence and
may thus be represented by a truth table as in (12):

(12)

$[\![$ Homer likes donuts $]\!]_s$	$[\![(11)]\!]_s$
1	0
0	1

Unlike (1) and (4), (12) only has two rows: rather than connecting two sentences, negation only modifies one; it is **unary**, not **binary**.

In general, whenever a sentence S is true, '*not* S' is false, and when S is
false, '*not* S' is true. Like its syntactic counterpart, this operation of inverting
truth values is called **negation** and symbolized as '$\neg$'. We thus have:

(13) $[\![not]\!]_s = \neg$

To sum up the findings of this section, the extension of *and*, *or*, and *not* are
combinations of truth values, viz., conjunction ($\wedge$), disjunction ($\vee$), and negation ($\neg$), respectively. These combinations may be represented by truth tables,
which, for future reference, we put down in a general form:

(14)

$[\![S_1]\!]_s$	$[\![S_2]\!]_s$	$[\![S_1]\!]_s \wedge [\![S_2]\!]_s$
1	1	1
1	0	0
0	1	0
0	0	0

(15)

$[\![S_1]\!]_s$	$[\![S_2]\!]_s$	$[\![S_1]\!]_s \vee [\![S_2]\!]_s$
1	1	1
1	0	1
0	1	1
0	0	0

(16)

$[\![S]\!]_s$	$\neg [\![S]\!]_s$
1	0
0	1

In writing truth tables, we consider all possible combinations of truth values, no matter which order they come in; thus, for example, (17) is but an equivalent reformulation to the disjunction truth table (15):

(17)

$[\![S_1]\!]_s$	$[\![S_2]\!]_s$	$[\![S_1]\!]_s \vee [\![S_2]\!]_s$
0	0	0
0	1	1
1	1	1
1	0	1

Both (17) and (15) cover the four ways in which the truth values of S_1 and S_2 may be distributed; they just come in different orders. However, (15) is more "orderly" than (17) in that it has the four "cases" arranged by size, starting with 11, which is the largest two-digit number consisting only of 1s and 0s, all the way down to the smallest one, 0 (or 00, adding an extra zero to make it two-place). In what follows, we will stick to the policy of "orderly" truth tables as in (17-a). This will pay off in Section 5 when it comes to taking more sub-clauses into account than just S_1 and S_2—and thus more cases: this way it is easier to make sure we haven't omitted a case. However, before entering into these complications, let us first see how the truth values of simple sentences can be obtained from the extensions of their parts.

2.   Referential Subjects and Objects

Once the extensions of sentences have been identified as truth values, it is not hard to see how extensions can be combined in accordance with Frege's Principle:

(18)   *Principle of Extensional Compositionality:*
        The extension of a compound expression is a function of the extensions of its immediate parts and the way they are composed.

Note that we have slightly modified Frege's Principle, as already suggested in the introduction to this chapter: the difference from the general principle of compositionality stated earlier is that we now take only the *extensions* of the expressions involved into account (rather than their meanings). This is a simplification to which we return in Chapter 7.

    Let us now apply the principle to a simple sentence like (19):

(19)   *Paul schnarcht*
Paul snores
'Paul snores/is snoring'

The immediate parts are *Paul* and *schnarcht*. The extension of the proper name is the individual Paul; the extension of *schnarcht* is the set of snoring individuals (in a certain situation). Can we determine a truth value by looking at these extensions? Yes, we can: Having adopted the framework of set theory, we only need to say that the sentence is true if the extension of *Paul* is an element of the extension of *schnarcht* (= the set of individuals snoring). If Paul is not an element of that set, the sentence is false. The same is true for *Tim schnarcht*. And for *Paul schläft* (Paul is sleeping), *Tim schläft*, etc. Therefore, a general pattern is at work here:

(20)   The extension of a sentence of the form "proper name + verb" is the truth value 1 if the extension of the proper name is an element of the extension of the verb; otherwise its extension is 0.

In a similar way we can 'calculate' the extensions of a simple clause whose subject is not a proper name but a definite description or any expression whose referent is an individual. As to descriptions, the following is an English example:

(21)   The president of the USA snores

The only thing our truth conditions require is this: Whoever should turn out to be the president (e.g., Barack Obama, at the time of writing), check if this individual, namely the extension of 'the president of the USA,' is among the snorers (at the time of writing). If so, the sentence is true; if not, the sentence is false. We thus have:

(22) $[\![$ the president of the USA snores $]\!]_s = 1$ if
$[\![$ the president of the USA $]\!]_s \in [\![$ snore $]\!]_s$, otherwise
$[\![$ the president of the USA snores $]\!]_s = 0$

In (22) we have used a common abbreviation for set-theoretic membership: "$X \in Y$" means that X (which may or may not itself be a set) is among the elements of the set Y. Generalizing from these examples, we may now state the following rule of extensional composition:

(23)   The extension of a sentence of the form "referential subject + verb phrase" is 1 if the extension of the referential subject is an element of the extension of the verb phrase; otherwise, its extension is 0.

Although (22) only involves a lexical verb, the rule (23) is general enough so as to also cover the case of complex predicates (like *show the Vatican to the president*), which also have sets of individuals as their extensions, as we have seen in the previous chapter. The term *verb phrase* (or "VP", for short) is meant to cover all sorts of predicates whether lexical or more complex.

In (23) the qualification *referential* is meant to apply (at least) to proper names and definite descriptions, but not to quantificational phrases such as *every child*, to which we will turn in due course.

Let us now look at sentences with transitive verbs and referential objects. As before, we would like to be able to calculate the extensions of sentences of the form "subject + verb + object":

(24)   *Paul liebt Mary*
        Paul loves Mary

We already know the extensions of the names, namely the individuals called *Paul* and *Mary*, and we also know the extension of *liebt*, which is a set of n-tuples, namely the set of ordered pairs $\langle x, y \rangle$, where x loves y. For (24) to be true, it must therefore be the case that the pair $\langle \text{Paul}, \text{Mary} \rangle$ is an element of the extension of *liebt*.

(25) $[\![\textit{Paul liebt Mary}]\!]_s = 1$ if and only if $\langle [\![\textit{Paul}]\!]_s, [\![\textit{Mary}]\!]_s \rangle \in [\![\textit{liebt}]\!]_s$

At this point, however, we encounter a difficulty: (25) requires us to consider $\langle [\![\textit{Paul}]\!]_s, [\![\textit{Mary}]\!]_s \rangle$, i.e., the pair consisting of the subject and the object. However, when looking at the syntactic structure of (25), it turns out that the subject and the object do not form a constituent. Rather, we learned that in order to derive (24) two transformations were needed, namely topicalization and verb-second movement. In order to simplify things a bit, let us assume that these movements are undone, so that we now have to interpret the still simplified structure in (26):

(26) | Paul | Mary liebt |

Equivalently, the structure for English would be (27):

(27)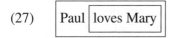

It is easy to see that the pair consisting of the subject and the object mentioned in (25) still does not form a constituent in either structure. Is that a problem?

Well, yes and no. "Yes," because the rule (25) does not conform to the Principle of Compositionality, and "no" because it's easy to find a way around the problem so as to still conform to the principle. Taking (18) seriously means that the extension of the sentence, its truth value, must be calculated from its *immediate* constituents. These are *Paul* and the embedded box containing the verb phrase. Accordingly, we first have to calculate the extension of the VP *loves Mary/Mary liebt* before we can determine whether the sentence is true or false. The main question therefore reduces to the problem of assigning extensions to the VPs in (26) (or (27)). The problem seems to be that our original encoding of transitive verbs as two-place relations does not fit with the syntax.

The good news is that it is quite easy to overcome this problem. The key to an understanding of the method of compositional interpretation is to look at the set-theoretic objects that correspond to the syntactic categories. As mentioned in the previous section, the VP has a set as its extension—but which set? Of course this must be the set of Mary's lovers. So Paul loves Mary if and only if Paul is an element of the set of Mary's lovers, which is the extension of the VP.

Now the only remaining problem is to determine that set on the basis of the extension of *love*. But again, this is not too difficult. We only have to look at those pairs in $[\![\textit{liebt}]\!]_s$ (or $[\![\textit{love}]\!]_s$) whose second component is Mary; these tuples represent that someone loves Mary. Now out of this set of pairs, we collect all the first components in a new set. This of course is the set of Mary's lovers, i.e., the extension of the VP.

What remains to be done is to state a general rule that interprets complex verb phrases along these lines:

(28)   The extension of a VP of the form "verb + referential term" (or "referential term + verb" for German) is the set of all individuals such that any pair consisting of that individual and the extension of the referential term is an element of the extension of the verb.

The abstractness of this rule may be unfamiliar, so let us demonstrate the method by way of a small example. First recall that by a *referential term* we mean something like a proper name or a definite description, e.g., the subject and object in *The pope loves Mary*. Now suppose the relation of loving—i.e., the extension of the English word *love* or rather the German stem form *lieb-* can be represented by the following set of ordered pairs:

(29) $[\![\text{love}]\!]_s = [\![\text{lieb-}]\!]_s = \{\langle a,b\rangle, \langle b,c\rangle, \langle b,d\rangle, \langle b,e\rangle, \langle d,d\rangle, \langle e,d\rangle\}$

Note that this extension is merely stipulated; any other two-place relation would do the same job. Technically speaking, what we did by stipulating a certain (arbitrary) extension like (29) is to assign a particular **interpretation** to the verb in question; any other set of pairs would have done the same job and would also be an interpretation. The idea is that instead of specifying the true extensions in the real world, which is often impossible because we lack knowledge about the real extensions, we simply choose a representation that acts as a proxy for that extension. Any such collection of extensions is called a **model** for a language. Thus, a model contains the extensions of all expressions of a language—stipulated extensions of course, as is the entire model. In our case, the very small model contains just the extension of the predicate *love* and the extensions of proper names.

Let us assume that in our model (29) *d* is the extension of *Dorothy*, and *a* is the extension of *Albert*. Is it true (in our model) that Albert loves Dorothy? Of course we could inspect (29) directly by looking for a pair $\langle a,d\rangle$. But this is not the point of the exercise. Rather, we want to proceed compositionally, following syntactic structure, at the same time testing (or understanding, as the case may be) our rules (23) and (28). So we first need to calculate the extension of the VP *love Dorothy*, and thus look at all pairs containing *d* as their second component (corresponding to the object), viz.:

(30) $\langle b,d\rangle, \langle d,d\rangle, \langle e,d\rangle$

Now each of *b*, *d*, and *e* in (30) loves Dorothy; collecting them in a set we obtain

(31) $\{b,d,e\}$

This is the set of Dorothy's lovers and thus the extension of the VP, according to (28), but also according to the considerations of the previous chapter, where we assumed that the extension of any "predicate" (VP) is the set of those individuals of which it can be truly said. Now, is Albert an element of the set

(31)? Obviously not. Therefore the sentence *Albert loves Dorothy* comes out as false (in this model) according to (23). Again, this is as it should be.

Now, after having seen an example, you should return to (28); the condition sounds rather complicated, but we hope that by having gone through an example, its content has become much clearer. Nonetheless, the wording of the rule still looks cumbersome. We can, however, simplify (28) enormously if we are allowed to use a little bit of set theory. Some bits of terminology and notation will be introduced in the following digression.

3. Sets and Set-Theoretic Notation

As already explained in the previous chapter (Section 3.2), a set is any collection of objects. There are a number of ways to characterize sets. According to one such method, we simply list the members of a set, as we already did in an earlier example:

(32)   {Madrid, Venice, Berlin, Tübingen, Rome ... }

The dots here say that this characterization is not quite complete.

Another way to characterize sets is by stating a property that is common to all and only the members of a set. This is a property that qualifies an individual as a member of that set. For this one normally uses a special notation:

(33)   a. $\{x : x$ is a city in Europe$\}$
        b. $\{x : x$ is a natural number that can be divided by 5$\}$

The letter "x" in (33) is a variable. As usual, variables function as a kind of place holder standing in for objects without specifying which. The colon following the variable x is read 'such that'. The whole expression now reads: "the set of those x such that x is ...". The use of these auxiliary symbols is highly conventionalized; as variables one normally uses letters from the end of the alphabet. Thus, instead of saying (34-a), we will write (34-b):

(34)   a.   Let A be the set of all cats.
        b. $A := \{x : x$ is a cat$\}$

Read (34-b) as "A is defined as the set of all x such that x is a cat". Hence $A = [\![$ cat $]\!]_s$. Note that $A = \{x : x \in A\}$; in fact, this equation holds for any set A.

When every member of a set A is also a member of a set B, we call A a
subset of B. This is formally written as $A \subseteq B$. The notation already suggests
that for $A \subseteq B$ to hold it is not necessary that the sets be different. If every
member of A is also a member of B this does not exclude the possibility of A
and B having exactly the same members.[3]

We also say that if A is a subset of B, then B is a **superset** of A. These
relations are often visualized by using so-called ☞ **Venn diagrams**, as shown
in (35):

(35)

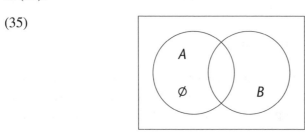

The symbol "$\emptyset$" in (35) indicates that the corresponding sector—in this case
the set of elements of A that are not in B—is empty, just as the defining
criterion of subsethood has it. However, the absence of a $\emptyset$-marking does not
mean that the corresponding sector of the diagram represents a non-empty
set; in this respect (non-annotated) areas of Venn diagrams are neutral.

The particular subset situation in (35) is frequently depicted in a somewhat
more suggestive way, viz., by leaving out the empty sector, as in (36):[4]

(36)

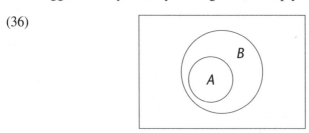

---

3   The notation $\subseteq$ is actually composed out of $\subset$ and $=$, which suggests that $\subset$ is the *proper*
subset relation, whereas $A \subseteq B$ means A is either a proper subset of B or equal to B.
According to the **extensionality axiom** of set theory, A and B are identical if and only if
$A \subseteq B$ and $B \subseteq A$.

4   Strictly speaking, such diagrams are no longer Venn diagrams, but are instead known as
Euler diagrams.

Note that, as in (35), the remaining sectors do not come with a bias as to representing empty sets or not.

Taken together, the subsets of a given set A again form a new set called its *power set* and written as $\wp(A)$. For example, if $A = \{a, b, c\}$ then:

(37) $\wp(A) = \{\emptyset, \{a\}, \{b\}, \{c\}, \{a, b\}, \{a, c\}, \{b, c\}, \{a, b, c\}\}$.

Note that in (37) we counted $\emptyset$ among the subsets of A. This is so because for any set B to be a subset of A, everything that is in B is also in A—or, in other words: *nothing is in B without being in A*. Now, the empty set B certainly satisfies this last condition; for nothing at all is in B, let alone anything that is also in A. Obviously, this argument does not depend on which set A is. Consequently, the empty set turns out to be a subset of every set!

In order to describe the composition of meanings in terms of set theory, we will introduce two simple yet important operations on sets. Both take pairs of sets as input and yield another set as output.

The first is **union** of sets. The union of A and B is defined as the set whose members are precisely the members of A together with the members of B. These are just the objects which are elements of A or B (or both). The notation for this is $\cup$:

(38) $A \cup B = \{x : x \in A \text{ or } x \in B\}$

Intersection of two sets is the second operation; it's written as $\cap$ and defined as:

(39) $A \cap B = \{x : x \in A \text{ and } x \in B\}$

Intersection produces a set whose members are just the members of both A and B. As an example, take the sets of socks and shirts. Since nothing is both a shirt and a sock the intersection is the empty set. As another example, consider the set of red entities and the set of socks. Then the intersection of these sets is the set of red socks.

Note that if A is a subset of B, then $A \cup B = B$ and $A \cap B = A$.

Both the union and the intersection of sets are often visualized by using Venn diagrams:

(40)   a.

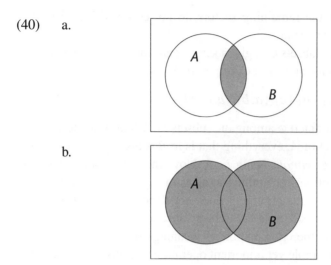

   b.

In each diagram, the shaded region represents the set that results from performing either operation on A and B. Diagram (40-a) is meant to represent intersection, (40-b) union.

It is important to realize that, while union and intersection are *operations* on sets, subsethood (or supersethood, for that matter) is not, because it does not output anything when applied to a pair of sets A and B. Rather, subsethood either holds or does not hold between A and B; it is a *relation* rather than an operation. The difference between set-theoretic relations and operations is analogous to that between arithmetical operations (like addition and multiplication), which output numbers, and arithmetical relations like < and ≠, which hold between pairs of numbers. The algebraic analogies between arithmetic and set theory, which go deeper than we can discuss here, show most clearly in the structure of power sets, which is also known as *Boolean Algebra*, from which derives the term *Boolean operations*, under which we will subsume set-theoretic intersection and union.[5]

Note also that the concept of a power set presupposes that sets may themselves have sets as their members. Here are some further examples of sets having sets as members:

---

5   The term derives from the English mathematician George Boole [1815–1864], one of the founding fathers of modern logic.

(41) $\{\{a,b\},\{b,c\}\}$
        $\{\{a,b,c\}\}$
        $\{a,b,c,\{d,e\}\}$
        $\{\{a\},\{a,b\},\{a,b,c\}\}$
        $\{\emptyset\}$
        $\{\emptyset,\{\emptyset\}\}^6$
        $\{\{a,b,c\},\{a,b,c,d\},\{a,b,c,e\},\{a,b,c,d,e\}\}$

Note that the numbers of elements in these sets are 2, 1, 4, 3, 1, 2, and 4, respectively. Note also that in the last example, all sets contained in this set are supersets of $\{a,b,c\}$. If our model contains exactly five individuals, namely a,b,c,d, and e, the last set described in (41) consists of *all* supersets of its smallest element, $\{a,b,c\}$. Using the notation introduced earlier, this set can also be described as shown in (42):

(42) $\{X:\{a,b,c\}\subseteq X\}$

The variable X does NOT range over individuals, rather, its values must be sets. The general convention is to use capital letters from the end of the alphabet as variables standing in for sets, whereas small letters are used as variables for individuals. Thus, $\{X:\{a,b,c\}\subseteq X\}$ is the set of all supersets of $\{a,b,c\}$.

To complete our discussion of Boolean operators, let us introduce another operation that will come in handy much later in this book (viz., in Chapter 9). It is called set-theoretic difference and is defined as follows:

(43) $A\backslash B=\{x:x\in A \text{ and } x\notin B\}$

For example, the set of bachelors is the difference $Y\backslash M$, where Y is the set of male adults and M is the set of married persons. (Well, maybe not—is the Pope a bachelor?)

A special constellation ensues if A is a subset of some larger set X. For example, let X be the set of human beings, and A the subset of X that contains all and only married people. Then $X\backslash A$ is the set of unmarried people. In a

---

6   This set has two members, namely the empty set and the set containing only the empty set. Such sets may look weird, but they do play an important role in mathematics. In fact, this very specimen happens to be the set-theoretic surrogate of the natural number 2, according to von Neumann's construction (cf. footnote 8, p. 74). Why, if it were not for sets themselves having sets as their members, the notion of a set would be totally boring and irrelevant for mathematics (and linguistics).

way, then, set-theoretic difference corresponds to the negative morpheme *un-* in natural language.

EXERCISE 13:

> Represent the set-theoretic difference between two sets by a Venn diagram in the style of (40).

4.   Referential Arguments and Functional Nouns

Given the set-theoretic notation introduced in the previous section, we may now reformulate our compositional rules for the extensions of referential subjects and objects in a more perspicuous way. To begin with, we may simplify (28) considerably, reformulating it as:

(44) $[\![\text{TV} + \text{referential term}]\!]_s := \{ x : \langle x, [\![\text{referential term}]\!]_s \rangle \in [\![\text{TV}]\!]_s \}$

The category TV makes it explicit that the verb is transitive so that its extension is a set of ordered pairs, as we have been assuming all along. Rule (44) presupposes that this verb precedes the object. As we have seen, the reverse is true in German, where a corresponding rule is required that looks as follows:

(45) $[\![\text{referential term} + \text{TV}]\!]_s := \{ x : \langle x, [\![\text{referential term}]\!]_s \rangle \in [\![\text{TV}]\!]_s \}$

Rules (44) and (45) only differ in the order of the constituents in the semantic input. In fact, it is often assumed that this order is immaterial for semantic considerations, so that (44) and (45) would be considered as equivalent. Although we will not follow this assumption here, we will briefly turn to some relevant considerations in Chapter 6, Section 3. In any case, when stating further rules for the combination of extensions, we will continue to use the same kind of notation as in (44) and (45).

According to (44) and (45), the result of combining the extension of a transitive verb with that of a proper name is a set of individuals (not a truth value!), i.e., something that could be the extension of an intransitive verb. The advantage of this procedure can be seen by looking at a ditransitive (three-place) verb that allows three proper names as arguments. A sentence like *(that) Paul introduces Bernadette to Geraldine* can be expressed in German as (46):

(46)   *(dass) Paul Bernadette Geraldine vorstellt*

Paul is the subject, Bernadette is the direct object, and Geraldine the indirect object. The syntactic structure is straightforward, namely (47)

(47)   dass | Paul | Bernadette | Geraldine vorstellt

If we try to account for the extension of (47) compositionally, the challenge is that this time the verb denotes a three-place relation (a set of 3-tuples) rather than a set of pairs. How can we design a semantics for this case?

The key to a simple solution lies in the fact that when combining a ditransitive verb like *vorstellt* with its first object *Geraldine* we reduce the valency of the verb by one and we then get a two-place relation, namely one that has the same kind of extension as a TV (transitive verb). This means that once we have a rule that applies to the innermost box, we get a "TV" and we can then go on with the rule we already have, namely with (45). That is, we only need one additional rule for DTVs (ditransitive verbs). The reader is asked to explicitly formulate this rule in an exercise.

In (44) and (45), the extension of the VP is constructed from a binary relation R—the extension of the transitive verb—and an individual y—the referent of the object, viz., the set of individuals x that stand in the relation R to y. This procedure is a special case of what logicians sometimes call a **plugging operation**, because it reduces the number of places of a relation (from 2 to 1, in this case) by "plugging in" one particular component (viz. the referent y). More precisely, there are two (binary) plugging operations, depending on whether y is plugged in as the first or the second component:[7]

(48)   If R is a binary relation (i.e., a set of ordered pairs) and y is any object, then $y * R$ and $R * y$ are defined as the following sets:
$$y * R = \{x : \langle y, x \rangle \in R\}$$
$$R * y = \{x : \langle x, y \rangle \in R\}$$

Using this notation, we may (but don't have to) restate the VP extensions in (44) and (45) as $[\![\text{TV}]\!]_s * [\![\text{referential term}]\!]_s$.

---

7   More generally, plugging operations are defined for any n-place relation R, object y, and number $i \le n$, by plugging in y at the i-th place of R. Since we will not make use of this general concept, we won't bother to define it here.

As a combination of extensions, plugging in is not only encountered in the domain of verbs but can also be seen at work in the realm of nouns. In Section 3.3 of the preceding chapter we took a quick look at functional nouns, whose extensions came out as sets of ordered pairs, i.e., similar to those of transitive verbs. And like a TV, a functional noun like *capital* combines with a referential noun phrase like *Italy*, the result being a complex noun—*capital of Italy*, in this case.[8] Now, what is the extension of this complex noun? Given that the extension of the noun *capital* is a function that can be applied to the referent of the name *Italy*, one may think that this is precisely what happens when the two get combined. In that case, however, the extension of the complex noun *capital of Italy* would be the value the function $[\![\text{capital}]\!]_s$ assigns to the country Italy. This would be odd, because $[\![\text{capital}]\!]_s$ (Italy) is Rome, i.e., an individual, not a set of individuals—as it ought to be given that *capital of Italy* is a (complex) noun. In fact, just like a non-functional lexical noun, it can be combined with the definite article to produce the noun phrase *the capital of Italy*, which does refer to Rome. So, just like any non-functional lexical noun, the complex noun *capital of Italy* ought to have a set as its extension, viz., the set of Italy's capitals. Of course, that set is a singleton; but then so are the extensions of *Pope*, *universe*, or, indeed, *desk* in many situations. Now, in order to construct this set from the extensions of *capital* and *Italy*, one may scan the ordered pairs in the former for those that have the latter as their first component and then collect the second components in a set. The general procedure is strongly reminiscent of (45):

(49) $[\![\text{functional noun + referential term}]\!]_s :=$
        $\{ y : \langle [\![\text{referential term}]\!]_s , y \rangle \in [\![\text{functional noun}]\!]_s \}$

In fact, apart from matters of ordering the constituents and components, the extensions of complex nouns are determined from those of their constituents in the same fashion as those of complex verb phrases are. So again, plugging in is at work and we could restate the extension of the complex noun in (49) as: $[\![\text{referential term}]\!]_s * [\![\text{functional noun}]\!]_s$. Note that this is the first of the two plugging operations defined in (48), whereas (44) and (45) made use of the second.

---

8   We assume that for semantic purposes, the complex noun *capital of Italy* consists of the functional noun *capital* and the proper name *Italy* only, the preposition *of* merely indicating the (syntactic) function of the latter. At the beginning of the next section we will see how such "semantically inactive" material may still be taken into account in the compositional interpretation process.

That this approach to functional nouns and their referential arguments is on the right track is confirmed when we turn to definite descriptions. Now, whatever the precise meaning of the definite article may be, it is obvious that the referent of any noun phrase of the form *the N* is itself an element of the extension of *N*:

(50) $[\![\text{the N}]\!]_s \in [\![N]\!]_s$

According to (50), the referent of *the Pope* is an element of the extension of *Pope*, i.e., the set of popes in the situation *s*; and similarly for any other definite description, as long as it has a referent at all. (Otherwise we continue to ignore it.) So by the same token, the referent of *the capital of Italy* is an element of $[\![\text{capital of Italy}]\!]_s$. Now, if the latter is determined according to (49), it contains those individuals *y* that are second components in a pair in the extension of *capital* whose first component is Italy. Since that extension is a function relating each country with its capital (in the current historical situation, say), there is just one such *y*, viz., Rome—the referent of *the capital of Italy*. Hence, (50) does come out right. In fact, whenever *F* is a functional noun and *N* is a referential noun phrase, the extension of *the F of N* will be the singleton containing the value that the extension of *F* assigns to the referent of *N*:

(51) $[\![\text{the F of N}]\!]_s = [\![F]\!]_s ([\![N]\!]_s)$

And this is as it should be: *the capital of Italy* refers to Rome, which is the value the extension of *capital* assigns to the referent of the name *Italy*. The verification of (51) is left to the reader as an exercise.

As a condition on the meaning of the definite article, (50) is as trivial as it is important. In particular, according to (50), the referent of a definite description *the N* will be the sole member of the extension of *N*, whenever the latter happens to be a singleton. Still, (50) is a far cry from a full-fledged semantic analysis of the definite article—it does not even account for its extension. According to one classic analysis, going back to Frege (1904), the extension of the definite article is a function whose domain consists exclusively of singletons:[9]

(52) $[\![\text{the}]\!]_s = \{ \langle X, y \rangle : X = \{ y \} \}$

---

9   For set-theoretic reasons, the variable *X* in (52) cannot stand for arbitrary sets but should be restricted to sets of individuals.

Equation (52) obviously satisfies condition (50), provided that the extension of a definite description is obtained by applying the function in (52) to that of the "head" noun:

(53) $[\![\text{the N}]\!]_s = [\![\text{the}]\!]_s ([\![\text{N}]\!]_s)$

However, the "Fregean" interpretation of definite descriptions according to (52) and (53) is plagued with a number of problems that we do not want to go into at this point. In fact, describing the meaning of *the* is a very delicate and controversial matter, to which we will return at the beginning of Chapter 9.

Equation (51) shows how a noun that refers to a function can be combined with the name of an argument so as to refer to the corresponding value. However, we have seen that the extensions are combined in a somewhat roundabout way, by first forming a set and then pulling out its sole member. However, there is a more direct alternative, the so-called **Saxon genitive**, as in *Paul's birthplace*. Here, it seems, we do have a natural language analogue of the mathematical notation '$f(x)$'. Again assuming (as in (49)) that the possessive marker is semantically inactive, we thus arrive at the following straightforward rule: [10]

(54) $[\![\text{referential term + functional noun}]\!]_s :=$
        $[\![\text{functional noun}]\!]_s ([\![\text{referential term}]\!]_s)$

Rule (54) can be used to resolve a puzzle briefly mentioned in Section 3.3 of the previous chapter: why do *Paul's birthplace* and *Paul's place* have different extensions—viz., Liverpool and Peasmarsh, respectively? After all, any place (of sufficient size) is somebody's birthplace and so any place would seem to be *a* birthplace. Part of the solution is, of course, that the extension of *birthplace* is a function, while that of *place* is a set of individuals; and only functional nouns enter the possessive construction in the way described in (54). Yet this cannot be the whole story: the fact that *place* is not functional does not make the Saxon genitive *Paul's place* ungrammatical or meaningless. Even though the precise mechanisms at work in the interpretation of this construction would lead us too far astray, let us briefly indicate the direction

---

10   The attentive reader will note that the respective syntactic inputs of (49) and (54) only differ in their order although the semantic outputs are not the same. This would cause a (mild) problem for a so-called type-driven approach to semantic combination as addressed in Chapter 6, Section 3. One way to get around it is to dissect the Saxon genitive into a definite article and a possessive rest, thus bringing the two possessive constructions into line after all ....

in which one analysis goes. According to it, any non-functional count noun N has an alternative functional reading the precise extension of which is a matter of context dependence (and thus outside the realm of this book). Roughly, the extension of this functional reading of N assigns to any individual x in its (context-dependent) domain the most obvious (prominent, salient) object in the extension of N that is suitably related to x, where the suitability of the relation again is a matter of context. In many cases in which the domain consists of persons, the pertinent relation is ownership, giving the impression that genitives have to do with possession. In the case at hand, though, the functional extension of *place* will typically assign to every person the place where (s)he lives. This is why the noun phrase *Paul's place* may be understood as referring to (a farmhouse in) an East Sussex village—and not the Merseyside city that the (context-independent) extension of *birthplace* assigns to Sir Paul.

EXERCISE 14:

> Try to formulate the semantic rule that takes a proper name plus a DTV so that the result is the denotation of a TV.

EXERCISE 15*:

> Show that (51) follows from (49), (52), and (53).
> (HINT: Recall that, quite generally, "$f(x)$" means "that z such that $\langle x, z \rangle \in f$".)

EXERCISE 16:

> Use the Fregean analysis (52) to derive the extension of *the capital of Italy* in a compositional way.

EXERCISE 17*:

> In the following sentences the nouns *surface* and *mother* are used as count nouns:
>
> (55)   I would have bought the table, but the surface was scratched
>
> (56)   The regulation applies to mothers only
>
> What are the extensions of these count noun readings (in a given situation)? Describe them in terms of the ordinary extensions of the two functional nouns. What is the general pattern?

5.   Analyzing Structural Ambiguities

In this section we will bring together a number of issues discussed on the fly in previous sections. Our principal aim is to provide explicit formal accounts of some of the structural ambiguities encountered in Chapter 3.

5.1.   *Logical Connectives:* and *and* or

In Section 1 we briefly discussed the semantics of *and* and *or*. These words are also called **sentential**, **propositional** or **logical connectives**. In grammar, sentential connectives belong to the category of "conjunctions" (other examples being *but, although, since, because*) whereas in logic the term "conjunction" is reserved for the word *and* and its truth table. The corresponding term for the word *or* is "disjunction". These terms may also be applied to coordinated sentences of the forms 'S_1 *and* S_2' and 'S_1 *or* S_2', respectively. Moreover, 'S_1 and S_2' are said to be "conjoined" in 'S_1 *and* S_2', or "conjuncts"; similarly, in 'S_1 *or* S_2', they are said to be "disjoined", or "disjuncts".

An implicit assumption behind our analysis of connectives in Section 1 was that it works regardless of which sentences are connected. In other words, the fact that the conjunction (or, for that matter, the disjunction) of two sentences 'S_1 and S_2' is true or false holds regardless of which sentences S_1 and S_2 are. The rule is completely general; in particular, it ignores all additional semantic relations that might hold between S_1 and S_2. As a case in point, consider (57):

(57)   a.   John visited Mary and Mary (she) became angry
        b.   Mary became angry and John visited Mary (her)

Both sentences are of the form 'S_1 *and* S_2'. An inspection of the pertinent truth table (p. 87) reveals that the order of the two conjuncts is immaterial; (57-a) and (57-b) have the same truth conditions:

(58)

$[\![S_1]\!]_s$	$[\![S_2]\!]_s$	$[\![S_1]\!]_s \wedge [\![S_2]\!]_s$	$[\![S_2]\!]_s \wedge [\![S_1]\!]_s$
1	1	1	1
1	0	0	0
0	1	0	0
0	0	0	0

Nonetheless it seems that the respective meanings of (57-a) and (57-b) differ. Sentence (57-a) seems to suggest that the visit temporally precedes Mary's becoming angry, and (57-b) has it the other way around. Moreover, it is plausible that there is a causal relation between the sentences, so that John's visiting Mary is the reason for her anger in (57-a). None of this is part of the truth conditions imposed by *and*, because these additional conclusions do not generalize but depend on the particular contents (or meanings) of S_1 and S_2 in relation to each other.

Propositional logic abstracts away from these additional aspects of meaning by treating all connectives as **truth functional**, which means that all that matters in (58) for determining the truth value of 'S_1 *and* S_2' is the respective truth values of S_1 and S_2. In other words, the connective *and* is treated as denoting a function called "$\wedge$" that takes two truth values as arguments, yielding a truth value as a result. The same holds for the connective *or*, which corresponds to the function represented as "$\vee$".

Many of the ambiguities we considered above were designed by analogy to potential ambiguities in propositional logic. For example, more complex combinations of $\wedge$ and $\vee$ are ambiguous, as we will see below. In syntax, the ambiguity reveals itself in different ways to analyzing the scope of logical the corresponding connectives, as exemplified in (59):

(59)   a. | S_1 *and* | S_2 *or* S_3 |
       | --- | --- |

       b. | | S_1 *and* S_2 | *or* S_3 |
       | --- | --- | --- |

In compositional semantics, the ambiguity shows up in different tables. In order to draw a truth table for a sentence containing S_1, S_2 and S_3, we will have to consider all possible combinations of truth values for them. It so happens that there are eight such combinations,[11] which means that our truth table needs eight different rows:

---

11   In fact, the number of cases (= truth value distribution) is always 2^n, where n is the number of clauses considered, i.e., three in the case at hand.

(60)

$[\![S_1]\!]_s$	$[\![S_2]\!]_s$	$[\![S_3]\!]_s$
1	1	1
1	1	0
1	0	1
1	0	0
0	1	1
0	1	0
0	0	1
0	0	0

In order to fill (60) in with the distribution of truth values of the constellations in (59), we proceed compositionally. That is, we first calculate the truth values of the innermost (non-compound) constituents. In the case of (59-b), we thus need to start with 'S_1 *and* S_2' and put in the values according to the truth table for conjunction: in each line, the value is determined by the corresponding argument truth values for S_1 and S_2 given in the leftmost columns. The result is (61):

(61)

$[\![S_1]\!]_s$	$[\![S_2]\!]_s$	$[\![S_3]\!]_s$	$[\![S_1]\!]_s \wedge [\![S_2]\!]_s$
1	1	1	1
1	1	0	1
1	0	1	0
1	0	0	0
0	1	1	0
0	1	0	0
0	0	1	0
0	0	0	0

The next step is to connect this result with S_3 by disjunction. Hence, in each case (= line), the disjunction table must be applied to the value obtained in (61) (as the left argument) and the truth value of S_3, which is given in the third row. We thus arrive at (62), where the rightmost column finally represents the truth value distribution of (59-b):

(62)

$[\![S_1]\!]_s$	$[\![S_2]\!]_s$	$[\![S_3]\!]_s$	$[\![S_1]\!]_s \wedge [\![S_2]\!]_s$	$([\![S_1]\!]_s \wedge [\![S_2]\!]_s) \vee [\![S_3]\!]_s$
1	1	1	1	1
1	1	0	1	1
1	0	1	0	1
1	0	0	0	0
0	1	1	0	1
0	1	0	0	0
0	0	1	0	1
0	0	0	0	0

The brackets in the top line of the rightmost column reflect the way in which the resulting truth value is computed; they have been added to avoid ambiguity. This kind of ambiguity can hardly be tolerated in formal languages used for mathematical reasoning, which is why all such languages incorporate a little bit of overt syntactic structure by using brackets (instead of boxes). Such languages are called **disambiguated**. In a disambiguated language, '$[\![S_1]\!]_s \wedge [\![S_2]\!]_s \vee [\![S_3]\!]_s$' is not a well-formed expression; rather we have to insert some brackets—just as in (62).

Let us now turn to the structure in (59-a), where 'S_2 *or* S_3' is a constituent. Again we proceed compositionally, starting with (60) and determining the value of 'S_2 *or* S_3' according to the disjunction table:

(63)

$[\![S_1]\!]_s$	$[\![S_2]\!]_s$	$[\![S_3]\!]_s$	$[\![S_2]\!]_s \vee [\![S_3]\!]_s$
1	1	1	1
1	1	0	1
1	0	1	1
1	0	0	0
0	1	1	1
0	1	0	1
0	0	1	1
0	0	0	0

Next we calculate the truth values of (59-a) case-wise, applying conjunction to $[\![S_1]\!]_s$ and the result in (63):

(64)

$[\![S_1]\!]_s$	$[\![S_2]\!]_s$	$[\![S_3]\!]_s$	$[\![S_2]\!]_s \vee [\![S_3]\!]_s$	$[\![S_1]\!]_s \wedge ([\![S_2]\!]_s \vee [\![S_3]\!]_s)$
1	1	1	1	1
1	1	0	1	1
1	0	1	1	1
1	0	0	0	0
0	1	1	1	0
0	1	0	1	0
0	0	1	1	0
0	0	0	0	0

We may now compare the results of our two calculations. This is done in (65):

(65)

$[\![S_1]\!]_s$	$[\![S_2]\!]_s$	$[\![S_3]\!]_s$	$[\![(59\text{-}a)]\!]_s$	$[\![(59\text{-}b)]\!]_s$
1	1	1	1	1
1	1	0	1	1
1	0	1	1	1
1	0	0	0	0
0	1	1	0	1
0	1	0	0	0
0	0	1	0	1
0	0	0	0	0

There is a difference in the fifth and in the seventh row; thus, the two structures may give rise to different truth values—and thus reflect different meanings.

We will return to propositional logic in Chapter 7, Section 4.1.

5.2. Nominal Modification

The complex VPs we have looked at so far consist of a verb and an object (or two). Of course, there are other types, in particular those that contain a predicate which selects an adjective instead of a nominal constituent:

(66)   Paul is dead

Under the assumption that the extension of *dead* is the set of dead individuals, (66) says that Paul is an element of that set. It seems, then, that the verb *be* in this context is semantically inactive.[12] This is exactly what (67) says:

(67) $[\![\,\text{is} + \text{adjective}\,]\!]_s := [\![\,\text{adjective}\,]\!]_s\ (= \{x : x \in [\![\,\text{adjective}\,]\!]_s\})$

Of course, (67) only covers the so-called *predicative* use of adjectives. The semantic function of *ad-nominal* adjectives, as in *the old man*, is different. In fact, we have already come across this constellation on p. 95, when we illustrated the set-theoretic operation of intersection intuitively by examples like *red socks*: given that both the noun *sock* and the adjective *red* have sets as their extensions—the set of socks and the set of red objects, respectively— the idea is that the combination of adjective and noun denotes the intersection $[\![\,\text{red}\,]\!]_s \cap [\![\,\text{sock}\,]\!]_s$. Assuming that the term **noun phrase** (**NP**) covers simple nouns like *sock* as well as complex expressions like *red sock*, we may thus formulate the underlying rule as in (68):

(68) $[\![\,\text{adjective} + \text{noun phrase}\,]\!]_s := [\![\,\text{adjective}\,]\!]_s \cap [\![\,\text{noun phrase}\,]\!]_s$

Note that the rule is **recursive** in that it allows us to apply it to ever more complex NPs, as in *holey red sock*, *old holey red sock*, *beautiful old holey red sock*, etc.

The above semantic combination of extensions by intersection also applies in other syntactic contexts, e.g., when NPs are modified by relative clauses or by prepositional clauses as in *woman from Berlin*. Let us discuss this more closely.

To begin with, it is natural to assimilate prepositions to transitive verbs by interpreting a preposition like *from* as having a binary relation as its extension, viz., the set of pairs $\langle a, b \rangle$, where (person or object) a is, i.e., comes or originates, from place b. Given this assimilation of (some) prepositions with transitive verbs, we may then employ the same semantic mechanisms to combine them with their complements, thereby arriving at:

(69) $[\![\,\text{from Berlin}\,]\!]_s$
= $[\![\,\text{from}\,]\!]_s * [\![\,\text{Berlin}\,]\!]_s$
= $\{x : \text{in } s, x \text{ is from Berlin}\}$

Then the extension of the modified NP can be obtained by intersection:

---

12   This is a simplification since the finite verb form carries temporal information, which is ignored throughout this text.

(70) $[\![\,\text{woman from Berlin}\,]\!]_s$
= $[\![\,\text{woman}\,]\!]_s \cap [\![\,\text{from Berlin}\,]\!]_s$
= $\{x : \text{in } s, x \text{ is a woman}\} \cap \{x : \text{in } s, x \text{ is from Berlin}\}$
= $\{x : \text{in } s, x \text{ is a woman and } x \text{ is from Berlin}\}$
= $\{x : \text{in } s, x \text{ is a woman from Berlin}\}$

As an illustration, let $\{a, b, c\}$ be the set of women and $\{a, x, y\}$ the persons from Berlin in s. Then accordng to (70), $[\![\,\text{woman from Berlin}\,]\!]_s = [\![\,\text{woman}\,]\!]_s$ $\cap [\![\,\text{from Berlin}\,]\!]_s = \{a, b, c\} \cap \{a, x, y\} = \{a\}$.

We leave it to the reader to analyze NPs like *smart woman from Berlin* by a combination of (68) and (70).

Before putting this formalization to work in the analysis of ambiguities, a short remark on modification by adjectives is in order. Above, we stated the rule for predicate adjectives on the assumption that the adjective denotes a set of things, and we also illustrated the recursiveness of the mechanism. Because $A \cap B \cap N = B \cap A \cap N$, this implies that the order of adjectives is immaterial. But this is not necessarily the case, since many adjectives simply do not denote sets. To see this, consider a small model, consisting of a row of circles and boxes: ○□□□○□○□. Now assume that some of the boxes and circles are painted black: ●□□■●□○□. Now pick out the rightmost black circle. This is the 5th element in the row. Next pick out the black rightmost circle. But now we are stuck. The rightmost circle is the 7th element in the row. However, this one is not black. But then, the description does not refer. The reason for this is that the adjective *rightmost* does not simply denote the set of "rightmost" things; rather it contains an implicit superlative that takes scope over the rest of the NP and thereby makes the order of adjectives relevant.

Other adjectives, even quite normal ones, pose similar difficulties. Consider the following sentences:[13]

(71)   a.   Jumbo is a small elephant
       b.   Jumbo is a big animal
       c.   Jumbo is big and small

Sentences (71-a) and (71-b) may both be true (in a given situation). Yet according to the above treatment of adjectives, they seem to jointly imply

---

13   A full compositional analysis of these sentences requires a treatment of indefinites and a more sophisticated interpretation of the verb *to be*, which will not be given until the next chapter.

(71-c), which sounds contradictory. The trouble is that adjectives like *small* and *big* require a standard of comparison—someone is small *for an elephant*, but not small *for an animal*—for which there seems to be no place if adjective extensions are merely sets.

There are additional problems with other adjectives like *alleged murderer* and *former president*, where it is obvious that the adjective on its own does refer to a set. Since we cannot go into the details here, the interested reader may consult Heim and Kratzer (1998), pp. 68ff. and pp. 300ff., for further discussion.

EXERCISE 18:

> Formulate the general rule behind (70). Show that the analysis of *smart woman from Berlin* involves a syntactic but not a semantic ambiguity.

5.3.   Calculating an Attachment Ambiguity

Ambiguous constellations of Boolean operations also show up below the sentence level, as in the following attachment ambiguity:

(72)   the women and the children from Berlin

In Chapter 3 ambiguities of this sort were analyzed as

(73)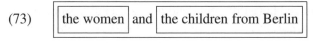

vs.

(74)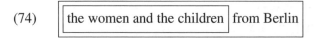

The ambiguity is due to *from Berlin* having different scope. In (73), *from Berlin* modifies *the children*, whereas in (74) the modified phrase is *the women and the children*.

Turning to semantics, let us first analyze (74). The crucial task is to supply an extension for the coordinated descriptions *the women and the children*. At this point it will help to recall the semantic operation called set union defined in (38) on page 95. So far, this operation has not played any role in our analyses. But now, it will come in handy. Intuitively, *the women and the children* form a set that contains all of the children plus all of the women.

As the former is $\{x : x$ is a child$\}$ and the latter is $\{x : x$ is a woman $\}$, we accordingly have:

(75) $[\![$ the women and the children $]\!]_s$
   $=$ $\{x : x$ is a woman$\} \cup \{x : x$ is a child$\}$
   $=$ $\{x : x$ is a woman or x is a child$\}$

If this is correct, it seems that by compositional reasoning, the following equivalences can be derived from the first equality in (75):

(76) $[\![$ the women $]\!]_s = [\![$ woman $]\!]_s = \{x : x$ is a woman $\}$, and
        $[\![$ the children $]\!]_s = [\![$ child $]\!]_s = \{x : x$ is a child$\}$

This equivalence of a plural description with a singular NP is somewhat puzzling; we will return to the point at the end of the next section.

Let us now account for the ambiguity. Semantically, *and* is represented as $\cup$ and modification via attachment of a prepositional phrase is represented as $\cap$.[14] We can therefore symbolize the ambiguity schematically as:

(77)   a. $\boxed{\boxed{A \cup B} \cap C}$ (= high attachment of C = (74))

        b. $\boxed{A \cup \boxed{B \cap C}}$ (= low attachment of C = (73))

In order to show that the ambiguity is "real" we may construct a model such that (77-a) and (77-b) indeed have different denotations. Let us assume therefore that

(78) $A = [\![$ child $]\!]_s = \{a, b, c\}$
        $B = [\![$ woman $]\!]_s = \{x, y, z\}$
        $C = [\![$ from Berlin $]\!]_s = \{a, x, y, d, e\}$
        a.   High attachment:
             $A \cup B = \{a, b, c, x, y, z\}$
             $\{a, b, c, x, y, z\} \cap C = \{a, b, c, x, y, z\} \cap \{a, x, y, d, e\} = \{a, x, y\}$
        b.   Low attachment:
             $B \cap C = \{x, y\}$
             $A \cup \{x, y\} = \{a, b, c\} \cup \{x, y\} = \{a, b, c, x, y\}$

---

14   Note that *and* as set-theoretic union must be restricted so as to not apply to sentences: as we will see later (cf. Section 4.1 of Chapter 7) the conjunction of sentences corresponds to intersection rather than union.

As $\{a, b, c, x, y\} \neq \{a, x, y\}$ we have shown that the construction is really ambiguous.

5.4.   Plural NPs*

Let us now come back to the surprising equations in (76). Due to the semantic equivalence of *child* with *the children* it would seem that the the definite article and the plural morphology are semantically vacuous. But this is extremely implausible, given the clear semantic difference between:

(79)   a.   John cares for children
   b.   John cares for the children
   c.   John cares for the child

Sentence (79-a) shows that the lack of an article implies that it is children in general that John cares for. This is called the generic interpretation of *children*; let us ignore this reading. We still need to account for the difference between (79-b) and (79-c), which could not be explained if the plural did not contribute to the meaning of the description *the children*. On the other hand, the equations seem to indicate that the semantic contribution of pluralization and that of the article cancel each other out. To see this, we must briefly go into the semantics of plural NPs.

   Without much justification, we will follow the literature on plural semantics (cf. Schwarzschild (1996)) in assuming that all plural NPs denote sets of sets. For instance, the denotation of *men* is the set of all non-empty sets of men. This is the set of all non-empty subsets of the extension of *man*. In the same way, the plural of *child* denotes all (non-empty) sets of children, etc.

   You might wonder why the denotation of a plural noun is allowed to contain elements that are not at all "plural", since it also contains sets with only one element. The reason for this can be derived by inspecting the following alternative dialogues:

(80)   Do you have children?
   a.   Yes, I have a daughter
   b.   No, I don't have children

The answer (80-a) is affirmative, although I might have only one child. But if *children* always referred to two or more of them, then I would be entitled to reply (80-b) in the case that I only have one child. As this is absurd, it makes

more sense to include the one-child case in the definition of *children*. On the
other hand, in plain sentences like (81) (uttered out of the blue),

(81)   I have children

we *do* understand *children* as referring to more than one child. The choice
between singular and plural phrases must therefore be regulated by considerations that belong to pragmatics.

Plural denoting sets can be quite large and not easy to handle. Therefore
we have done a little bit of cheating: in the previous section we ignored the
plural morphology entirely and tried to keep to the denotations we already
had at hand. But now that we have the more complicated entities, we can
describe the semantic effect of the definite article *the* when combined with
a plural noun or NP. Its function is to pick out the largest set of the NP-
extension.[15] For example, assume that $[\![\text{child}]\!]_s = \{a, b, c\}$; then $[\![\text{children}]\!]_s$
$= \{\{a\}, \{b\}, \{c\}, \{a, b\}, \{b, c\}, \{a, c\}, \{a, b, c\}\}$, and $[\![\text{the children}]\!]_s = \{a, b, c\} =$
$[\![\text{child}]\!]_s$. This way, the effect of pluralization and the semantics of the article
neutralize each other.

Having entered the realm of plural descriptions like *the children*, we would
now have to adjust the entire remainder of the grammar in order to integrate
the new objects in combination with predicates, i.e., in sentences like *the children hide behind the trees*. This would require a more complicated semantics
for the verb *hide*, namely its "pluralization", and also for the two-place relation *behind*. This could be done in a very systematic way similar to the
technique of type shifting discussed in Section 2 of the next chapter, but we
refrain from going into any detail here.

---

15   Hence the meaning of the plural definite article does not seem to have much in common
with its singular counterpart, briefly discussed in Section 4 above. Somewhat surprisingly, though, as the American philosopher Richard Sharvy [1942–1988] pointed out
(cf. Sharvy (1980)), the two may be seen as instances of the same maximization operation.

Chapter 6
Quantifiers

1. Determiners and Quantifiers

The grammatical subjects of the following sentences are neither proper names nor descriptions nor any other kinds of referential expressions:

(1)   a.   Every student snored
        b.   A woman snored
        c.   No fly snored

In logic and philosophy of language such expressions are known as quantifying expressions, or **quantifiers** for short, and so are the words *every, a,* and *no* they contain. Though we will also use these terms here, when it comes to stating semantic rules, we prefer the standard syntactic terminology according to which the function words *every, a,* and *no* are called **determiners**, and complex expressions such as *every/a/no man* are **determiner phrases**, or **DPs**.

Since there is no relevant difference here between German and English, we will continue our discussion with reference to English only. In order to exclude unwanted (generic) readings (as for *a woman snores*), we switched to the past tense of the verb in the examples above, but this detail is otherwise immaterial and will also be ignored in what follows, continuing with the present tense in many of the sample sentences discussed below.

The problem with quantifying expressions already mentioned earlier is that they do not refer to anything and that, therefore, the subjects in (1) do not seem to have extensions. If so, how can we determine whether the sentences are true or false, given that these extensions (the truth values) are to be calculated by reference to the extensions of the subject-DP and the verb? Fortunately, Frege found a way to systematically relate quantifying expressions to certain abstract objects that may serve as their extensions. To see how this goes, we will continue to assume that the extensions of nouns and verbs are sets. Thus, for instance, whereas in a normal nighttime situation the predicate *snore* might contain a lot of individuals, during the daytime—and in particular during a lecture—the extension should rather be the empty set. And even if we don't know the extension precisely, we can say *under what conditions* these sentences are true and false. We know that the extension of the entire clause is a truth value, so the question is this: given the two sets corresponding to the predicate *snore* and the predicate *student*, what is the compositional role of *every* in determining the truth value of the sentence *Every student snores*? The question would be similar for sentences (1-b) and (1-c).

The trick here is to think about what must be the case for the sentences to become true *in terms of a comparison between the extensions of the two predicates*. Conceived of this way, we may say that

(2)   *Every student snores* is true if and only if the set of snoring individuals contains the set of students.

Clearly, the relevant kind of containment is the **subset** relation. In fact, we can formulate the truth conditions of all three sentences in (1) in terms of set-theoretic relations:

(3)   a.   (1-a) is true if and only if the extension of *student* is contained in the extension of *snore*; that is: the set of students is a **subset** of the set of snoring individuals. —
         Formally: $[\![\,\text{student}\,]\!]_s \subseteq [\![\,\text{snore}\,]\!]_s$

        b.   (1-b) is true if and only if the extension of *woman* and the extension of *snore* have a common element; that is: the set of women and the set of snoring individuals **overlap**. —
         Formally: $[\![\,\text{woman}\,]\!]_s \cap [\![\,\text{snore}\,]\!]_s \neq \emptyset$

        c.   (1-c) is true if and only if the extension of *fly* and the extension of *snore* have no common element; that is: the set of flies and the set of snoring individuals are **disjoint**. —
         Formally: $[\![\,\text{fly}\,]\!]_s \cap [\![\,\text{snore}\,]\!]_s = \emptyset$

At this point readers are strongly advised to carefully scrutinize these conditions and convince themselves that they are intuitively correct.

Having stated (3), it seems that the analysis of (1) is complete. However, this is not quite right. First observe that in (3) we are talking about particular sentences. What we want to formulate, however, is a general rule. So what we want so say is something like:

(4)   a. $[\![\,\text{every} + \text{Noun} + \text{VP}\,]\!]_s = 1$ if and only if $[\![\,\text{Noun}\,]\!]_s \subseteq [\![\,\text{VP}\,]\!]_s$
        b. $[\![\,\text{a} + \text{Noun} + \text{VP}\,]\!]_s = 1$ if and only if $[\![\,\text{Noun}\,]\!]_s \cap [\![\,\text{VP}\,]\!]_s \neq \emptyset$
        c. $[\![\,\text{no} + \text{Noun} + \text{VP}\,]\!]_s = 1$ if and only if $[\![\,\text{Noun}\,]\!]_s \cap [\![\,\text{VP}\,]\!]_s = \emptyset$

So far, so good. But although we've made some progress, the rules in (4) still do not conform to the Principle of Compositionality.

There are in fact two problems to be solved. The first is that we have not yet defined an extension for the determiners *every*, *a*, and *no* themselves. That is, we still need to say what $[\![\text{every}]\!]_s$, $[\![\text{a}]\!]_s$, and $[\![\text{no}]\!]_s$ are. The second problem is to harmonize the observations in (4) with syntactic structure.

Turning to the first problem, we may observe that the quantifiers in (4) serve to compare the extensions of two sets and thereby describe a relation between them: one might say that *every* denotes the subset relation, whereas *no* and *a* correspond to the relations of overlap and disjointness, respectively. Thus, we can indeed assign some sort of extension to each of the determiners in (1), namely a particular relation between sets:

(5) $\quad [\![\text{every}]\!]_s := \{\langle X, Y \rangle : X \subseteq Y\}$
$\quad\ \ [\![\text{a}]\!]_s := \{\langle X, Y \rangle : X \cap Y \neq \emptyset\}$
$\quad\ \ [\![\text{no}]\!]_s := \{\langle X, Y \rangle : X \cap Y = \emptyset\}$

A closer look at the above list reveals that the extensions of determiners are relations of a rather special kind. For one thing, they do not really seem to depend on the situation to which they are applied. True, different situations may contain different individuals, and so maybe also different sets of individuals; but the way these sets are related by the determiner extensions remains stable from one situation to the other.

While this may not be anything to write home about (in fact, the same is true of proper names), the fact that all three determiner extensions relate sets according to general set-theoretic criteria—and not, say, by the properties of the individuals they contain—is somewhat more remarkable: the decision as to whether or not a given pair of sets N and V (thought of as noun and verb extensions, respectively) is in the extension of a given determiner always boils down to **counting** elements in certain set-theoretic combinations of N and V. More specifically, and as the interested reader may verify, $\langle N, V \rangle$ is in the extension of *every* if the number of individuals that are in N but not in V is 0; the pair $\langle N, V \rangle$ is in the extension of *a* if the number of individuals in $N \cap V$ is larger than 0; and it is in the extension of *no* if the number of individuals in $N \cap V$ is 0.

As it turns out, this is not a peculiarity of the above three words; the extensions of determiners in general correspond to arithmetical relations in this sense. In logical terminology, this means that they are (permutation-) **invari-**

ant or **logical constants**, a feature they share with the Boolean connectives, but one that we cannot define here. Apart from this, determiner extensions share an additional property known as **conservativity**: whenever a pair $\langle N, V \rangle$ is in the extension of a determiner, then so is the pair $\langle N, N \cap V \rangle$. Roughly, this means that sentences of the forms "Determiner Noun Verb" and "Determiner Noun *is a* Noun *and* Verb" boil down to the same thing. Readers are invited to check this on their own, since we will not go into the matter any further.[1]

Having settled this, we can now state the semantic analysis of the sentences in (1) as in (6):

(6) $\langle [\![\text{student}]\!]_s, [\![\text{snore}]\!]_s \rangle \in [\![\text{every}]\!]_s$
        $\langle [\![\text{woman}]\!]_s, [\![\text{snore}]\!]_s \rangle \in [\![\text{a}]\!]_s$
        $\langle [\![\text{fly}]\!]_s, [\![\text{snore}]\!]_s \rangle \in [\![\text{no}]\!]_s$

However, there is a certain mismatch now between these truth conditions and the—rather straightforward—syntactic structuring, viz.:

(7) | every student | snores |

It is obvious that the ordered pairs in (6) do not correspond to any constituents in the syntactic analysis. Rather, together with the relation itself, the first components correspond to the subject, which then forms the sentence with what corresponds to the second component, i.e., the VP. The attentive reader will have noted that we have encountered this kind of constellation before, namely when combining transitive verbs with their objects, or functional nouns with their possessors. Here, as before, the solution is to supply the components incrementally by **plugging** them in. Let us repeat (the relevant case of) the general procedure from the previous chapter:

(8)   If R is a binary relation (i.e., a set of ordered pairs) and y is any object, then $y * R$ is defined as the following set:
        $y * R = \{x : \langle y, x \rangle \in R\}$

---

1   The universality of the properties just mentioned was first conjectured in an influential paper co-authored by the American mathematician Jon Barwise [1942–2000] and the British linguist Robin Cooper. Published in 1981, it became the starting point of the interdisciplinary field of **generalized quantifier theory**, which brings together researchers from linguistic semantics and philosophical and mathematical logic. The literature on the subject is vast; see, for example, Keenan and Westerståhl (1997) for a survey.

As it turns out, this form of plugging is exactly what we need here too, with the determiner extension playing the role of the relation R and the extension of the noun supplying the first component y. We thus arrive at the following compositional analysis of quantifying determiner phrases (to mix syntactic and semantic nomenclature):

(9) $\llbracket D + \text{Noun} \rrbracket_s = \llbracket \text{Noun} \rrbracket_s * \llbracket D \rrbracket_s$
    $= \{ X : \langle \llbracket \text{Noun} \rrbracket_s, X \rangle \in \llbracket D \rrbracket_s \}$

It should be noted that (9) not only applies to lexical nouns but also covers complex expressions like *every tall man, a former student, no brother of mine*, etc.

Two details are noteworthy about (9) in relation to the general pattern (8). The first, rather superficial difference concerns notation: in describing the resulting set, we have chosen a different variable (viz. "X"). This is, of course, because the elements of that set are themselves sets; in any case this switch of notation from (8) to (9) should not bother the reader, for the names of variables are arbitrary anyway. And secondly, the fact that the objects related by the determiner extension $\llbracket D \rrbracket_s$ are sets of individuals is quite in accordance with (8), where no restriction as to the nature of the objects related by R is imposed; but it is different from the application of (8) to the extensions of VPs and nouns, where only relations between individuals were at stake.

With the help of (9), then, we have finally managed to find extensions for the quantifying subjects of (1):

(10)   a. $\llbracket \text{every} + \text{Noun} \rrbracket_s = \{ X : \langle \llbracket \text{Noun} \rrbracket_s, X \rangle \in \llbracket \text{every} \rrbracket_s \}$
    b. $\llbracket a + \text{Noun} \rrbracket_s = \{ X : \langle \llbracket \text{Noun} \rrbracket_s, X \rangle \in \llbracket a \rrbracket_s \}$
    c. $\llbracket \text{no} + \text{Noun} \rrbracket_s = \{ X : \langle \llbracket \text{Noun} \rrbracket_s, X \rangle \in \llbracket \text{no} \rrbracket_s \}$

Obviously, unlike the individuals referential nouns refer to, these extensions are highly abstract objects, viz., sets of sets of individuals. To see what precisely these sets are, one may call in the determiner extensions given in (5) and reformulate the equations in (10) as follows:

(11)   a. $[\![\, \text{every} + \text{Noun} \,]\!]_s = \{X : [\![\, \text{Noun} \,]\!]_s \subseteq X\}$
      b. $[\![\, \text{a} + \text{Noun} \,]\!]_s = \{X : [\![\, \text{Noun} \,]\!]_s \cap X \neq \varnothing\}$
      c. $[\![\, \text{no} + \text{Noun} \,]\!]_s = \{X : [\![\, \text{Noun} \,]\!]_s \cap X = \varnothing\}$

From (11-a) we can see that the extension of *every man* contains all supersets of the extension of *man*.

Equation (11-b) implies that the extension of *a man* contains all sets that overlap with the extension of *man*; in other words, it is the set of all sets (of individuals) that contain at least one man. And according to (11-c), the extension of *no man* contains all sets that are disjoint from the extension of *man*; in other words, it is the set of all man-less sets of individuals. Given that extensions in general are there to explain reference and that none of these DPs refer to anything in particular, one may not have expected them to have extensions in the first place; and it is certainly a surprise to discover what their extensions are, viz., abstract set-theoretic constructions. However, the precise choice of these extensions is far from arbitrary; rather, it is motivated by the fact that on the basis of these extensions, the contribution of quantifying DPs to the truth values of the sentences in which they occur can be accounted for in a compositional way. In fact, we are nearly there.

So far we have reached our first goal and found an extension for the immediate constituents of sentences like (1) above. Now this extension still needs to be combined with the verb phrase. This, however, is not a big deal. In fact, again the situation is quite similar to that of transitive verbs: once the referent of the object has been plugged in, the resulting extension is a set containing the referents of subjects that make the sentence come out true; thus, for example, John will be in the extension of the VP *loves Mary* if, and only if, *John loves Mary* is true. Quite analogously now, once the extension of the noun has been plugged into that of the determiner, the resulting extension will consist of the extensions of precisely those VPs that form a true sentence together with the quantifying subject. Thus, for instance, the extension of the VP *snores* will end up in the extension of the quantifier *every man* just in the case that the sentence *Every man snores* happens to be true (in a given situation). We thus arrive at the following general compositional rule:

(12) $[\![\, \text{DP} + \text{VP} \,]\!]_s = 1$ if and only if $[\![\, \text{VP} \,]\!]_s \in [\![\, \text{DP} \,]\!]_s$

With (12) we are finally in a position to give a fully compositional analysis of sentences like (1). Let us illustrate this with one, leaving the other two to the reader, for practice. As usual in this kind of exposition, we proceed by a sequence of equivalences that unravel the truth conditions of the sentence under scrutiny. The equivalences are expressed by "iff", which is the common abbreviation for "if and only if". The justification for the individual steps will be given immediately afterwards:

(13) $[\![\text{no fly snored}]\!]_s = 1$
iff $[\![\text{snored}]\!]_s \in [\![\text{no fly}]\!]_s$
iff $[\![\text{snored}]\!]_s \in [\![\text{fly}]\!]_s * [\![\text{no}]\!]_s$
iff $\{ x : x \text{ snored in } s \} \in \{ x : x \text{ is a fly in } s \} * \{ \langle X, Y \rangle : X \cap Y = \emptyset \}$
iff $\{ x : x \text{ snored in } s \} \in \{ Y : \{ x : x \text{ is a fly in } s \} \cap Y = \emptyset \}$
iff $\{ x : x \text{ is a fly in } s \} \cap \{ x : x \text{ snored in } s \} = \emptyset$

Obviously, the last line expresses the intuitively correct conditions under which (1-c) is true, viz., that the set of flies does not overlap the set of (former) snorers; so only the chain of equivalences remains to be justified. The very first step is a direct application of our compositional rule (12) of quantifying subjects. The next one applies the rule (9) that plugs the noun extension into that of the determiner. In the third step we have simultaneously specified the extensions of the three lexical expressions, thereby making use of the analysis of the determiner *no* given in (5). Next, the ∗-notation is undone, applying the definition of (the pertinent case of) plugging repeated in (8) above. The final step reduces the penultimate line by a set-theoretic principle that undoes the notation introduced at the beginning of Section 3 of the previous chapter: for an object a to be a member of a set $\{ z : \ldots z \ldots \}$ means satisfying the condition $\ldots a \ldots$. Readers are urged to check each of these justifications in detail (and taking their time) and then write up the analogous chains of equivalences for the other two sentences in (1).

Before closing this section, let us briefly discuss the denotation of German *nichts* (*nothing*). This is a DP that can be paraphrased as *no object*. So the extension of *nichts* is:

(14) $[\![\textit{nichts}]\!]_s = \{ X : [\![\text{object}]\!]_s \cap X = \emptyset \}$

But now, if the set of entities comprises all the things there are, then

(15) $[\![\text{object}]\!]_s \cap X = X$

Therefore, the only X that gives the empty set as a result is the empty set itself, so that we have: [2]

(16) $[\![\,nichts\,]\!]_s = \{\emptyset\}$

It thus follows that the extension of *nichts* is not nothing (*nichts*), but a set with an element that turns out to be the empty set.

EXERCISE 19:

What is the extension of the DP *etwas* (= something)?

2.   Names as Quantifiers

Compositional and adequate though it may be, our account of quantifying DPs leads to problems in the architecture of semantic theory. Since these kinds of problems come up frequently in semantics, we take the opportunity to present and discuss them, along with a well-known and general solution strategy known as **type shifting**. To see what is at stake, let us recall how the extensions of subjects and predicates (VPs) are to be composed to arrive at the truth values of the sentences they form. You probably have noticed that we actually need to stipulate two different rules here: one that applies to names and descriptions, to the effect that, for the sentence to be true, $[\![\,\text{subject}\,]\!]_s$ must be an element of $[\![\,\text{predicate}\,]\!]_s$ (cf. Chapter 5, (23)); and another one that applies to quantifying DPs and according to which $[\![\,\text{predicate}\,]\!]_s$ must be an element of $[\![\,\text{quantifying subject}\,]\!]_s$ (cf. (12) above). Let us repeat the two rules in a slightly different formulation that highlights the difference between the two:

(17)   a.   If N is a referential noun phrase and V is a verb phrase, then:
$[\![\,N+V\,]\!]_s = 1$ iff $[\![\,N\,]\!]_s \in [\![\,V\,]\!]_s$; and
$[\![\,N+V\,]\!]_s = 0$ iff $[\![\,N\,]\!]_s \notin [\![\,V\,]\!]_s$.
    b.   If Q is a quantifying phrase and V is a verb phrase, then:
$[\![\,Q+V\,]\!]_s = 1$ iff $[\![\,V\,]\!]_s \in [\![\,Q\,]\!]_s$; and
$[\![\,Q+V\,]\!]_s = 0$ iff $[\![\,V\,]\!]_s \notin [\![\,Q\,]\!]_s$.

---

[2]   It may be noted in passing that according to (16), *nichts* comes out as having the same extension as any true sentence; of course, this is purely coincidental.

This duality may appear artificial, and one may justly wonder whether it is really necessary. Couldn't we do with one "subject-predicate" rule, despite the two distinct modes of semantic composition?

In fact, there are popular strategies of unifying the two rules in (17). One is to treat proper names and descriptions like quantifying DPs, instead of simply identifying their extensions with their referents. So their extensions would have to come out as sets (of sets of individuals). Which sets could do the job? Following the strategy of analysis pursued in the previous section, the extension of a name would have to consist of the extensions X of all those (possible) VPs that can form a true sentence with that name in subject position. Thus, the extension of *snore* is in the extension of *Paul* (as a quantifier) just in the case that it counts Paul (the bearer of the name *Paul*) among its elements. In general, then, the extension of *Paul* is the set of sets that contain Paul as an element. To the extent that properties correspond to the sets of their bearers, one may think of this extension as the set of all the properties Paul has: that Paul snores thus amounts to saying that the extension of *snore* is among Paul's properties, i.e., an element of the set of all his properties.

Once proper names have been recast as DPs, we can eliminate the rule for names. This solves our problem, because there is only one rule now for the combination of subjects with predicates. Assume that the extension of Paul is defined as in (18), and let us for a change switch to German to avoid the appearance of circularity in the truth condition:

(18) $[\![Paul]\!]_s = \{X : \text{Paul} \in X\}$

The following calculation shows that we get the correct truth conditions:

(19) $[\![Paul\ schnarcht]\!]_s$ is true
iff $[\![schnarcht]\!]_s \in [\![Paul]\!]_s$ (by application of rule (17-b))
iff $[\![schnarcht]\!]_s \in \{X : \text{Paul} \in X\}$ (by (19))
iff $\text{Paul} \in [\![schnarcht]\!]_s$ (by set theory)
iff $\text{Paul} \in \{y : \text{in } s, y \text{ is snoring}\}$ (by the meaning of *schnarcht*)
iff   Paul is snoring in s (by set theory again)

We still need to account for definite descriptions. These, like names, denote things in the universe, not sets. But unlike names, we do not have a finite list of definite descriptions in the lexicon. We cannot assume, as we did in (19), that there is a complicated lexical entry for each description. Rather, we presuppose that there are semantic rules that allow us to pick out an individual that satisfies the description. Given that individual, we now have to apply a rule that shifts the extension of the description (an individual) to the extension of a DP (a set of sets). Such rules that replace the extension of an expression with a more complex one are called **type shifting** rules, because they change the set-theoretic type of the extension without affecting its substance.[3] In the case at hand, the pertinent type shift is known as **Montague Lifting** and can be stated as in (20): [4]

(20) $\text{LIFT}(a) := \{X : a \in X\}$

To illustrate, assume that the extension of a proper name is an individual and that its syntactic category is PN (= proper noun). Let us encode the syntactic category of a meaning as a superscript on the double brackets. Then

(21) $[\![Paul]\!]_s^{PN} = \text{Paul}.$

Application of type shifting now yields the quantifier extension of *Paul*, as defined in (18):

(22) $[\![Paul]\!]_s^{DP} := \text{LIFT}([\![Paul]\!]_s^{PN})$
$= \quad \{X : [\![Paul]\!]_s^{PN} \in X\}$
$= \quad \{X : \text{Paul} \in X\}$

In a similar way, we may now convert the extension of a definite description, say *the Pope*, into the more complicated extension of a DP: [5]

(23) $\text{LIFT}([\![der\ Papst]\!]_s)$
$= \quad \{X : [\![der\ Papst]\!]_s \in X\}$
$= \quad \{X : \text{the pope in } s \in X\}$
$= \quad [\![der\ Papst]\!]_s^{DP}$

Given this modification, we now have a unique rule (24) applying to all kinds of subject-predicate combinations alike:

(24) $[\![DP + VP]\!]_s = 1$ iff $[\![VP]\!]_s \in [\![DP]\!]_s$; and
$[\![DP + VP]\!]_s = 0$ iff $[\![VP]\!]_s \notin [\![DP]\!]_s$

---

3   The pertinent notion of a *type* will be made more precise in Section 3.
4   The term alludes to Richard Montague, who introduced (18) and (20), writing LIFT(*a*) as '*a**'.
5   In case the reader wonders what (23) says about pope-less situations: we will return to this question in Chapter 9.

In fact, (24) employs the same combination of extensions as (17-b). So by **type shifting** the simple extension of an individual to the more complicated one of a quantifier we have found an an elegant way to unify rules of semantic composition. Instead of distinguishing the two subject-predicate rules as in (17), we may now do with (24) alone.

In the next section, we will briefly explore an alternative to type shifting, one that leaves the extensions of referential DPs unscathed.

3. Type-Driven Interpretation

The unified treatment of referential and quantifying subjects comes with a price: extensions, which are meant to determine reference, only do so in a rather roundabout way. After all, proper names merely refer to their bearers, whereas their type-shifted extensions encode the latter by set-theoretic means. The same point applies to definite descriptions, personal pronouns, and other referential expressions once they undergo type shifting. Hence while type shifting decreases the number of rules at the syntax/semantics interface, it tends to create complex and artificial extensions. The trade-off between the complexity of extensions and the number of rules can be evaded by having the semantic rule itself decide which combination of extensions is appropriate:

(25)   If VP is a verb phrase and α is the subject of the sentence "$\alpha + $ VP",
        then: $[\![\alpha + \mathrm{VP}]\!]_s = 1$ iff

$$\text{EITHER (a)} \quad [\![\alpha]\!]_s \in [\![\mathrm{VP}]\!]_s$$
$$\text{OR} \quad\ \ \text{(b)} \quad [\![\mathrm{VP}]\!]_s \in [\![\alpha]\!]_s$$

        otherwise, $[\![\alpha + \mathrm{VP}]\!]_s = 0$.

To avoid distracting complications, let us assume that only the extensions of quantifying DPs contain any sets as their members, and neither the extensions of referential subjects nor those of predicates do. Hence for sentences with referential subjects, option (b) fails, and thus (25) boils down to (17-a) on p. 122: the sentence is true in the case that (a) is. Similarly, for sentences with quantifying subjects, option (a) fails, and thus (25) boils down to (17-b): the sentence is true just in the case that (b) is. Taken together, then, (25) boils down to the combination of the two rules in (17).

The unified composition opens up an interesting perspective on the syntax/semantics interface in general. Loosely speaking, (25) is self-regulating in that it has the extensions of the expressions combined decide on the way they are combined. General mechanisms of self-regulating semantic combination have been developed in the tradition of **type-driven interpretation**, where different kinds of extensions are assigned specific labels known as *types* that determine appropriate modes of combination. In the following we briefly indicate the basic tools and mechanisms. For further details, we refer the reader to the pertinent literature, and especially to the standard textbook by Heim and Kratzer (1998).

The method is based on a particular way of encoding sets in terms of so-called *characteristic functions*, which explicitly distinguish membership and non-membership by truth values. To see how this works, let us assume we are given a fixed domain of individuals which, taken together, form a (non-empty) set U. Then any subset A of U is *characterized* by a function f that assigns 1 to A's members and 0 to all other individuals in U:

(26)

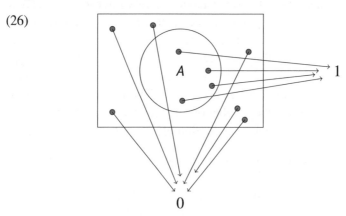

The arrows depict a relation between individuals and truth values that can be defined in set-theoretic terms, as a set of ordered pairs. What makes this relation a *function* is the very fact that each member x of U is associated with, or *assigned*, precisely one object, the *value* (for x); what makes it a *characteristic* function is the fact that the value always happens to be a truth value; what makes it the characteristic function *of* the set A is the fact that the truth value assigned to any given $x \in U$ happens to be 1 if and only if x is a member of A. In general, the characteristic function of a set of individuals consists of all pairs $\langle x, 1 \rangle$ where $x \in A$ plus all pairs $\langle x, 0 \rangle$ where x is an individual but not a member of A. It is easy to see that, no matter what we take to be our universe U, its subsets stand in a one-to-one correspondence to their characteristic functions: the empty set corresponds to the function that assigns 0 to all members of U; the singletons $\{x\}$ correspond to functions that assign 0 to all individuals but x; etc. Given this correspondence, sets may as well be replaced by their characteristic functions—which is precisely what happens in type-driven interpretation.

In order to arrive at a self-regulating system of extensions, the extensions are classified according to their *types*. If the extension of an expression is an individual (as in the case of names and definite descriptions), it is said to be of type e; if it is a truth value (as in the case of declarative sentences), it is said to be an extension of type t; if it is the characteristic function of a set of individuals, then its type is $\langle e, t \rangle$, thus indicating that it assigns a truth value to each individual.[6] So after replacing sets by their characteristic functions, intransitive verbs and verb phrases turn out to have extensions of type $\langle e, t \rangle$, and so do common nouns. Now, since the extensions of quantifier phrases are sets of predicate extensions, it is not hard to guess what their type would be, viz., $\langle \langle et \rangle, t \rangle$. In fact quite generally, $\langle a, b \rangle$ is the type of functions that assign values of type b to arguments (or *inputs*) of type a.

Replacing sets by their characteristic functions has immediate consequences for semantic combination. Simple sentences consisting of subject and predicate are cases in point. If the subject is referential, its extension is an individual to which the predicate extension assigns a truth value. Obviously, this truth value is the truth value of the sentence; it is 1 if and only if the subject extension is in the set characterized by the extension of the predicate, which is the truth condition of a predicational sentence. Similarly, if the subject is quantificational, its extension assigns a truth value to the predicate extension. Again, this truth value is the truth value of the sentence; it is 1 just in case the predicate extension is in the set characterized by the extension of the subject, which is the truth condition of a quantificational sentence. Thus in both cases, the truth value of the sentence ensues as the value the extension of one of the constituents assigns to the extension of the other one. In mathematical parlance, determining the value of a function is called *applying* it. Hence, in both kinds of subject-predicate combinations, the relevant semantic combination turns out to be **functional application**, the only difference being which of the two constituents provides the function. And it is precisely this piece of information that is encoded by the types of their extensions. For if the subject is referential, its extension will be of type e and thus fits the

---

6   e abbreviates the philosophical term *entity*. The notation originates with Montague's 1970 *Universal Grammar*, but the classification itself can be traced back to Bertrand Russell's work on the foundations of mathematics at the beginning of the 20th century. Type-driven interpretation was developed in the 1980s in extension of Montague's work.

type of the predicate extension, $\langle e, t \rangle$, in that the former forms the input to the latter. Otherwise, i.e., if the subject is quantificational, its extension is of type $\langle \langle e, t \rangle, t \rangle$, to which the predicate type $\langle e, t \rangle$ forms the input. Hence, it is easy to decide in which way the extensions of the two constituents, subject and predicate, combine *by just looking at the types of their extensions*: if one is of the form $\langle a, b \rangle$, where the other is of the form a, then the former gets applied to the latter to output a value of type b.

Type-driven interpretation now generalizes the strategy of reading off the pertinent semantic combination from the types of the extensions involved. To this end, functions are also used to replace relational extensions like those of transitive and ditransitive verbs, using a technique known as **Currying**, which allows plugging to be simulated by functional application.[7] Instead of going into the general mechanism, we'll just look at an example, the extension of the transitive verb *kiss* (in a given situation), which we have taken to be a set of ordered pairs $\langle x, y \rangle$ of kissers x and kissees y. Let us imagine a situation in which John and Mary kiss and Jane also kisses John (though not vice versa), and no one else is involved in any kissing. Hence the extension of *kiss* contains precisely three pairs of persons. Currying now turns this relation into a function that can be combined with the extension of the (referential) object by functional application. The idea is that this function assigns to any object extension the corresponding extension of the ensuing verb phrase. Thus, for example, the Curried extension of *kiss* will assign to John (the characteristic function of) the set of persons that kiss him, i.e., Mary and Jane, and it will assign to Mary (the characteristic function of) the singleton set containing John; etc.

(27) $\{ \langle \text{John}, \langle \text{Mary}, 1 \rangle \rangle, \langle \text{John}, \langle \text{Jane}, 1 \rangle \rangle, \langle \text{John}, \langle \text{John}, 0 \rangle \rangle,$
        $\langle \text{John}, \langle \text{Bill}, 0 \rangle \rangle, \langle \text{John}, \langle \ldots, 0 \rangle \rangle,$
        $\langle \text{Mary}, \langle \text{John}, 1 \rangle \rangle, \langle \text{Mary}, \langle \text{Jane}, 0 \rangle \rangle, \langle \text{Mary}, \langle \text{Mary}, 0 \rangle \rangle,$
        $\langle \text{Mary}, \langle \text{Bill}, 0 \rangle \rangle, \langle \text{Mary}, \langle \ldots, 0 \rangle \rangle,$
        $\langle \text{Jane}, \langle \ldots, 0 \rangle \rangle,$
        $\langle \text{Bill}, \langle \ldots, 0 \rangle \rangle,$
        $\langle \ldots, \langle \ldots, 0 \rangle \rangle \}$

---

7   The popularity of the "lambda operator", already mentioned in footnote 4 on p. 68, is a result of this ubiquity of functions in type-driven interpretation; see the final section of the last chapter (Chapter 10) for more on this. The term "Currying" alludes to the American mathematician Haskell Curry [1900–1982]; incidentally, the German term for the technique is *Schönfinkelei*, after the Russian mathematician Moses Schönfinkel [1889–1942].

We leave it to the reader to check that the Curried version of the extension preserves all information about who kisses whom. Since the Curried extension assigns characteristic functions (of sets of individuals) to individuals, its type is going to be $\langle e, \langle e, t \rangle \rangle$. And once again, when it comes to combining the verb with its (referential) direct object e, the types reveal that their extensions combine by applying the extension of the former to that of the latter.

In a similar (though not exactly parallel) way, determiner extensions also get replaced by functions whose rather complicated type turns out to be $\langle \langle e, t \rangle, \langle \langle e, t \rangle, t \rangle \rangle$. We will not go into this here but merely point out that at the end of the Currying day, many syntactic constructions (or branchings) surface as combining expressions with matching types of the forms $\langle a, b \rangle$ and a, ready to be combined into extensions of type b by functional application. Hence, if all goes well, we end up with a single rule of (extensional) semantic combination applicable to any syntactically well-formed binary structure [A B]:

(28)   If $[\![A]\!]_s$ is of some type $\langle a, b \rangle$ and $[\![B]\!]_s$ is of type a, then: $[\![[A\ B]]\!]_s$
         is the result of applying $[\![A]\!]_s$ to $[\![B]\!]_s$. Otherwise, $[\![[A\ B]]\!]_s$ is the
         result of applying $[\![B]\!]_s$ to $[\![A]\!]_s$.

The rule presupposes that in the second case too, the extensions of A and B match in type. Doubtlessly, a lot of work would have to be done to ensure this. However, we will not pursue this interpretation strategy any further, but once again invite the reader to consult the relevant literature.

4. Quantifying DPs in Object Position*

Let us now tackle a problem that arises with transitive verbs and quantifying expressions in object position. Looking back at the rule that combines a verb and an object ((28) and its variants discussed in Section 2 of the preceding chapter), we are in trouble: the rule seems to work only for names and descriptions, and not for quantifying objects as in (29).

(29)   Paul loves every girl

This is because our semantics of transitive verbs expects an individual as the extension of the object, not a set of sets, as denoted by quantifying DPs. Fortunately, there are several ways out of this quandery, a couple of which we will now look at.

The most straightforward strategy of interpreting (29) is by tampering with its syntactic structure. To see how this works, let us briefly consider a paraphrase:

(30)   Every girl is loved by Paul

Obviously, (29) and (30) have the same truth conditions. Moreover, there is nothing mysterious about the contribution the quantificational DP makes to arriving at these truth conditions; after all, it is in (surface) subject position and thus can be analyzed according to our rule (12) above (cf. p. 120). Now, by and large, (29) and (30) consist of the same lexical material; it is just arranged in different ways.[8] The reason why (30), unlike (29), presents no obstacle to semantic analysis is that in it the material is arranged in such a way that, as its subject, the quantifier is an immediate part of the sentence.

4.1.   Solution 1: Quantifier Raising

There are different methods that aim at interpreting the quantifier as an argument of being loved by Paul. A simple strategy for escaping our predicament has it that, for the purposes of semantic analysis, (29) must be carved up in the same way as (30), i.e., it must be assigned an LF that consists of the quantifier and the remainder of the sentence. This remainder, then, would have to receive an extension, too—viz., the extension of the remainder of (30), i.e., the VP *is loved by Paul*:

(31) $[\![$ Paul loves every girl $]\!]_s = \left[\!\!\left[\, \boxed{\text{every girl}}\, \boxed{\text{Paul loves \_\_\_}}\, \right]\!\!\right]_s = 1$

iff $[\![$ is loved by Paul $]\!]_s \in [\![$ every girl $]\!]_s$

The middle term in the above equation indicates (the extension of) a syntactic structure that derives from the original (surface) structure of (29) by an operation we already discussed in subsection 4.2 of Chapter 3 (pp. 48ff.), namely **Quantifier Raising**, or **QR**, for short. The exact formulation and nature of this syntactic transformation will not concern us here. Roughly, QR transforms a given structure by moving a quantifying DP upward to the left of a sentence, leaving a gap in its original position. The operation may be applied more than once within the same structure:

---

8   We are deliberately glossing over some details here, like the passive morphology and the preposition *by*.

(32)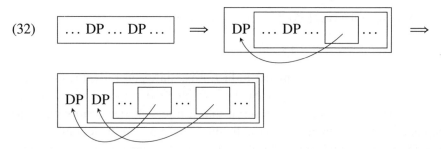

Instead of using arrows, a coindexing convention sees to it that each upwardly moved DP is connected with the gap it leaves behind; the convention also replaces the empty box with a place holder (a variable) that is coindexed with its matching DP:

(33) | DP$_x$ | DP$_y$ | ... x ... y ... |

In the case at hand, QR produces the following LF:

(34) | every girl$_y$ | Paul loves y |

Given its purpose as syntactic input to interpretation, we better make sure that the result (34) of applying QR is compositionally interpretable. As it turns out, this is not so easy. To begin with, (31) shows that the extensions to be combined at top level are the same as in (30); in other words, we have been assuming that not only the quantificational DPs but the remainders, too, are semantically equivalent:

(35) $\llbracket$ Paul loves y $\rrbracket_s$ = $\llbracket$ is loved by Paul $\rrbracket_s$

Following the strategy of Section 3.4 of Chapter 4, the right term in (35) is a set of individuals:

(36) $\llbracket$ is loved by Paul $\rrbracket_s$ = {y : in s, y is loved by Paul}

Since any individual y is loved by Paul if and only if Paul loves y, we may reformulate the latter term so as to avoid the passive voice:

(37) {y : in s, y is loved by Paul} = {y : in s, Paul loves y}

Our chain of equations (35)–(37) thus adds up to:

(38) $[\![\text{Paul loves } y]\!]_s = \{y : \text{in } s, \text{Paul loves } y\}$

Now this looks pretty systematic; in fact, it is: quite generally, the extension of a sentence with a (single) gap can be characterized as the set of individuals that **satisfy** the sentence in the sense that a true sentence results once the gap is filled with a name for that individual.[9] Given (38), the complete truth conditions amount to saying that the extension described there is an element of the extension of the quantifying DP. Thus, it follows that:

(39) $\left[\!\left[\boxed{\text{every girl}_y} \; \boxed{\text{Paul loves } y} \right]\!\right]_s = 1$

iff	$\{y : \text{in } s, \text{Paul loves } y\} \in [\![\text{every girl}]\!]_s$
iff	$\{y : \text{in } s, \text{Paul loves } y\} \in \{X : [\![\text{girl}]\!]_s \subseteq X\}$
iff	$[\![\text{girl}]\!]_s \subseteq \{y : \text{in } s, \text{Paul loves } y\}$
iff	$\{x : \text{in } s, x \text{ is a girl}\} \subseteq \{y : \text{in } s, \text{Paul loves } y\}$
iff	every z that is a girl in s is such that Paul loves z in s
iff	every girl in s is such that in s Paul loves her
iff	Paul loves every girl in s

One advantage of the QR-strategy is that it is very general, applying not only to direct objects but to all sorts of positions in which quantifying DPs may occur. Thus, as our readers are invited to verify for themselves, the following sentences can be treated along the same lines as (29):

(40)   a.   The assistant showed the shop to *a customer*
      b.   Mary looked behind *every door*
      c.   The janitor saw *no one* leave the building
      d.   A raindrop fell on the hood of *every car*

Since QR may apply to a given sentence more than once, it can also be used to deal with multiple quantification, which we will not go into, however. Moreover, QR also comes in handy in the analysis of so-called *bound pronouns*:

(41)   Every boy hopes that he will pass the test

---

9   Its systematicity notwithstanding, this characterization is a far cry from a compositional interpretation of gappy structures—a task we defer to Chapter 10.

In its most obvious reading, the pronoun in the embedded clause in (41) stands in for the schoolboy(s) quantified over in the main clause.[10] However, this does not mean that it is short for the quantifier, for the following sentence certainly means something entirely different:

(42)   Every boy hopes that every boy will pass the test

In order to capture the intended reading of (41) (and distinguish it from (42)), one may, however, treat the pronoun as if it were a gap left behind by the quantifier that would have had to be raised in the first place:

(43) | every boy$_y$ | y hopes | that y will pass the test |

Note that this structure contains two gaps—one for the original position of the subject, and one for the pronoun. Once dissected and indexed in this way, the sentence (42) comes out as true if the extension of the doubly gapped part is an element of the extension of the quantifier:

(44) $[\![$ Every boy hopes that he will pass the test $]\!]_s = 1$
iff $\{y$: in s, y hopes that y will pass the test$\} \in [\![$ every boy $]\!]_s$

Unfortunately, we are not in a position to justify these truth conditions beyond this point, partly because of the technical obstacles mentioned in fn. 9, and partly because (41) involves a kind of construction (clausal embedding) that will not be addressed until the next chapter. Even so, we hope that (44) does have some plausibility, if only as a sketch.[11]

4.2.   Solution 2: In Situ *Interpretation*

QR is not without alternatives (and not without its own problems either). In fact, our original example (29) could also be handled in a variety of ways that

---

10   Note that in (41), *he* may also refer to a particular person that had been mentioned before. We are not concerned with this reading here, which would call for a separate analysis (a simpler one, actually).

11   Actually, as it stands, (44) does not stand up to scrutiny for a third reason: the binding mechanism introduced in Chapter 10 does not square with the (simplified) semantics of clausal embedding of the next chapter: the latter is lacking the so-called *de se* aspect implicit in the pronoun, i.e., the fact that it relates to the students quantified over as being seen from their own perspectives (their selves, as it were) ....

do not involve a re-bracketing of the syntactic input. We will briefly go into one of them, and then leave the subject altogether.

To arrive at a so-called *in situ* interpretation of the VP in (29), let us return to the satisfaction set (38) that served as the extension of the remainder LF in (34). Since we are after the extension of the VP, this set may appear irrelevant—the more so because it depends on the extension of the subject, Paul. With a different name in subject position—*John*, say—we would have had a different satisfaction set, viz.:

(45) $\{y : \text{in } s, \text{John loves } y\}$

In general, whenever we replace the subject in (29) with a name or with a description of an individual x, the corresponding satisfaction set—the extension of the remainder after moving the object DP—would be:

(46) $\{y : \text{in } s, x \text{ loves } y\}$

And in general, such a replacement sentence would be true if this set (46) were an element of the extension of the object, $[\![\text{every girl}]\!]_s$. Now, the extension that we are after, $[\![\text{loves every girl}]\!]_s$, consists of precisely those individuals x that make (29) true if the subject *Paul* is replaced by (a name of) x. Hence that extension collects all those individuals x whose corresponding satisfaction set (46) is an element of $[\![\text{every girl}]\!]_s$. We may thus characterize the extension of the VP in the following way:

(47) $\{x : \{y : \text{in } s, x \text{ loves } y\} \in [\![\text{every girl}]\!]_s\}$

Note that (47) can be rewritten in terms of the extension of the transitive verb:

(48) $\{x : \{y : \langle x, y \rangle \in [\![\text{love}]\!]_s\} \in [\![\text{every girl}]\!]_s\}$

Crucially, now, (48) shows how the extension of the VP is composed of the extensions of its immediate parts, the verb *love* and the object *every girl*. As it turns out, the combination is independent of the particular example and generalizes to (almost) arbitrary quantificational DPs in direct object position. We thus arrive at the following compositional alternative to the above QR-treatment:

(49)   If TV is a transitive predicate and DP its (quantifying) object, then
        $[\![\text{TV} + \text{DP}]\!]_s := \{x : \{y : \langle x, y \rangle \in [\![\text{TV}]\!]_s\} \in [\![\text{DP}]\!]_s\}$.

The same rule also works for much simpler sentences like *Paul loves Mary*, if we assume that *Mary* is type-shifted, as explained in Section 2. Then, according to (49), being loved by Paul must be one of the properties Mary has, which is exactly how it should be.

4.3. Discussion

Obviously, the semantic combination (49) avoids the compositionality issue mentioned in connection with QR because it avoids any gaps and co-indexing in the syntactic input. This may be seen as a price worth paying for the somewhat opaque and *ad hoc* character of (49). However, it should be noted that it is also less general and principled than the QR-strategy in that it only applies to DPs in direct object position. For different environments (e.g., indirect objects of ditransitive verbs), additional rules would have to be formulated in the spirit of (49). While in many cases these rules may be subsumed under a general pattern, more complex phenomena like multiple quantification and bound pronouns appear to require more involved techniques. At the end of the day, then, the *in situ* strategy might turn out to be too restrictive, and if extended to other cases more complicated than it appears from (49) alone.

On the other hand, although the mechanism of QR can be made precise quite easily, it leads to a massive overgeneration of readings. An example may illustrate the point:

(50)   His mother loves every boy

(50) cannot have the same reading as

(51)   Every boy is being loved by his mother

with the pronoun *his* being interpreted like a gap. But this would be predicted by applying QR in the manner introduced above.

Finally, consider:

(52)   A man ate an apple from every basket

Applying QR to *every basket* would yield a reading that is paraphrased in (53):

(53)   For every basket there is an apple and a man who ate that apple

Such a reading (with different men and different apples for each basket) is intuitively unavailable, but nonetheless generated by QR. Likewise, in more complex situations, QR generates multiple ambiguities, many of which are intuitively unavailable. It follows that QR must be subjected to severe restrictions that seem to have an *ad hoc* character in many cases. The tricky and complicated part here is to find a principled way to rule out unwarranted applications of QR. As already announced, we will leave it at that, inviting the readers to consult the relevant literature (e.g., May (1985), Reinhart (1997), or Cechetto (2004).)

EXERCISE 20:

> Give a precise account of *Paul loves Mary* by explicitly stating each step of the calculation of truth conditions with respect to a scenario s where $[\![\text{Paul}]\!]_s = p$, $[\![\text{Mary}]\!]_s = m$, and $[\![\text{love}]\!]_s = \{\langle a,b \rangle, \langle p,p \rangle\}$.

EXERCISE 21:

> Design a new *in situ* rule for quantifying objects of three-place verbs, exemplified by *every boy* in:

(54)   John | bought | every boy | a toy

EXERCISE 22:

> Describe a situation s for which (55-a) is true and (55-b) is false:

(55) a. Mary kisses a doll
     b. Mary kisses every doll

> Now calculate the truth conditions according to (49), thereby stating a formal proof that s does indeed verify (55-a) and falsify (55-b).

5.   The Verb *to be*

One of the most vexing problems in the analysis of natural language is the verb *be* (also called the copula). Above (on p. 108) we considered sentences like

(56)   Paul is alive

and decided that *is* has no meaning of its own. However, there are other uses of *is*, attested in the following examples:

(57)   a.   Obama is the president of the USA
        b.   Paul is a nerd

In (57-a), *Obama* and *the president of the USA* each denote an individual, so it is obvious that the semantic content of *is* is the identity relation =. In this case, *is* is not meaningless but denotes the set of all pairs $\langle x, x \rangle$. It thus follows that *is* expresses two different verbs, depending on whether it combines with an adjective or a definite description (or a proper name).

(57-b) represents a different case. Here *is* combines with a DP whose grammatical function is that of a so-called predicative noun. Recall that we have already calculated the meaning of *a nerd* as the set of all (non-empty) X that overlap with the set of nerds. But this type of denotation does not easily fit with the denotation of the subject. It seems, then, that we need yet another type of *is* that combines a quantifying DP with a subject. Such a denotation for *is* has indeed been proposed in the literature, but it is rather complex.[12]

A simpler solution would be to postulate that in such constructions neither the copula *be* nor the indefinite article *a* have any meaning of their own. Instead of postulating another ambiguity of *be* we now postulate one of *a*. Thus, in ordinary constructions, *a* still denotes a quantifier, but in predicative constructions it does not. These constructions are syntactically characterized as combining an indefinite DP with verbs like *be* or *become*.[13] If so, $[\![\text{nerd}]\!]_s$ = $[\![\text{a nerd}]\!]_s$ = $[\![\text{is a nerd}]\!]_s$, and the rule for combining a subject with a VP may apply as usual.

---

12   The interested (and ambitious) reader may want to check that the following relation between individuals x and DP-denotations Q does the job:

(i) $[\![\text{is}]\!]_s = \{ \langle x, Q \rangle : \{ x \} \in Q \}$

The idea behind this analysis of the copula can be traced back to W. V. O. Quine's 1960 book *Word and Object*, a classic in philosophy of language and logical semantics.

13   Some evidence for this alternative way of treating the indefinite article as vacuous can be gained from the fact that the German analogue *ein* in these contexts is optional. Thus, the following pairs of sentences are identical in meaning:

(i)   a.   *Mindestens ein   Deutscher ist ein Weltmeister*
                at least   some German   is a   world champion
        b.   *Mindestens ein Deutscher ist Weltmeister*

(ii)   a.   *Jeder Weltmeister   ist ein Medaillengewinner*
                every world champion is a   medal winner
        b.   *Jeder Weltmeister ist Medaillengewinner*

The optionality of the indefinite article *ein* thus suggests that it is as meaningless as the copula verb *ist* in these constructions.

Chapter 7
Propositions

Extensions concern that part of a theory of meaning that ensures that linguistic expressions can be used to refer to objects in the world. It should be obvious from the previous chapter that this cannot be the whole story about meaning. If the meaning of an expression were equated with its extension, then in particular, all true sentences would have the same meaning, and so would all false sentences. In the present chapter, we will fill in some of the gaps deriving from the extensional analysis of meaning.

1. Intensional Contexts

In this section we will show how the compositionality of meaning provides additional motivation for going beyond extensions. So far we have been relying on extensional compositionality, i.e., the assumption that the extension of an expression is a function of the extensions of its (immediate) parts. As it turns out, however, this principle cannot hold in full generality: in order for compositionality to work throughout language, a broader concept of meaning is called for. This part of the theory of meaning is concerned with the *information* conveyed by a sentence.

Consider the following two sentences:

(1)   a.   Hamburg is larger than Cologne
        b.   Pfäffingen is larger than Breitenholz

It so happens that both sentences are true,[1] which means that they have the same extension; indeed their extensions can be calculated from the extensions of the names and the relation *larger than* (the set of pairs $\langle x, y \rangle$ where x is larger than y). But now consider so-called *propositional attitude* reports, i.e., sentences that tell us something about a person's information state:

(2)   a.   John knows that Hamburg is larger than Cologne
        b.   John knows that Pfäffingen is larger than Breitenholz

---

1   Pfäffingen and Breitenholz are districts in the municipality of Ammerbuch; ☞
    http://de.wikipedia.org/wiki/Ammerbuch#Gemeindegliederung.

There is no reason to doubt that the extensions of the words *John*, *knows*, and *that*—whatever they may be—are exactly the same in (2-a) and (2-b). Moreover, no structural ambiguity is detectable. We also know that the embedded sentences of (2) (identical to the sentences in (1)) have the same extensions. Now, regardless of what exactly the extensions of *know* and *that* are, given the Principle of Extensional Compositionality, we would have to infer that the extensions of the more complex sentences in (2) must also be identical, simply because the extensions of (1-a) and (1-b) and those of all other relevant lexical items and constructions are the same. But now we face an obvious dilemma. It is surely not the case that anyone who knows that Hamburg is larger than Cologne also knows that Pfäffingen is larger than Breitenholz. In particular, suppose that John knows (1-a) but not (1-b). As a consequence, (2-a) is true, whereas (2-b) is false in the same situation. Still, our theory of extensional compositionality predicts identical truth values, contrary to fact. What went wrong?

It seems intuitively clear that the complement (the object) of a verb like *know* cannot just denote a truth value. If this were the case, then any piece of knowledge would imply omniscience. This means that extensional compositionality fails in a context like ... *know that* ... . In plain words: the principle cannot hold in full generality; there must be exceptions. Such environments in which extensional compositionality fails are called **intensional contexts**. If we embed an expression (e.g., a subordinate clause) in an intensional context, then the contribution of the embedded expression cannot be its extension. But what else could it be?

2. Cases and Propositions

The difference in truth conditions between the sentences in (2) seems to be due to the state of information John is in. More precisely, what the sentences claim is that John's state of information comprises the information expressed by the embedded sentences. But the embedded sentences convey different information; they report different facts. Hence the truth value of the entire sentence depends on the information expressed by the embedded sentence. In semantics, the technical term for this information is the **proposition** expressed by the sentence. The truth values in (2) may differ because the propositions expressed in (1) do.

What is a proposition? What is the information contained in, or conveyed by, a sentence? To answer this question consider the following sample sentences:

(3)   Four fair coins are tossed

(4)   At least one of the 4 tossed coins lands heads up

(5)   At least one of the 4 tossed coins lands heads down

(6)   Exactly 2 of the 4 tossed coins land heads up

(7)   Exactly 2 of the 4 tossed coins land heads down

Sentence (3) is the least informative of the five sentences, because it does not tell us anything about the result of the tossing. The other sentences are more informative in this respect. Sentence (4) is less informative than (6), though; and (7) is more informative than (5). Presupposing that each coin lands either heads up or heads down (thereby excluding a third possible outcome of the tossing), (6) and (7) are equally informative. Whether (4) and (5) are also equally informative, depends on our understanding of "informative": in a certain sense, both contain the same *amount*, or *quantity*, of information. But qualitatively, they are of course totally different. To see this, assume that all four coins land heads up. Then (4) is true, but (5) is false. According to the so-called **most certain principle of semantics** (from p. 28), repeated in (8),

(8)   If a (declarative) sentence S_1 is true and another sentence S_2 is false in the same circumstances, then S_1 and S_2 differ in meaning.

we must conclude that although the *amount* of information might be the same, the meanings are still different. And so are the propositions expressed by the two sentences, if the propositions are what makes up the contribution of the embedded sentence in an attitude report. To see this, consider John again:

(9)   John knows that at least one of the 4 tossed coins lands heads up

(10)   John knows that at least one of the 4 tossed coins lands heads down

If (4) and (5) expressed the same proposition, then a substitution argument along the lines of the previous section would show that (9) and (10) coincided in their truth values—which they do not have to. For imagine that John can

2. *Cases and Propositions* 141

see only one coin. If (9) is true, (10) will be false. Hence, to be on the safe side, we better make sure that the propositions expressed by (4) and (5) differ even though the sentences seem to carry the same *amount* of information. In other words: when it comes to propositions, it is *quality* of information that counts, rather than quantity.

The coin-tossing example is reminiscent of probabilities, and this is not accidental. As one can easily verify, the quantitative informativity of these sentences corresponds to the probability of a certain event taking place. This probability can be measured by counting the positive outcomes in relation to all possible cases. More specifically, a sentence S_1 is *more* informative than a sentence S_2 if the *number* of cases that make S_1 true is *smaller* (!) than the *number* of cases that make S_2 true.

On the other hand, the *qualitative* differences between the sentences depend on the *kind* of situations that make sentences come out true or false. Thus, the qualitative difference between (4) and (5) consists in the fact that the positive outcomes, i.e., the cases that make the respective sentence true, are not the same, although their number may be. Generalizing from the example we may say that two sentences that are qualitatively equally informative apply to exactly the same cases; their **informational content** can be identified with the set of cases that make the sentence true:

(11)   The **proposition** expressed by a sentence is the set of possible cases of which that sentence is true.

Returning to the coin-tossing scenario, let us chart the possible cases according to the outcome for each of the four coins c_1-c_4, with 1 and 0 standing for "heads up" and "heads down", respectively:

(12)

possible cases	c_1	c_2	c_3	c_4
1	1	1	1	1
2	1	1	1	0
3	1	1	0	1
4	1	1	0	0
5	1	0	1	1
6	1	0	1	0
7	1	0	0	1
8	1	0	0	0
9	0	1	1	1
10	0	1	1	0
11	0	1	0	1
12	0	1	0	0
13	0	0	1	1
14	0	0	1	0
15	0	0	0	1
16	0	0	0	0

The table lists all possible outcomes of a tossing; each of the sixteen different rows represents one type of situation. Now, the informational content of, and hence the proposition expressed by, the sentences (4) to (7) can be identified with the following sets of possibilities:

(13) a. At least one coin lands heads up: $\{1,\ldots,15\}$
      b. At least one coin lands heads down: $\{2,\ldots,16\}$
      c. Exactly 2 coins land heads up: $\{4,6,7,10,11,13\}$
      d. Exactly 2 coins land heads down: $\{4,6,7,10,11,13\}$
      e. Exactly one coin lands heads down: $\{2,3,5,9\}$

EXERCISE 23:

   Continue:

   (14) a. Exactly one coin lands heads up: ?
        b. Exactly one coin lands heads down: ?
        c. Coin c_3 lands heads down: ?
        d. All coins land heads down: ?

3. Logical Space

It would now seem that the propositions expressed by (13-c) and (13-d) are identical. But this is not really so. In order to fully capture the meaning of the sentences, we need to consider more possibilities. Above, we simply didn't take enough cases into account; we only looked at scenarios with exactly 4 coins being tossed. In a situation with 5 (or more) coins being tossed, the set of outcomes to be considered is much larger, although the quantitative amount of information expressed by the two sentences still remains the same. In such a situation, the propositions expressed by the sentences differ, which can easily be checked by imagining a possible situation in which (13-c) is true and (13-d) is false.

The point just made is much more general, which becomes clear when we turn to sentences like:

(15)   a.   Four coins were tossed when John coughed
          b.   Four coins were tossed and no one coughed

Again, (15) shows that, in general, we need to distinguish more cases—not only according to the outcome of coin tossings but also according to who happens to be coughing. Hence, it would seem we need to add more and more columns to the table—one for each potentially coughing person—thereby dramatically increasing the number of rows, i.e., cases, and their length. Since the examples (15) were quite arbitrarily chosen, it is clear that the number of cases needed to distinguish any two non-synonymous sentences by the cases they apply to must be very large indeed. And the cases themselves must be differentiated in quite varied and arbitrary ways. In fact, the cases needed appear unlimited in their fine-grainedness and scope, thus amounting to complete descriptions of arbitrary **states of affairs**. Any such complete description must take into account anything we can conceive of: the number of hairs on your head; the names of all your ancestors; the position of all atoms in our world; etc. Such a completely specified possible state of affairs is called a **possible world**. In effect then, we can say that only sufficiently many cases can capture all potentially relevant aspects of (literal) meaning. We therefore identify the meaning of a sentence with a sufficiently large set of possible worlds, namely the set of **all** possible worlds of which the sentence is true.[2]

---

2   The attentive reader must have noticed that we say of a sentence that it is true or false *of*, rather than *in*, a world (or case, or situation). This is to avoid the unwelcome impression

In sum, then, **propositions are sets of possible worlds**. And possible worlds are highly specific, completely specified (and very big) situations in which every possible case is determined. As Wittgenstein put it: "*Die Welt ist alles, was der Fall ist*" (*The world is all that is the case*).[3]

The switch from situations to worlds induces a change in notation. From now on, we use 'w' (for world) rather than 's' (for situation) as an index on the extensions $[\![...]\!]$. By definition, then, $[\![S]\!]_w$ is the denotation or extension of sentence S in a world w, namely its truth value at w. We may now reformulate (11) as follows:

(16)   The **proposition** expressed by a sentence is the set of possible worlds of which that sentence is true.

(17)   A sentence S is true of a possible world w if and only if $[\![S]\!]_w = 1$.

(18)   By $[\![S]\!]$ we mean the proposition expressed by S:
$$[\![S]\!] := \{w : [\![S]\!]_w = 1\}$$

Hence it follows that

(19)   A sentence S is true of a possible world w if and only if $w \in [\![S]\!]$.

Or symbolically:

(20) $[\![S]\!]_w = 1$ iff $w \in [\![S]\!]$.

This is basically the definition of *Wittgenstein (1921)* (= Wittgenstein (1922)) and Carnap (1947). Adopting Wittgenstein's terminology, we may say that all possible combinations of circumstances (*Sachverhalte*) make up a **Logical Space** (*logischer Raum*) and each sentence cuts this space into two parts: in one part, *A*, the sentence is true, and in the other part, *not A*, the sentence is false.

---

that, in order to be true or false, a sentence needs to be uttered in that world (or case, or situation). As a matter of fact, it does not even have to exist; or it may exist as a sound form carrying a different meaning.

3   This is the first sentence in ☞ Ludwig Wittgenstein's [1889–1951] *Tractatus logico-philosophicus*, arguably the origin of (16) below.

(21)

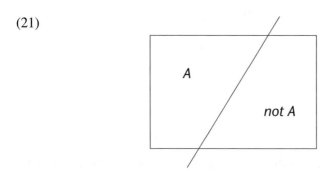

In diagram (21) Logical Space (as represented by the rectangle) is cut into two parts, the A-worlds and the not-A-worlds.

Actually, Wittgenstein identified possible worlds (his *possible states of affairs*) with sets of certain *elementary sentences* of an idealized language of science; Carnap followed him, but was more liberal as to the choice of language. The idea is that the sentences determining a world constitute a *state description* (Carnap's term) that leaves no (describable) facts open. Later advocates of Logical Space proposed recognizing possible worlds as independently given objects. Nevertheless there is considerable disagreement among philosophers about the ontological status of Logical Space: should we imagine possible worlds as abstract units of information or should we conceive of them as made up of atoms, in analogy to our real world? The most extreme (and provocative) position has been taken by the American philosopher David Lewis [1941–2001] in his 1986 book *On the Plurality of Worlds*.[4] Luckily, semantic analysis can proceed without resolving these difficult matters. So we will leave it at that.

4. Propositional Logic as the Logic of Propositions

4.1. Venn Diagrams and Truth Tables

In the previous section we represented a proposition inside the Logical Space box (21) by a region produced by a "cut". In fact, however, the shape of that region plays no role when considered in isolation; we could equally well represent the division between worlds (the *A*-worlds and the *not-A*-worlds) as the difference between the region inside *A* and the region outside *A* in a drawing like (22):

---

4   Cf. also ☞ *http://www.zeit.de/1999/44/199944.lewis1_.xml.*

(22)

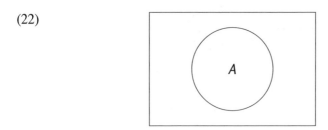

Suppose A is the proposition that S, i.e., the set of worlds of which some sentence S is true. Then $A = [\![\,S\,]\!]$, whereas the region outside A is the proposition expressed by the negation of S, i.e., $[\![\,\text{not }S\,]\!]$.

As a side effect of defining propositions as sets, we can now define the proposition expressed by a conjunction 'S$_1$ *and* S$_2$' as an operation on sets, namely the intersection of $[\![\,S_1\,]\!]$ with $[\![\,S_2\,]\!]$. This gives us a neat semantics for the conjunction of sentences in terms of the propositions they express:

(23) $[\![\,S_1 \text{ and } S_2\,]\!] := [\![\,S_1\,]\!] \cap [\![\,S_2\,]\!]$

That is, the set of worlds where 'S$_1$ *and* S$_2$' holds is precisely the intersection of all worlds of which S$_1$ is true and all worlds of which S$_2$ is true. These set-theoretic truth conditions can be visualized by using a Venn diagram as shown in (24):

(24)

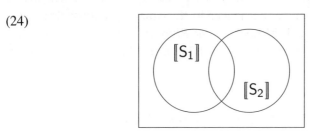

The diagram divides Logical Space into four regions corresponding to the four possibilities listed in the truth table of conjunction: worlds with S$_1$ true and S$_2$ false, S$_2$ true and S$_1$ false, both true, and both false. No world, i.e., no possibility, is excluded; moreover, the diagram does not tell us anything about what the actual world looks like.

Now, by shading regions of the diagram, we **exclude** certain situations that are incompatible with the truth of a sentence under discussion. For example, by asserting that S$_1$, we exclude situations in which S$_1$ is false. Shading thus means excluding possible situations; asserting S$_1$ is thus represented as:

(25)

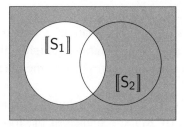

And likewise if only S_2 is asserted, we get:

(26)

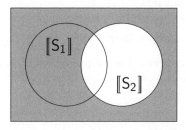

With both S_1 and S_2 being true, the diagram corresponding to 'S_1 *and* S_2' results from shading the regions that are incompatible with S_1 and in addition shading those incompatible with S_2:

(27)

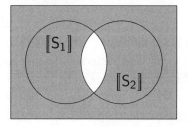

So this diagram represents *and* in an obvious way: a representation for the conjunction *and* should pick out the worlds where 'S_1 *and* S_2' hold, and this means that we must shade all the situations that are incompatible with 'S_1 *and* S_2' being true. That is, the remaining white space represents the situations where 'S_1 *and* S_2' is true. We may therefore say that this graphic represents the truth conditions for 'S_1 *and* S_2'.[5]

---

5   Hence there is a sharp contrast between the uses of *and* as a sentential connective and
    as (forming and) modifying plural NPs, discussed in Chapter 5, p. 112: while the former
    expresses intersection (on the level of propositions), the latter corresponds to union (of
    extensions). This semantic disparity of *and* and its cognates in other languages is as

Note that we have switched our graphical representation vis-à-vis earlier graphic representations of sets. The shading is now meant to *eliminate* possibilities, whereas in earlier Venn diagrams it highlighted the set represented. Of course, whether or not a color represents set membership is purely a matter of convention.

Disjunction, too, can be represented by a Venn diagram. According to the relevant truth table (p. 87), a sentence of the form 'S$_1$ *or* S$_2$' is true of precisely those worlds w that satisfy one of the following conditions:

1. S$_1$ and S$_2$ are both true of w;
2. S$_1$ is true of w and S$_2$ is false of w;
3. S$_1$ is false of w and S$_2$ is true of w.

Hence the only worlds excluded are those of which both S$_1$ and S$_2$ are false. This can again be represented in a Venn diagram:

(28)

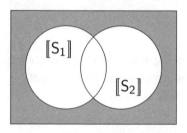

The diagram only excludes situations where neither S$_1$ nor S$_2$ is true. Describing the construction of Venn diagrams in procedural terms, disjunction of S$_1$ and S$_2$ forces white space for both $[\![\,S_1\,]\!]$ and $[\![\,S_2\,]\!]$.

In a similar way, one we may now represent the truth conditions of 'S$_1$ *but not* S$_2$' by a Venn diagram, excluding all $[\![\,S_1\,]\!]$ worlds:

(29)

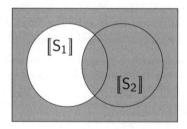

---

widespread as it is ill-understood. See, however, Winter (1996) for a heroic attempt of unifying the two.

Likewise, 'S$_1$ *but not* S$_2$' is represented as:

(30)

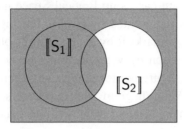

Here is another Venn diagram:

(31)

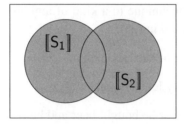

You may wonder how the situation described in this picture could be expressed in natural language. Your answer should be that (31) corresponds to '*neither* S$_1$ *nor* S$_2$'. This could of course also be expressed by using a truth table:

(32)

$[\![S_1]\!]_w$	$[\![S_2]\!]_w$	$[\![S_1]\!]_w$ NOR $[\![S_2]\!]_w$
1	1	0
1	0	0
0	1	0
0	0	1

(32) shows that *neither–nor* is a truth functional connective corresponding to a combination truth values aptly called 'NOR'.

The correspondence between truth tables and Venn diagrams is far from accidental. In fact, both represent the very same aspects of Logical Space. Each row in a truth table stands for one way the world might be (or might have been) in terms of the propositions $[\![S_1]\!]$, $[\![S_2]\!]$, ... corresponding to the (leftmost) columns. In a sense, each row "locates" the world relative to these propositions. If it contains a "1" in a particular row, then the world is in the corresponding proposition; otherwise the pertinent cell contains a "0". Similarly, a Venn diagram carves up Logical Space into the regions defined by certain propositions represented by circles, leaving a region white if the corresponding truth table marks it by 1s. As it turns out, the method of truth tables and the representation by Venn diagrams are equivalent. In particular, as readers may want to figure out for themselves, there are 16 different possibilities of shading a Venn diagram with two circles, and there are also 16 corresponding truth tables, some of which will be discussed further below.

4.2.   *Logical Connectives Revisited*

Let us now apply this technique to a kind of ambiguity already discussed in Chapter 5 and exemplified in (33):

(33)   He bought wine or beer and chips

For the sake of simplicity let us replace (33) by:

(34)   He bought wine or he bought beer and he bought chips

and abbreviate this by:

(35) S_1 or S_2 and S_3

Like the constellation extensively discussed in Chapter 5, Section 5, p. 105, (35) is structurally ambiguous, and this ambiguity can be represented by different trees:

(36)   a.

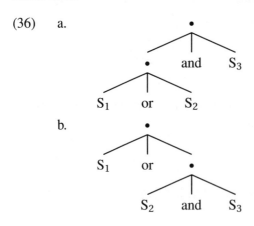

b.

It is quite obvious that in (36-b) the conjunction *and* is in the domain of *or*, whereas in (36-a) it's the other way around. It follows that scope relations also differ. In (37-a) the disjunction *or* has narrow scope with respect to the conjunction *and*, and in '(S_1 *or* S_2) *and* S_3', it's just the other way around.

(37)   a.   (S_1 or S_2) and S_3
       b. S_1 or (S_2 and S_3)

Is this difference in bracketing also accompanied by a difference in meaning? If not, then (37-a) and (37-b) would be synonymous. Thinking about it for a while, you should agree that from the truth of (37-a) we can infer that S_3 must also be true, but this conclusion cannot be drawn on the basis of (37-b), because we do not know whether (S_2 *and* S_3) is true. Constellation (37-b) could be true just on the basis of S_1 alone being true, while both S_3 and possibly S_2 are false.

This sort of reasoning exploits the following idea: the sets of conclusions that can be drawn from each of two sentences X and Y are identical if and only if X and Y are synonymous. We have just demonstrated that (37-a) and (37-b) do not allow exactly the same conclusions. This implies that the meaning of the complex expressions must be different, which suggests that (35) is ambiguous.

If so, the Venn diagrams for (37-a) and (37-b) must differ, and so must the truth tables in at least one row (i.e., at least one assignment of truth values to the sentences S_1, S_2, and S_3). Above, we looked at only two sentences and considered all combinations of truth values for them. Now we have to consider all possible combinations of three sentences S_1, S_2, and S_3. That is, we have to look at a Venn diagram like this:

(38)

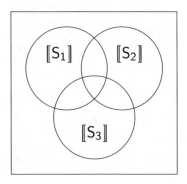

Or a table with eight different rows and three columns, one for each sentence:

(39)

$[\![S_1]\!]_w$	$[\![S_2]\!]_w$	$[\![S_3]\!]_w$	...
1	1	1	...
1	1	0	...
1	0	1	...
1	0	0	...
0	1	1	...
0	1	0	...
0	0	1	...
0	0	0	...

To represent (37-a) in a Venn diagram, we first look at (S_1 *or* S_2):

(40)

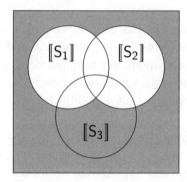

We then have to add S_3 by conjunction, which means that we have to shade in addition everything outside $[\![S_3]\!]$. The result is shown in (41):

(41)

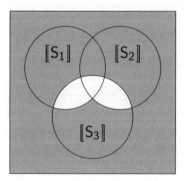

Turning next to (37-b), we first look at the embedded clause 'S$_2$ *and* S$_3$':

(42)

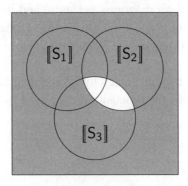

Now adding '*or* S$_1$' means that we have to remove (!) the shaded space inside $[\![\,S_1\,]\!]_w$. The result is given in (43):

(43)

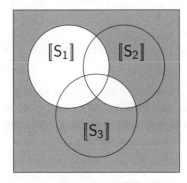

Since the diagrams obviously differ, we have thus established the ambiguity.

EXERCISE 24:

Calculate the same ambiguity by using truth tables.

EXERCISE 25:

What about 'S$_1$ *and* S$_2$ *and* S$_3$'? Do we have a semantic ambiguity?

EXERCISE 26:

Design a truth table and a Venn diagram for '(S$_1$ *and* S$_2$) *or* (S$_3$ *and* S$_4$)'.
(It might be useful to check the web for a Venn diagram for four sets.)

Summarizing the above demonstration, we have shown that a simple ambiguity at the level of sentence coordination can be calculated by using diagrams or truth tables. In the long run, it seems to us that truth tables are easier to handle. In particular, Venn diagrams get more and more complex and confusing the more different propositional variables a formula consists of; check Wikipedia for a method to produce Venn diagrams for arbitrarily many variables.

Negation, too, may be represented by a Venn diagram. In fact, this is easy: if S is any sentence, then the proposition expressed by its negation 'not S' is depicted in (44):

(44)

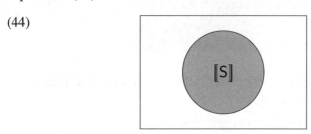

Negation plays a crucial role in complex formulae. Consider:

(45)   Not S_1 and S_2

and observe that (45) is structurally ambiguous. The scope of negation could be either S_1 alone, or the entire conjunction. Syntactically, this corresponds to two different trees:

(46)   a.

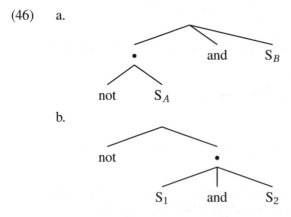

b.

Now we can represent the ambiguity in (46) in the linear notation used by logicians:

(47) a. $(\neg [\![S_1]\!]_w) \wedge [\![S_2]\!]_w$
      b. $\neg ([\![S_1]\!]_w \wedge [\![S_2]\!]_w)$

By a general convention, the brackets in (47-a) may be omitted. The brackets in (47-b), however, are essential. Let us now prove the ambiguity by calculating the truth tables for (47-a) and (47-b). We begin with (47-b), where we apply the negation truth table (p. 87), replacing the variable S by the truth value of the sentence 'S$_1$ *and* S$_2$', i.e., $[\![S_1]\!]_w \wedge [\![S_2]\!]_w$, as calculated in (47). Doing this yields the opposite truth value of 'S$_1$ *and* S$_2$':

(48)

$[\![S_1]\!]_w$	$[\![S_2]\!]_w$	$([\![S_1]\!]_w \wedge [\![S_2]\!]_w)$	$\neg([\![S_1]\!]_w \wedge [\![S_2]\!]_w)$
1	1	1	0
1	0	0	1
0	1	0	1
0	0	0	1

Next assume that negation only has scope over S$_1$. The resulting truth table is the following:

(49)

$[\![S_1]\!]_w$	$[\![S_2]\!]_w$	$\neg [\![S_1]\!]_w$	$(\neg [\![S_1]\!]_w \wedge [\![S_2]\!]_w)$
1	1	0	0
1	0	0	0
0	1	1	1
0	0	1	0

In (49) we first calculated $\neg [\![S_1]\!]_w$. In the second step we applied the truth value chart for conjunction to $\neg [\![S_1]\!]_w$ and $[\![S_2]\!]_w$.

EXERCISE 27:

Draw two different Venn diagrams that illustrate the ambiguity.

4.3. *Material Implication and Valid Inferences*

As mentioned at the end of subsection 4.1, there are 16 different possibilities to draw Venn diagrams or truth table charts given two propositions A and B. So there might be many more connectives besides *and* and *or*. A case in point has already been discussed: *neither ... nor* (cf. p. 149). However, most of the additional operators have no analogue in natural language. The reason for this is quite obvious. Consider the following truth tables:

(50)

$[\![S_1]\!]_w$	$[\![S_2]\!]_w$	
1	1	1
1	0	1
0	1	1
0	0	1

$[\![S_1]\!]_w$	$[\![S_2]\!]_w$	
1	1	1
1	0	1
0	1	0
0	0	0

Neither of them is expressed in natural language, and the reason for this seems clear: the resulting columns do not in any way depend on the truth values of S_1 and S_2 together. In the first table, S_1 and S_2 play no role whatsoever in the result, and in the second table, S_2 does not influence the outcome: it would thus simply be possible to say S_1 instead of something like 'S_1 *regardless of* S_2'. So there is not much practical use for those potential connectives.[6]

Considerations like these drastically reduce the number of meaningful candidates for natural language connectives. Two of the remaining possibilities are captured by the following truth tables:

(51) a.

$[\![S_1]\!]_w$	$[\![S_2]\!]_w$	
1	1	1
1	0	0
0	1	1
0	0	1

b.

$[\![S_1]\!]_w$	$[\![S_2]\!]_w$	
1	1	1
1	0	1
0	1	0
0	0	1

These may indeed be relevant to natural language semantics (and certainly are to logic). An inspection of the truth table in (51-b) reveals that it merely reverses (51-a), so there is no need for a particular natural language connective for both tables. Let us therefore concentrate on the first table, which corresponds to a connective called **material implication**, represented by an arrow:

---

6   Or perhaps *regardless of* itself is the wanted connective? Meaning that S_2 has no logical connection with or causal impact on S_1? But see below for the influence of pragmatics in cases where truth values alone do not capture the meaning of expressions.

(52)

$[\![S_1]\!]_w$	$[\![S_2]\!]_w$	$[\![S_1]\!]_w \to [\![S_2]\!]_w$
1	1	1
1	0	0
0	1	1
0	0	1

The corresponding Venn diagram is:

(53)

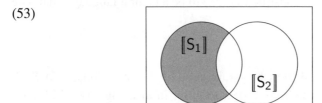

Note that unlike the tables or diagrams for conjunction and disjunction, (52) is not symmetric in that $[\![S_1]\!]_w$ and $[\![S_2]\!]_w$ cannot be swapped: as the reader may verify, the truth table for $([\![S_1]\!]_w \to [\![S_2]\!]_w)$ is different from that for $([\![S_2]\!]_w \to [\![S_1]\!]_w)$.

One way of reading (53) is by interpreting it as an instruction to combine the diagrams for the assertion of S_1 and S_2. Recall that the composition of diagrams is simply addition of shaded space in the case of conjunction, while white space is added up with disjunction. These operations are symmetrical. The asymmetry of implication is due to the following instruction for implication: first form the negation of the antecedent S_1 (white space outside $[\![S_1]\!]$, shading of $[\![S_1]\!]$) and then add S_2 by disjunction (adding the white space of $[\![S_2]\!]$). These coloring conditions are identical with the diagram for the disjunction '*not* S_1 *or* S_2'. And indeed the truth values $([\![S_1]\!]_w \to [\![S_2]\!]_w)$ and $(\neg [\![S_1]\!]_w \vee [\![S_2]\!]_w)$ are always the same, as can be checked by calculating the respective truth tables.

The Venn diagram (53) clearly illustrates that material implication leaves only those $[\![S_1]\!]$-worlds that are also $[\![S_2]\!]$-worlds. Hence if the proposition $[\![S_1]\!]$ happens to be a subset of $[\![S_2]\!]$, $([\![S_1]\!]_w \to [\![S_2]\!]_w) = 1$ throughout Logical Space! It is this fact that makes material implication a cornerstone in valid inferences, a topic to which we briefly turn in a minute.

Before doing so, however, we need to get clear on how material implication is expressed in natural language. An inspection of the truth table (52) reveals that precisely one of the rows is excluded as a possibility: the sole 0 in the second row means that the only case in which it comes out false is the one in which S_1 is true and S_2 is false. It thus turns out that material implication can be expressed as in (54):

(54)   It is not the case that both S_1 and not S_2

Instead of (54), many logicians and philosophers, as well as some semanticists, take the conditional construction (55) to be a natural language analogue of material implication.

(55)   If S_1, [then] S_2

Indeed, in many cases (54) may be paraphrased by the conditional (55). Still, in general the two constructions appear to differ in meaning. We will briefly look into this in Section 5.1. For the time being, though, let us stick to the traditional paraphrase (55) of material implication. We will also follow logical terminology, according to which S_1 and S_2 are called the **antecedent** and the **consequent** of conditionals like (55), respectively.

As we have demonstrated above, formal semantics is not only concerned with the meaning of sentences in isolation but also with semantic relations *between* sentences. Traditionally, i.e., before semantics turned into a branch of linguistics, the study of meaning of natural language sentences was confined to such *intersentential* aspects of meaning, in a quest for so-called ☞ **laws of thought**. In this tradition (dating back to ancient Greek philosophy), the main objective of study has been to characterize **valid inferences**—correct conclusions from sets of sentences, called the premises. Here are some examples:

(56)   Every cat is black
        Fred is a cat
$\vDash$ Fred is black

(57)   Fred is a black cat
$\vDash$ Fred is black

(58)   Fred is a black cat
$\vDash$ Fred is a cat

(59)   Fred is black and Fred is a cat
$\vDash$ Fred is black

(60)   Fred is black and Fred is a cat

⊨   Fred is a cat

(61)   Fred is black and Fred is a cat

⊨   Fred is a black cat

In each of the above examples the final sentence of the sequence is marked by the sign ⊨. We will refer to this as the **conclusion**, and to the one(s) preceding it in the sequence as the **premises**; the sequence as such will be called an **inference**. In each of the above inferences the conclusion obviously follows from the premise(s); if all of the premises are (or were) true, then so is (or would be) the conclusion: given that Socrates is a man, and given that every man is mortal, Socrates cannot fail to be mortal too; given that Fred is a black cat, Fred has got to be a cat; etc. The very fact that the last sentence cannot fail to be true once the preceding ones are reflects an important semantic relation between the sentences, one that is at the core of all deductive reasoning. It is precisely this feature—that the truth of their last member can be concluded from the (purported) truth of the initial ones—that makes the above inferences **valid**.

An inference is valid if and only if it is impossible that the premises are true and the conclusion is false. But this is precisely what is excluded by the material implication consisting of (the conjunction of) the premises (as the antecedent) and the conclusion (as the consequent). This is why material implication can be used to *define* a valid inference. But doing so requires an additional notion: a (proposition expressed by a) sentence S is a **tautology** if and only if it spans Logical Space. For example, any sentence of the form 'S *or not* S' is such a tautology, because there is no way to draw a Venn diagram for it where any region is (or remains) shaded. Equivalently, in each row of a truth table for 'S *or not* S', the output is 1. Now, for an inference from premises $P_1, P_2, \ldots P_n$ to a conclusion C to be valid, there should be no way to make all the premises simultaneously true (by conjoining them) and the conclusion C false, which is the case if and only if (*if* P_1 *and* P_2 … *and* P_n, *then* C) is a tautology. Accordingly:

(62)   An inference from P_1 *and* P_2 ... *and* P_n to C is valid if and only if, for any possible world w,
$$((\llbracket P_1 \rrbracket_w \wedge \llbracket P_2 \rrbracket_w \cdots \wedge \llbracket P_n \rrbracket_w) \rightarrow \llbracket C \rrbracket_w) = 1.$$

A classic inference pattern is exemplified by:

(63)   If Gromit likes cheese, then he wants to fly to the moon
        Gromit likes cheese
$\vDash$ Gromit wants to fly to the moon

This inference is valid, and it is so regardless of the content of the non-logical material, which therefore gives rise to the general pattern in (64):

(64)   If S_1 then S_2
        S_1
$\vDash$ S_2

In logic, this (valid) inference goes by the Latin name of **modus ponens**, which is actually short for *modus ponendo ponens*, which may be loosely translated as "way of concluding an affirmative (the conclusion S_2) by affirming (the premise S_1)". A less obscure (but also less current) term for the same pattern is **implication elimination**.

    Let us now see why the *modus ponens* pattern (64) is indeed valid. In order to do so, consider the Venn diagram (53) for the first premise, using material implication. If we now add the second premise S_1 by conjunction, we have to exclude all $\llbracket$ not $S_1 \rrbracket$-worlds:

(65)

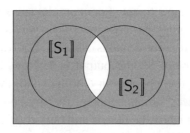

The diagram represents the premises $P_1, P_2, ..., P_n$ in rule (62), where of course, $P_1 =$ '*if* S_1 *then* S_2', $P_2 = P_n = S_1$, and $C = S_2$. Now the rule (62) for valid inferences applies and tells us to draw a diagram for:

(66) $(((\llbracket S_1 \rrbracket_w \rightarrow \llbracket S_2 \rrbracket_w) \wedge \llbracket S_1 \rrbracket_w) \rightarrow \llbracket S_2 \rrbracket_w)$

As a shortcut, we may recall from our discussion of (53) on page 157 that

(67)   If $[\![P]\!] \subseteq [\![C]\!]$, then, for any world w, $([\![P]\!]_w \rightarrow [\![C]\!]_w) = 1$.

In the case at hand, the role of $[\![P]\!]$ in (67) is played by the white space in (66) (the premises of (53)), and the role of C is played by S_2. Given the coloring in (65), the antecedent is indeed a subset of the consequent, and hence (66) comes out true (i.e., is represented by white space) throughout Logical Space, which means that it is a tautology, and so by (62) the inference turns out to be valid indeed.

To make the argument more explicit, we may also apply the operations that govern the construction of (53). This means that we first have to form the negation of the antecedent, shown in (68):

(68)

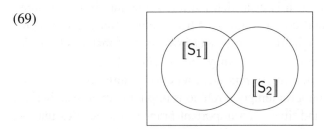

The final step is to whiten $[\![S_2]\!]$, which brings about the desired result (69) in a more detailed fashion.

(69)

5. Limits and Limitations of Propositional Logic

5.1. *Beyond Truth Functionality*

What we have done so far is to define the meaning of conjunction, disjunction, negation, and implication by looking at a Venn diagram or an entire truth table. For example, when looking at the two sentences in (70),

(70)   a.   I have two daughters and I am a professor
        b.   I have two daughters or I am a professor

one might assume that both *I have two daughters* and *I am a professor* are true, and therefore so are both (70-a) and (70-b). But this does not imply that (70-a) and (70-b) are synonymous, i.e., have the same meaning! In order to get at the meaning, we must consider all possible combinations of truth values, and this is exactly what truth conditions, as represented by Venn diagrams and truth tables, do: they provide values for all possible cases.

An inspection of the truth tables for conjunction and disjunction will reveal that they make no difference whatsoever between "A and B" on the one hand, and "B and A" on the other. Hence, the sentences in (70) should not differ in meaning from the respective sentences in (71):

(71)   a.   I am a professor and I have two daughters
        b.   I am a professor or I have two daughters

Yet, as already observed on p. 104, there are sentences in natural language that appear to be counterexamples to this symmetry:

(72)   a.   She married and (she) got pregnant
        b.   She got pregnant and (she) married

The relevant difference seems to be due to the influence of time, a topic we have been ignoring so far. It is clear that there is something in the meaning of *and* that goes beyond considerations of truth values alone; there seems to be a—presumably pragmatic—component involved that matches the order of sentences with the order of events they report. Thus, the meaning of *and* seems to turn into the meaning of *and then*; and, to be sure, the use of *then* indicates a need to account for temporal relations implicitly expressed in (72). The analysis of tense and time is an important branch of semantics that we will not be able to go into in any detail. However, some general considerations can be found in Section 7 of the next chapter. Nonetheless the "iconic" effect of *and*—the match between (order of) event-reporting speech and (order of) reported events—will not be addressed there since it is generally regarded as belonging to that part of pragmatics that deals with the proper organization of a discourse.

A similar asymmetry is felt in examples like:

(73) a. You leave the room or I shoot you
      b. I shoot you or you leave the room

The truth-functional paraphrases would be:

(74) a. If you don't leave the room, then I will shoot you
      b. If I don't shoot you, you will leave the room

There is an aymmetry here due to the fact that only in the (a)-sentences is it understood that shooting you is caused by not leaving the room. This is not the case in the (b)-sentences. Rather, (74-b) seems to say something like "shooting you is the only way to prevent you from leaving the room". All this is not contained in the truth conditions alone, which are symmetrical for all cases.

It seems that it is precisely the truth-functional character of material implication that insufficiently captures our understanding of *if . . . (then)* in natural language. Consider (75):

(75) If it rains, (then) the street is wet

Sentence (75) is readily understood as making a law-like statement, expressing a causal relation between rain and wetness. However, this additional meaning component cannot be accounted for by so-called truth-functional connectives (like material implication or disjunction and their truth conditions as stated above), although it is precisely these expressions that are used to convey this additional non-truth-functional component of meaning.

Closely connected to this failure of truth functionality is the fact that a conditional is true as soon as the antecedent is false. This seems counterintuitive; in fact, falsity of the antecedent is felt to be irrelevant for the conclusion. Thus, the sentence

(76) If it rains, (then) the moon will melt

comes out true (counterintuitively) in any world at any time when it does not rain. Intuitively, however, (76) expresses a causal relation between raining and melting, and therefore the sentence is judged false, even if there is no actual rain. Such a relation is not represented by material implication, nor do any of the 15 remaining connectives do the job. The reason is that, in line with the Principle of Extensional Compositionality, all connectives considered so far work truth-functionally, which means that for each, the resulting meaning of the complex expression can be calculated by looking at the truth values in each row. Unfortunately, however, most connectives of natural language are more complex in that they do not work in a truth-functional manner. So the method of analyzing sentence connectives in terms of propositional logic is severely limited in its range.

As a case in point, consider the connective *because*. A simple substitution argument like the one at the very beginning of the present chapter shows that the truth value of 'S_1 *because* S_2' cannot be captured by only looking at the respective truth values of S_1 and S_2 alone. For example, suppose that S_1 = *The street is wet*, S_2 = *I feel sick*, S_3 = *It is raining*, and that all of S_1, S_2, and S_3 are true in a given situation. Then assume further that the sentence *the street is wet because it is raining* (= 'S_1 *because* S_3') is true, whereas the sentence *the street is wet because I feel sick* (= '$S1$ *because* $S2$') is false. Now, if the meaning of *because* were truth functional, this would be impossible: since S_2 and S_3 are both true in the situation described, the result of applying the (purported) truth table for *because* to S_1 and S_2 should be exactly the same as applying it to S_1 and S_3. But surely, the result cannot be both 1 and 0! Once again we find that the truth value of a complex sentence is not always a *function* of the truth values of its parts. More is needed to determine the truth and falsity of *because* connections, namely a *causal* connection between the *propositions* expressed by the sentences connected. This is why conjunctions like *because* are not **truth functional**.[7] What makes the "logical" connectives special is that they are indeed truth functional, whereas most connectives in natural language are not.

EXERCISE 28:

> Discuss which aspect of the meaning of *or* in (77) makes the connection between the sentences S_1 and S_2 not truth functional:
>
> (77) a. I get my beer now (S_1) or I'm leaving (S_2)
>   b. I get a pay raise (S_1) or I'm quitting (S_2)

---

7   Finding an adequate semantic account of *because* is a matter of much debate, especially since causation seems a problematic notion in itself; cf. Lewis (1973*a*), the article "Counterfactual Theories of Causation" in the ☞ Stanford Encyclopedia of Philosophy, or Pearl (2009) for a recent discussion.

5.2. *Exclusive* or

The alert reader will have realized that the above treatment of *or* does not always square with linguistic intuition. For example, in cases like the following, it is understood that the addressee will not get two birthday presents:

(78)   You get a bicycle or you get an iPod

In other words, we conclude from (78) that (79) is false:

(79)   You get a bicycle *and* you get an iPod

This reasoning, however, does not conform to the truth table of disjunction: rather, one would expect 'S1 *or* S_2' to be if when S_1 and S_2 are both true:

(80)

$[\![S_1]\!]_w$	$[\![S_2]\!]_w$	$[\![S_1]\!]_w$ XOR $[\![S_2]\!]_w$
1	1	0
1	0	1
0	1	1
0	0	0

A connective with the meaning shown in (80) has also been called **exclusive** *or* (sometimes written as "XOR", as in (80)), for the obvious reason that it excludes the possibility of both S_1 and S_2 being true. By contrast, the connective corresponding to the function ∨, i.e., disjunction, is called **inclusive'** *or* . Inclusive *or* allows both S_1 and S_2 to be true, while exclusive *or* only allows one or the other to be true, but never both. Here is the Venn diagram for exclusive *or*:

(81)

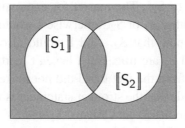

It has been claimed that *or* is ambiguous between inclusive and exclusive *or*. Such an ambiguity would be surprising, especially since it seems to occur in the majority of the world's languages. Also, it would have to be explained why natural language has not developed two different expressions in order to disambiguate the truth conditions.

In fact, and partly for reasons we cannot discuss here in detail, linguists have argued that there is no real ambiguity involved. One motivation for this claim comes from the observation that we are not free to choose either meaning. For example, consider:

(82)   If John shows up (S_1) or Mary starts singing (S_2), I will leave the party (S_3)

Clearly, the possibility that both S_1 and S_2 are true at one time cannot be excluded, and it is equally clear that in such a case this would definitely not lead to my staying at the party. This implies that *or* in (82) is understood as having an inclusive meaning. But could *or* also have the exclusive reading? We would then expect that I will stay if both S_1 and S_2 are true! But in that case we still would claim that (82) is false. The problem is that (82) simply has no such reading with S_1 and S_2 being true and me staying at the party (i.e., S_3 being false): only the inclusive reading is available in this kind of construction. The question is, of course, why this should be so if *or* is truly ambiguous.

Semanticists have therefore tried to attribute the difference between exclusive and inclusive *or* to pragmatics. Roughly, the answer pragmatics provides is the following: in fact, there is no ambiguity of *or* (and no pressure to resolve an ambiguity) because *or* unambiguously means inclusive *or* (in agreement with our intuitive understanding of (82)). The fact that *or* is nonetheless understood in an exclusive way in *some* contexts (but, as we saw, not in all) is due to additional pragmatic considerations of the following sort:

Suppose I say 'S_1 *or* S_2'. The reason for expressing myself this way is that I don't know whether S_1 or S_2, otherwise I would just say S_1 if I know that S_1, and S_2 if I know that S_2. And I would also say 'S_1 *and* S_2' if I know that both S_1 and S_2 are true. But I haven't made any of these 3 alternative utterances. So, from the fact that I did not make a (logically) stronger claim, one may conclude that the stronger statement is false—where *(logical) strength* relates to asymmetric entailment: 'S_1 *and* S_2' entails 'S_1 *or*, but not vice versa. But then, if 'S_1 *or* S_2' is true but the stronger 'S_1 *and* S_2' is false (because I did not make that claim), we just described exactly the truth conditions for exclusive *or*. We thus arrived at the conditions for XOR without having uttered a connective with exactly these truth conditions.

This also explains why we do not need a separate expression for exclusive *or*: there is no need for an additional expression because the job of expressing exclusiveness is already done in the pragmatic component of natural language.

On the other hand, there are a number of steps in the above argumentation that deserve closer examination (and elaboration), which would lead us into the field of (formal) pragmatics. Moreover, it still needs to be explained why there is no exclusive reading for (82). Roughly, the answer is that the exclusive reading is okay if it makes the entire proposition "stronger" in the sense explained above. But this would not happen in (82), because 'S$_1$ *or* S$_2$' is more deeply embedded into a conditional, so that '*if* S$_1$ *and* S$_2$, *then* S$_3$' is not stronger than (82). We leave it to the reader to make the required calculations.

As a result, the pragmatic inference to the stronger reading does not hold because the exclusive *or* would not make the entire statement logically stronger. Of course, the pragmatic tendency to strengthen an assertion is itself in need of an explanation, which we cannot go into here. In any case, the result of the discussion is that in natural language there is only one connective *or*, namely inclusive *or*.

There are many other additional inferences that come along with the use of connectives; most of them are discussed at length in the pragmatic literature. However, the reader is advised to read Chapter 9 on presuppositions first.

EXERCISE 29:

Is (83-a) equivalent to (83-b)?

(83) a. If S$_1$, then S$_2$
    b. If not S$_2$, then not S$_1$

EXERCISE 30:

Which of the following are tautologies?

(84) a. S$_1$ and not S$_1$
    b. S$_1$ or not S$_1$
    c. If (S$_1$ and S$_2$) or S$_3$, then S$_1$
    d. If S$_1$ and (S$_2$ or S$_3$), then S$_1$

5.3. Non-Clausal Connectives

Another limitation of truth-functional connectives is that they can only be used to combine or modify clauses. Yet, in natural language the same expressions are much more flexible as they are also used as a means to combine or modify all kinds of phrases, as exemplified for DPs and VPs in (85):

(85)   a.   At the zoo, we saw [DP penguins *and* bears]
          b.   One of the girls is *not* [VP sleeping]

On the other hand, one may try to avoid this flexibility by coming up with the following paraphrases:

(86)   a.   At the zoo, [we saw penguins] and [we saw bears]
          b.   One of the girls is such that it is false that [she is sleeping]

What is remarkable about these paraphrases is that they bring in the truth-functional connectives again: in going from (85-a) to (86-a) we replaced the *and* between two DPs by an *and* that connects sentences; in (b) we replaced the VP-modifying *negation* by an expression (*it is false that*) that takes a sentence as an argument and that can be interpreted as sentential negation.

The relation between (85) and (86) seems quite systematic. It is tempting, therefore, to design a semantic theory that takes advantage of such regularities in assuming that the semantic computation of the meaning of (85) in some way or other involves a calculation that applies to (86) (which might be considered the Logical Form of (85)). In particular, one might pursue the idea that the shift from (85) to the paraphrases in (86) should be accomplished by syntactic transformations. This would be a solution in the spirit of Generative Semantics, a theory that arose in the sixties of the 20th century. The task of the linguist is to define such transformations in a general rule-governed way.

Unfortunately, though, there are counterexamples that militate against such an idea. Let us illustrate the problem with reference to the zoo example (85-a). Consider (87):

(87)   In this zoo, penguins and bears live together in one enclosure

Here, the transformation that led us from (85-a) to (86-a) would yield the wrong result: (88) says that penguins live together on their own, as do bears, whereas (87) just says that bears and penguins share an enclosure.

(88)   In this zoo, penguins live together in one enclosure and bears live
        together in one enclosure

This shows that simple syntactic transformations won't do. What we need is
a semantic theory that can handle both cases; and it is by no means trivial
to come up with such a theory: there is more to the meaning of these words
than meets the eye. But once again, we cannot pursue these matters in an
introductory textbook.[8]

---

8   One might suggest that the following structure solves the problem:

    (i)   In this zoo, [penguins live together] and [bears live together] in
               one enclosure

    At least we conjoined sentences and so it seems that part of the (syntactic) problem is
    solved. But the reader should ask herself whether this is really an adequate (intuitively
    equivalent) paraphrase of (87). Observe also that the PP *in one enclosure* normally cannot
    modify a clause or, for that matter, a proposition, but seems to be dangling in both the
    syntactic and the semantic structure of (i). Hence (i) cannot in any way contribute to a
    solution of the problem. Rather, (i) seems to us to be an elliptic paraphrase of (88) rather
    than of (87).

Chapter 8
Intensions

1. From Propositions to Intensions

Recall that we identified the intension of a sentence S with the informational content of S. We will now show that the intension is practically the same as the proposition expressed by S, but for reasons that will become clear in a minute our formal definition of intension is a little bit more involved.

Our point of departure is again the box in (21) on p. 145, which we take to depict Logical Space—the vast set of all possible worlds W, among them our actual world. Using a method encountered in connection with type-driven interpretation (cf. Section 3 of Chapter 6), the proposition in (21) could also have been represented as a table in which every possible world is assigned a truth value:

(1)

world	truth value
w_1	1
w_2	0
w_3	1
...	...
w_n	0
...	...

This table represents the characteristic function of a proposition, i.e., a function assigning truth values to possible worlds. We will now declare the characteristic function of the proposition expressed by a sentence to be the *intension* of that sentence. For example, the intension of the sentence

(2)   Barschel[1] was murdered

---

1   Uwe Barschel [1944–1987] was a German politician who had to resign as the prime minister of Schleswig-Holstein under scandalous circumstances (comparable to the Watergate affair) and who was found dead in the bathtub of his hotel room a few days after his resignation. The circumstances of his death could never be fully clarified. Cf. *http://www.jurablogs.com/de/was-weiss-helmut-kohl-ueber-barschels-tod*.

is a function whose arguments are possible worlds and that assigns the value 1 to every world in which Barschel was murdered, and 0 to any other world.

The intension of a sentence shows how its truth value varies across Logical Space. Since the truth value of a sentence is its extension, we may say that *its intension is its extension in dependence of the world*. The most interesting aspect of this characterization is that it carries over from sentences to arbitrary expressions like nouns, verbs, adjectives, etc., the extensions of which we determined in the previous two chapters. As we saw there, what the extension of a given expression is depends on the situation. Having replaced situations with points in Logical Space, we can now define the intension of any expression α to be its extension in dependence of the world, i.e., as the function that assigns to any world w in Logical Space the extension of α at w. As in the case of sentences, such functions may be represented by tables matching worlds (in the left column) with extensions (to their right). The tables (4)–(6) indicate what the functions may look like in the case of the expressions in (3):

(3)   a.   The president snores
       b.   the president
       c.   snores

(4)

world	extension
w_1	1
w_2	0
w_3	1
...	...
w_n	the truth value 1 iff the president in w_n snores in w_n
...	...

(5)

world	extension
w_1	George
w_2	George
w_3	Hillary
...	...
w_n	the person who is president in w_n
...	...

(6)

world	extension
w_1	{George, Hillary, Kermit}
w_2	{Bill, Hillary}
w_3	{Bill, George, Hillary}
...	...
w_n	the individuals who snore in w_n
...	...

Table (4) characterizes the proposition expressed by (3-a). Table (5) shows how the extension of the description (3-b) varies across Logical Space: whereas George is the president in worlds w_1 and w_2, Hillary holds this office in w_3. Similarly, table (6) shows how the extension of the intransitive verb (3-c) varies across Logical Space. Hence the three functions indicated in tables (4)–(6) represent the intensions of the expressions in (3). It is important to realize that the values assigned by the intension in (4) are always truth values, whereas those assigned in (5) are individuals, and the intension described in (6) assigns sets of individuals to worlds. Of course, this is as it should be: the extensions of the expressions differ in type (to adopt a term from Section 3 of Chapter 6), and their intensions must reflect these differences in the values they assign. On the other hand, all intensions have the same input—the worlds of Logical Space.[2]

The upshot is that we may define the intension of an expression α as a function that assigns an extension to each possible world. More formally, we can build up intensions from extensions in the following way:

(7)   The intension of α, written as $[\![\,\alpha\,]\!]$, is that function f such that for every possible world w, $f(w) = [\![\,\alpha\,]\!]_w$.

According to (7), the intension of a sentence S is a function that assigns to S one of 1 or 0 depending on a possible world w. If the value of that function is 1 for a world w, then S describes a fact of w. If not, S does not describe a fact, and we say that S is false of w.

---

2   This is actually a simplification to be withdrawn in Chapter 9, where different expressions are seen to call for different inputs to their intensions. Still, the difference is independent of the type of expression and its extensions.

2. Composing Intensions

The above discussion has revealed that the concept of an intension applies to arbitrary expressions—as long as we can describe their extensions. Intensions can now be combined in order to form new intensions of complex expressions, in accordance with the

(8)   *Principle of Intensional Compositionality*
The intension of a complex expression is a function of the intensions of its immediate parts and the way they are composed.

Let us illustrate this with the following example:

(9)   *Paul schläft*
Paul sleeps
'Paul is sleeping'

The intension of (9) is a function that assigns to any world the truth value 1 if Paul is sleeping in that world, and 0 otherwise. How can this be calculated on the basis of the intensions of *Paul* and *schläft*? The intension of *schläft* works analogously to the intension of *snores* above: it is a function assigning the set of sleeping entities to each possible world. What is the intension of *Paul*? In reality, the name refers to a particular person, namely Paul.[3] But what about other possible worlds? Could someone else have been Paul? Hardly. Of course, another person could have been *called* "Paul", but calling her or him Paul wouldn't make this person Paul. Paul could have had another name, but he would still be Paul. When considering the possibility that Paul's parents almost called him "Jacob", we would have to say that Paul (and not Jacob) could have been given a different name from the one he actually has. Thus, with the name "Paul" we always refer to the same person—regardless of what this person would be called in other circumstances.[4] We conclude that the intension of *Paul* looks like this:

---

3   Of course, there are millions of people called "Paul". The convention is that if in a given situation only one person comes to mind, then we can use the name to refer to that person. In a textbook context, however, no such specific context is given. Here the convention is that *Paul* should really be understood as $Paul_i$, with the index i disambiguating between the millions of Pauls by indicating to which of them the expression is intended to refer.

4   This interesting observation about names was overlooked in many philosophical discussions prior to the pioneering work of Saul Kripke (1972). Alas, it has also been disputed, notably by the Dutch semanticist Bart Geurts (1997), who brought up the following example: *If a child is christened 'Bambi', then Disney will sue Bambi's parents.*

(10)

world	entity
w_1	Paul
w_2	Paul
w_3	Paul
...	Paul
w_n	Paul
...	Paul

This table of course reveals a certain redundancy because the extension of the name does not depend on any of the worlds. Still, for systematic reasons we assume that all names, like all other expressions, have an intension which determines the extension at every possible world. The only difference from other expressions is that this is a *constant* function that yields the same individual for each possible world. Such expressions are called *rigid designators*.

How can we combine these intensions in order to get a complex intension? This is quite simple. We only have to compute the extensions for every possible world. Having done so we get another table, which for each world w contains a row with the value 1 if and only if $[\![\mathit{Paul}]\!]_w \in [\![\mathit{schläft}]\!]_w$. This new table is again an intension, i.e., a function that assigns truth values to each possible world. This way, the combination of intensions is reduced to the combination of extensions, which has already been described in Chapter 5. It is only that the results of this computation for each possible world now make up a new intension, a function that assigns to each world w a truth value, namely the result of calculating the extension in w. The new intension is thus calculated in a "pointwise" manner, with the "points" being the extension at each point in the Logical Space (i.e., each possible world).[5]

Let us now, after this long detour, return to the analysis of the examples that initially gave rise to intensions:

(11)   a.   John knows that [Hamburg is larger than Cologne]
        b.   John knows that [Pfäffingen is larger than Breitenholz]

It is clear by now that the embedded sentences express different propositions. The Principle of Intensional Compositionality (8) says that the intensions of the embedded sentences are responsible for the difference in meaning of the

---

5   In fact, pointwise calculation is also at work in truth tables—with the additional twist that there the possible worlds come in "clusters" defined by the distribution of the truth values over the propositional variables.

entire sentences. Hence, the key to the solution of our problem must be that the object of *know* (the *that*-clause) is an intension (rather than an extension, i.e., a truth value).

What, then, is the extension of the verb *know*? Earlier we assumed that the extension of a transitive verb is a set of ordered pairs of individuals. For a verb like *know*, however, it ought to be obvious by now that we need a relation between an individual (the subject) and a proposition (representing the meaning of a sentence). In other words, for the sentences in (11) to be true, the extension of the verb *know* would have to contain the pair consisting of John and the intension of the embedded sentence. Quite generally, it would have to consist of pairs of persons and (characteristic functions of) propositions.

Now, given that the embedded sentences in (11) are not synonymous, we can easily imagine a possible world of which (11-a) is true but (11-b) is false, so that John might know one proposition but not the other. In other words, what we proposed above as the truth conditions for *John knows that S)* is the following:

(12) $[\![\text{John knows that S}]\!]_w = 1$ iff $\langle [\![\text{John}]\!]_w, [\![\text{S}]\!] \rangle \in [\![\text{know}]\!]_w$

Now, if p and q are different propositions it might well be that

(13) $\langle [\![\text{John}]\!]_w, p \rangle \in [\![\text{know}]\!]_w$ and
        $\langle [\![\text{John}]\!]_w, q \rangle \notin [\![\text{know}]\!]_w.$

To arrive at (13), we still need a rule for constructing the extension of the VP *knows that S*:[6]

(14) $[\![\text{attitude verb + that + S}]\!]_w := \{ x : \langle x, [\![\text{S}]\!] \rangle \in [\![\text{attitude verb}]\!]_w \}$

Using (14), we may go on with our extensional subject-predicate treatment (23) from Chapter 5 (p. 89) and derive (13). We leave this to the attentive reader, who will have noticed that (14) is rather similar to (44)—also from Chapter 5 (p. 98)—where a transitive verb was combined with its object. Of course, this similarity is not coincidental. After all, both rules deal with transitive verbs and their complements, which only happen to be of a different kind. However, there is another, more interesting difference between the clausal case (14) and its nominal analogue (44): whereas the latter had the object feed its extension to the extension of the VP, in the former case the

---

6   Since the complementizer *that* does not seem to have a meaning of its own, we treat it as part of the attitude verb; this is done purely for convenience.

complement clause contributes its intension. This, then, is how the compositionality challenge from Section 1 is finally solved: whereas normally, i.e., in extensional environments, the extension of a compound expression can be obtained by combining the extensions of its parts, in intensional contexts one of the parts contributes its intension instead. It should be obvious that this does not affect the overall nature of the process of composing meanings, i.e., intensions: as in the extensional environment considered at the beginning of this section, (14) allows a pointwise calculation of the intension of the VP, by determining its extension world by world. But whereas both the verb and the object clause contribute their intensions, only part of the verb intension—viz., its extension—is relevant when it comes to determining the extension of the VP at a given point; in this respect the verb behaves like any constituent in an extensional environment. The complement clause, however, always, i.e., at each point (possible world), contributes its full intension, which is what makes the construction intensional.

EXERCISE 31:

> Imagine a possible world where all singing people are also dancing. Now, if (15-a) is true of that world, (15-b) might well be false, and vice versa:
>
> (15) a. Mary tries to sing
>   b. Mary tries to dance
>
> Account for this by a semantic rule similar to (14).

Summarizing so far, all we did was replace the extension of the complement of *know* with its intension. Therefore the extension of the complex sentence is not calculated on the basis of the extensions of its parts, but in the case at hand on the basis of the intension of the sentential complement. As we have seen in connection with clausal connectives in Section 5.1 in the preceding chapter, most natural language connectives are not truth functional, which means that their interpretation is based on the intensions of their complements, rather than on their truth values. This also applies to all verbs and adjectives that take sentences (or infinitives) as their complement.[7]

---

7   An exception is adjectives (and corresponding verbs) like those occurring in *it is **true** that . . .*, *it **holds** that . . .*, etc.

As another case in point, consider (16):

(16)   Paul is looking for an exciting German detective story

The problem is the following: assume that the actual extension of *exciting German detective story* is actually the empty set, so there is no exciting German detective story. Assume further that there is no cheap French Bordeaux wine either. Then the two predicates have the same extension, namely the empty set. Nonetheless we cannot conclude from (16) that (17) holds.

(17)   Paul is looking for a cheap French Bordeaux wine

This, however, should be the case if the Principle of Extensional Compositionality were applicable. From this we must conclude that the verb *look [for]* creates an intensional context, turning the (prepositional) object into something intensional (the different intensions of the properties mentioned above). This may then also explain the ambiguity of examples like the one discussed in section 4.3 of Chapter 3.[8]

3.   Intensions and Sense Relations

Sense relations were introduced above (Chapter 2, pp. 18ff.) long before sets were. However, now that the latter have entered the stage, it is easy to see that many sense relations are closely related to set-theoretic relations between extensions. For example, the hyponymy relation between *woman* and *human being* boils down to a subset relation between the extensions of $[\![\text{woman}]\!]_w$ and $[\![\text{human being}]\!]_w$. It is therefore tempting to say that a noun phrase A is a hyponym of a noun phrase B iff $[\![A]\!]_w \subseteq [\![B]\!]_w$.

However, we did not present things that way because there is a potential danger of misunderstanding: the correspondence between sense relations and relations between sets needs further qualification. For it could well be that $[\![A]\!]_w \subseteq [\![B]\!]_w$ without A being a hyponym of B. For example, more likely than not all professors are adults, though *adult* is not a hyponym of *professor*. The fact that there is no hyponymy here reveals itself in that it is not *inconceivable* that there are professors who were younger than adults. Hence sense relations are not a matter of extension. Rather they are a matter of Logical Space. Since it is conceivable that some professors are non-adults, this is re-

---

8   An explanation of the ambiguity along these lines can be found in Quine (1956).

flected in Logical Space in that some possible worlds are inhabited by under-age professors. Although it is clear that such worlds are purely hypothetical, their mere existence helps to block unwanted inferences. For example, from

(18)   Saul Kripke is a professor

we cannot *logically* infer

(19)   Saul Kripke is an adult

although this is more than probable. The reason is that one can well imagine fictional scenarios where Kripke was appointed professor before reaching adulthood.[9] This means that the set of possible worlds that validate (18) is not a subset of the worlds of which (19) is true. On the other hand, from

(20)   This is a bus

we can validly infer

(21)   This is a vehicle

The proposition (20) is a subset of (21), and this is so because this time there is no possible world in (20) that is not contained in (21). And this is so because there is no possible extension of *bus* that is not contained in the extension of *vehicle*. In consequence, when depicting sense relations as relations between sets, we must always additionally keep in mind that these relations between extensions must hold in all possible worlds:

(22)   *A* is a hyponym of *B* if and only if
        $[\![A]\!]_w \subseteq [\![B]\!]_w$ holds for all possible worlds w.

Definition (22) illustrates that sense relations are *intensional* relations, i.e., they hold between expressions because their intensions are related in certain ways—and not just their (actual) extensions. More specifically, a sense relation may be defined as a relation that holds between two (not necessarily lexical) expressions *A* and *B* if and only if extensions are always related in a certain characteristic way: subsethood in the case of hyponymy, disjointness in the case of incompatibility, etc. Now, without the qualification "always", this characterization would refer to extensions only; but given that qualification—which is, of course, meant to quantify over Logical Space—

---

9   Given that he had published one of his major works by the age of 18, this is less far-fetched than, say, the ☞ Doogie Howser show.

we speak about the extensions at arbitrary possible worlds, and thus about the intensions of the expressions in question. It is for this reason that we were reluctant to represent sense relations as relations between extensions.

Sense relations may hold between any kind of expressions; in particular, they may hold between sentences. Again, the subset relation is a case in point: if the *propositions* expressed by two sentences S_1 and S_2 stand in that relation, there is a particular semantic relation between them: S_1 cannot be true without S_2 being true as well. It is thus not without intuitive appeal that this particular relation is known as **entailment**. As a case in point, this relation holds between the following two sentences:

(23)   a.   Mary is a blind piano teacher
        b.   Mary is blind

In any possible world in which Mary (i.e., the referent of *Mary*) is in the intersection of the extensions of *blind* and *piano teacher*, she is also in the extension of *blind*; for the latter is a subset of the former. Hence, the set of worlds of which (23-a) is true is a subset of those worlds of which (23-b) is true; in other words, the proposition expressed by (23-a) is a subset of the proposition expressed by (23-b)—which means that (23-a) entails (23-b), in the above sense.

Entailment is a sense relation, in the sense indicated a couple of paragraphs ago. For, as the reader may care to verify, the relation holds between sentences S_1 and S_2 iff $[\![S_1]\!]_w \le [\![S_2]\!]_w$, for any possible world w. The reader will have observed that we have come across this sense relation before, if under a different guise. For obviously, a sentence S_1 entails S_2 iff the *inference* with S_1 as a single premise and S_2 as its conclusion is valid. No wonder this sense relation is particularly interesting and important. In fact, most, if not all, sense relations may be defined in terms of entailment.[10] Thus, for instance, disjointness of the propositions expressed turns out to be a sense relation that is aptly called **contradiction**. As a case in point, consider:

---

10   Whether *all* sense relations can be reduced to entailment is a matter of both the details of definition (which we are carefully avoiding here) and the expressive power of language under scrutiny, i.e., what precisely can be expressed in it. These matters are formally investigated in a branch of logic and semantics called **model theory**; cf. Zimmermann (2011) and the literature cited there.

(24)   a.   John has three daughters
        b.   John has no children

The two sentences under (24) mutually contradict each other: even though both may be false (if John has one child, a son, say), they certainly cannot both be true in the same circumstances. In other words, the propositions they express are disjoint. To see what this has to do with entailment, consider the following pair of sentences:

(25)   a.   John has three daughters
        b.   It is false that John has no children

Obviously, and as the reader may verify in detail, (25-a) entails (25-b) in the above sense; moreover, (25-b) is the negation of (24-b), whereas (25-a) is the same as (24-a). And these facts seem to be related: the fact that the sentences in (25) stand in an entailment relation merely reflects that the sentences in (24) contradict each other. Readers will be invited to see the general pattern behind the relation between (24) and (25) in an exercise.

In a similar vein, other sense relations between sentences may be reduced to entailment between related sentences. In fact, not just sense relations between *sentences* can be reduced to entailment. For instance, in illustrating the hyponymy between the nouns *bus* and *vehicle*, we made use of the sentences (20) and (21), which stand in an entailment relation. In fact, it has been suggested that we only have intuitive access to sense relations of this sort via entailment (or inference) relations between corresponding propositions. If certain inferences hold, this justifies the existence of certain sense relations. This way, the intuitive evaluation of inferences may take priority over that of sense relations: the justification of certain sense relations proceeds via that of inferences, and these in turn rest on our intuitions about conceivable possible worlds (or at least conceivable situations; but after all, worlds are only large situations and nothing prevents very small worlds; cf. ☞ www.bussongs.com/songs/its_a_small_world_after_all_short.php).

EXERCISE 32:

> Use the definitions of entailment as subsethood and contradiction as disjointness to show that whenever a sentence S_1 contradicts a sentence S_2, S_1 entails the negation of S_2, and vice versa.

4. Compositional vs. Lexical Semantics

The preceding section may suggest that compositional semantics, particularly with its approach to sentence meaning in terms of propositions, covers the area of lexical semantics, the study of the meaning of words. Consider a common noun like *dog*. Compositional semantics teaches us that its extension is a set of individuals and that its intension is a function from Logical Space to the corresponding extensions. Hence the intension of *dog* is a function that assigns to each possible world a certain set, viz., the set of dogs. This way, then, compositional semantics seems to settle matters of lexical semantics. However, this impression is largely misguided. The relation between the two fields is far less straightforward.

To see this, let us first recall (from Section 3.2 of Chapter 4) that the extension of an expression in a given situation is not always known to the speaker; that is, the speaker does not always know of every expression just what its extension is.[11] In particular, we may not be able to point to, or even describe, every element of the extension of *dog*, and we may not even know how many elements it has. Still, there are quite a few extensions we do know, and in sufficiently constrained situations, they may even include that of *dog*. However, in all such cases it is crucial that we are part of the world relative to which the extensions are determined: in order to know what the extension of *dog* (or, for that matter, any other expression) at a given world is, one needs to be in that world; in other words, one cannot know the extension of *dog* at a world that one does not inhabit. The reason is that, in order to know what the extension of an expression at a particular world is, one would have to be in a position to somehow single out that world in the first place. However, this is impossible in the case of worlds one does not inhabit: one may try to characterize a foreign world by the facts that obtain in it, or by specifying how it differs from one's own world, but given the maximal specificity of worlds—which,

---

11   There is a distracting but interesting ambiguity lurking here, caused by the verb *know*.
By "knowing the extension of *dog*", we mean, of course, knowing *that* a certain set is the
extension of *dog*. However, there is also a sense of "knowing the extension of *dog*" as
being somehow acquainted with the set itself, though not necessarily *as* the extension of
the word *dog*. This is like the difference between knowing the capital of Italy by having
been to Rome (which one can do without even knowing that it is in Italy) vs. knowing the
capital of Italy in a geography test (for which one does not have to be acquainted with
Rome as a city). Since the latter reading, which is at stake here, describes the ability to
answer a question—*What is the extension of "dog"?*, or: *What is the capital of Italy?*—
semanticists have coined the term **concealed question** for it.

as the reader may remember from Section 3 of the previous chapter, is a crucial feature—one will never be able to complete this specification. The actual world is different in this respect because we may, as it were, point to it as *this* world.[12]

In sum, speakers do not know the actual extensions of the majority of expressions, and as to non-actual extensions, they cannot even know them. And why would semanticists be in a better position in this respect? This sounds like bad news for a theory of intensions, which after all largely consist of non-actual extensions. How could we ever account for the meaning of *dog* in terms of objects that we are unable to properly identify in the first place?

In reaction to this problem, some linguists would deny that a theory of meaning requires the identification of extensions at all possible worlds. In fact, they fall back on some minimal assumptions that do at least some work in a theory of meaning. One such assumption concerns the logical types of extensions and intensions of lexical items, which are specified somewhat along the following lines:

(26)   a. $[\![\,\text{dog}\,]\!]_w$ is a set of individuals.
        b. $[\![\,\text{cat}\,]\!]_w$ is a set of individuals.
        c. $[\![\,\text{animal}\,]\!]_w$ is a set of individuals.

Obviously, constraints like (26) (which are meant to hold for arbitrary possible worlds w) heavily underspecify the intensions of the words described. But they suffice to account for their compositional behavior, i.e., the way their extensions and intensions combine with those of other expressions. And this already covers a large variety of inferences, provided that the extensions of at least some "logical" expressions are explicitly specified. Thus, for instance, the validity of the following inference can be established without any assump-

---

12   Actually, some philosophers assume that particular non-actual worlds may be singled out in terms of their similarity (or "proximity") to the actual world, e.g., as the world that most closely resembles reality, except that Bizet and Verdi were compatriots; cf. Stalnaker (1981), or Warmbröd (1982). Arguably, however, this—highly debatable— so-called *limit assumption* is based on a somewhat different (less fine-grained) conception of worlds, and in any case it certainly does not suffice to characterize every member of Logical Space (nor is it supposed to). Also, some philosophers from Leibniz to Kristofferson (cf. ☞ http://www.cowboylyrics.com/lyrics/kristofferson-kris/best-of-all-possible-worlds-13012.html) have singled out a particular world by its overall quality— but then again this characterization as the "best of all possible worlds" is supposed to pick out the actual one anyway.

tions about the meanings of the words it contains—apart from the underlined ones:

(27) Tom is a̲ cat a̲n̲d̲ Tom is asleep

⊨ A̲ cat is asleep

Once the (world-independent) extensions of the indefinite article and conjunction have been specified (cf. p. 117 and 86, respectively), (27) follows by the pertinent rules of extensional composition and the general type constraints (26) (plus one for the name *Tom*, which is left to the reader to provide).

However, these very general, structural constraints on word meaning do not suffice when it comes to slightly more involved inferences like:

(28) Tom is a̲ cat

⊨ Tom is n̲o̲t̲ a̲ dog

If all that is known about *cat* and *dog* is their general extension type as laid down in (26), then (28) obviously does not follow; in fact, (26) is quite consistent with the assumption that all cats are dogs, or vice versa, or both! To make up for this lacuna, more assumptions on lexical meanings must be invoked. Thus, in addition to the specification of types in (26) further restrictions make up for a partial description of meanings. The relevant restriction in the case at hand is the requirement that the extensions of *cat* and *dog* do not overlap; moreover, these extensions (at every world w) must be subsets of the noun *animal*:

(29) a. $[\![\,\mathrm{dog}\,]\!]_w \cap [\![\,\mathrm{cat}\,]\!]_w = \emptyset$

   b. $[\![\,\mathrm{dog}\,]\!]_w \cup [\![\,\mathrm{cat}\,]\!]_w \subseteq [\![\,\mathrm{animal}\,]\!]_w$

These restrictions account for the fact that extensions are not distributed randomly across Logical Space. Rather, there is some uniformity in the way the extension of an expression depends on the particular world. In the simplest case it does not even vary. We have seen that proper names are **rigid** in this sense, and so are "logical words" like truth-functional connectives and determiners. Since the extensions of these expressions do not depend on the particular world, their intensions may be defined entirely in terms of their actual extension, without reference to any particular non-actual worlds, viz., as the function that assigns the actual extension to any world whatsoever. But even if extensions do vary, the way they do can be described without reference to any particular worlds. Given that (29) holds independently at every world

w, a (presumably rather long) list of statements like (29) partially captures word meaning by representing the sense relations addressed in the previous section: (29-a) is a clear case of incompatibility, whereas (29-b) represents hyponymy.

According to this theory, the role of lexical meaning in compositional semantics thus reduces to a blend of three components, which are meant to act as proxies for full meaning specifications of all words:

(30)   a.   Specifications of extensions of (a few) "logical words"
        b.   Extension type constraints for all lexical items
        c.   Specifications of sense relations between non-logical words

The specifications under (30-c) are also called **meaning postulates**.[13] Which meaning postulates are needed in a full-fledged semantic account depends on the inferences and sense relations to be captured. Ideally, a system of postulates ought to describe the entire semantic network determined by the lexical meanings of a language. However, whereas some sense relations, like hyponymy and incompatibility, can be directly expressed in terms of meaning postulates like (29), certain others are far harder to come by. More specifically, this holds for sense relations that are reflected in the *invalidity* of potential inferences. Compatibility and non-synonymy are cases in point. While postulates like (31) may still see to it that two *words* stand in these relations, it is much harder to establish the same relations above the lexical level.

(31)   a. $[\![\text{professor}]\!]_w \cap [\![\text{bachelor}]\!]_w \neq \emptyset$
        b. $[\![\text{dog}]\!]_w \neq [\![\text{animal}]\!]_w$

According to (31-a), the extensions of *professor* and *bachelor* in w overlap, as they should since the two nouns are compatible. More precisely, (31-a) must hold for *some* world(s) w, but certainly not for all: after all, it is still conceivable that all professors happen to be married. And the same goes for postulate (31-b), which expresses that *dog* and *animal* differ in meaning—something that the hyponymy postulate (29-b) still leaves open. In this respect, meaning postulates like the ones in (31) differ from those under (29), which are meant to hold for *all* worlds w. And it is such postulates that do not "project" beyond the lexical level. Consider:

(32)   John is both a professor and a bachelor

---

13   The term goes back to Carnap (1952), where it is introduced in a slightly different sense.

Sentence (32) certainly expresses something that could well be the case. So the proposition expressed by (32) is not the empty set. However, once lexical items are dealt with entirely in terms of the resources in (30), this is no longer obvious. In particular, (31-a) does *not* guarantee that (32) comes out as non-contradictory; as (31-a) is not about John (or about any individual in particular), it does not say that John, of all persons, ever ends up in the (at times non-empty) intersection of *professor* and *bachelor*. To be sure, there are ways around these problems, but no straightforward and principled ones, as far as we are aware.

In contrast to this partial characterization of meaning, a full-fledged account of word meaning would have it that statements like (33) are all we need for a theory of meaning:

(33) a. $[\![\, \mathrm{dog} \,]\!]_w = \{ x : x \text{ is a dog in } w \}$
      b. $[\![\, \mathrm{cat} \,]\!]_w = \{ x : x \text{ is a cat in } w \}$
      c. $[\![\, \mathrm{animal} \,]\!]_w = \{ x : x \text{ is an animal in } w \}$

Appearances to the contrary, our inability to refer to worlds other than ours does not militate against (33): rather than pinning down the individual worlds themselves, we have only described the way in which the respective extension depends on the worlds. Even if we cannot say what the truth value of a sentence like *Paul is blond* in a particular world is—again, merely for lack of means to refer to that world—we may well be able to specify the particular features of any world that this extension depends on, viz., the color of Paul's hair in that world. Similarly, we do know how the extension of *dog* depends on the particular facts of a possible world (including our actual one): it contains precisely those individuals in that world that are dogs. Hence if an individual happens to be a dog in a particular world, then it will be a member of the extension of *dog* at that world; otherwise it will not. Now, of course, this specification presupposes that we know what a dog is; but this we may safely assume to be part of our lexical knowledge of our meta-language.[14]

Our meta-linguistic knowledge may also be of help when it comes to matters internal to possible worlds. Thus, for instance, once we specify the extensions of *dog*, *cat*, and *animal* as in (33), we may conclude that, whichever world w we consider, the extensions of the first two nouns at w do not over-

---

14   The air of circularity of this explanation vanishes if it is translated into a different (meta-)language: a German description of the intension of the English noun *dog* does not depend on any previous knowledge of English (but it may make use of the German word *Hund*).

lap; and they will both be (not necessarily proper) subsets of the extension of the third one. In other words, the meaning postulates set up in (29) no longer have to be stipulated, but follow from (33). Thus, for example, the fact (29-a) that the extensions of *cat* and *dog* do not overlap (in any world w) can be proved indirectly by hypothetically assuming that (for some world w) they do have a common element x. Then, according to (33-a), x would have to be a dog (in w); and similarly, according to (33-b), x would have to be a cat (in w). But then x would have to be both a cat and a dog (in w)—which is impossible, and thus not the case in any possible world (w). We thus conclude that the hypothesis that the two extensions overlap cannot be upheld; hence (29-a) has been established. And by a similar kind of reasoning we could deduce (29-b).

The crucial step in the above argument for (29-a) involves the impossibility of there being anything that is both a cat and a dog. Where did that come from? How do we know? The answer is: from our own linguistic competence.[15] As speakers of English, we have mastered the meaning of *cat* and *dog*, and thereby know that these express incompatible properties. In fact, this very piece of lexical semantics of our meta-language closely corresponds to the object-linguistic fact described in (29-a). Again, there is nothing wrong or circular about this correspondence. However, it does show that when it comes to substantial claims about the lexical semantics of the object language, these may have to be derived by invoking our own linguistic competence of the meta-language.

Many semanticists have qualms about this kind of reasoning, because it does not sufficiently separate general or anecdotal background knowledge from linguistic theory. They propose making partial descriptions of lexical meanings by way of meaning postulates. One potential advantage the reductive strategy (30) has over "direct" specifications of lexical meanings along the lines of (33) ought to be kept in mind: the separation of semantic competence and background knowledge. To see why this is a feature of rather than a bug in the system of postulates, one should first note that sense-related matters are not as clear-cut as we have been presenting them. Consider (29-a) again. We have been assuming that the incompatibility of *cat* and *dog* is a matter of linguistic competence. Consequently, anyone who would even con-

---

15   In his highly readable essay *The Meaning of 'Meaning'*, American philosopher Hilary Putnam (1975) has argued that this kind of knowledge cannot be a matter of knowing the intensions of words like *cat* and *dog*—which is beyond ordinary speakers' grasp!

sider the existence of animals that are both cats and dogs a logical possibility would have to be classified as having insufficient mastery of English, rather than poor biological knowledge. Similarly, if someone tells a story in which it turns out that cats, which mankind had been thinking of as a species of animals, were actually robots extra-terrestrials had sent to earth as spies, the use of *cat* in that story would not be in line with its literal meaning, given (29-b).[16]

This may seem hard to swallow. Aren't the relations established in (29) matters of science rather than semantics? If so, then it would seem that the postulates in (29) would have to go, and presumably quite a few other postulates with them, given analogous considerations and scenarios. At the end of the day, this could leave very little for the lexical part of semantics—a few (if any) full descriptions of logical words, some differential postulates like (31-b) (or suitable principles to make up for their effects), and type constraints like (26), which would form the core part of lexical semantics. However, this does not seem quite right either: somebody who does not have the first idea of how the meanings of English words relate to each other could hardly be attributed mastery of the language, which (s)he would have to be if lexical intensions were only regulated by type constraints. The problem seems to be that there is no clear-cut border between linguistic and extra-linguistic knowledge.[17] Now, as a matter of fact, meaning postulates may actually help to account for this continuum of knowledge. For they make explicit which additional assumptions are needed in order to classify a relation between expressions as purely semantic. Roughly, the more postulates that have to be invoked to establish a sense relation or a valid inference, the further away the latter will be from semantic core knowledge. As far as we can see, this idea has not been systematically explored so far; so we leave it as a speculation for future research.

The disappointing message is that at the end of the day compositional semantics tells us next to nothing about the meaning of individual words. In particular, it cannot in full answer the question "What Is Meaning?". On the other hand, semanticists generally do not bewail this unfortunate state of affairs. Why not? For one thing, compositional semantics may still provide the tools for the analysis of interesting lexical items, e.g., modal verbs like

---

16   This thought experiment is inspired by Putnam's work mentioned in fn. 15, p 186.

17   This is a central concern of another classic essay in 20th century philosophy of language, Willard Van Orman Quine's *Two Dogmas of Empiricism* (1951).

must, can, ought, might, and others (cf. e.g. Lewis (1973*b*), Kratzer (1977), or Kratzer (1981)). And there are many more lexical items that reveal an interesting behavior even within the severe limitations compositional semantics may impose on a theory of meaning. As a prime example of the kind of semantic analysis we have in mind, let us, in the next section, consider the verbs *know* and *believe*.

5. Hintikka's Attitudes

In Section 2 we used a classic substitution argument to show that attitude verbs like *know* and *believe* create intensional contexts: instead of operating on the truth values of their object clauses, their extensions were taken to be relations between persons and propositions. But we did not say just which persons and propositions these extensions connect. An analogy to the realm of determiners may help to appreciate what is at stake here. Rather than just saying that their extensions relate two sets—viz., noun and VP extensions— we also specified what conditions two sets must fulfill in order to be related by a given determiner extension. This was done in terms of set theory: the extensions of *every*, *a*, and *no* turned out to be the relations of, respectively, subsethood, overlap, and disjointness between sets. In the current section we take a brief look at a semantic analysis of attitude verbs that uses Logical Space to spell out which persons are related to which propositions by the extension of a given verb. In other words, just like quantifiers have been analyzed as reporting relations holding in the realm of sets, so attitude verbs will be analyzed as reporting relations holding between possible worlds. The approach is known as **Hintikka semantics**.[18]

To see how Logical Space enters the picture of attitudes, let us concentrate on a particular specimen, the verb *think*, in a particular reading, according to which the sentence (34) does not report a mental activity of its subject but rather a general state that she may be in even when she is not actively thinking about John:

(34)   Mary thinks that John is in Rome

---

18   After the eminent Finnish logician Jaakko Hintikka (*1929), who put it forward in his 1969 paper *Semantics for Propositional Attitudes*, which heavily builds on insights from his own earlier work in Hintikka (1962). Incidentally, what is called *Hintikka semantics* in linguistic semantics should not be confused with the quite unrelated *game-theoretic* account of quantification to which Hintikka has turned in his later work.

Suppose Mary takes John to the airport, then goes home and later talks to John over the phone, who tells her he has just arrived at Rome. Given such a scenario, (34) is likely to be true and continues to be so, as long as Mary has no reason to believe that John may have left Rome. In particular, (34) does not become false simply because Mary gets distracted or falls asleep: the sentence reports an attitude, which disposes her to judge true that John is in Rome if her mind turns to this question. The mental state that Mary is in and which causes her to think that John is in Rome rather than Los Angeles, that it is Sunday night and not Monday morning, that her name is *Mary*, not *Harry*, etc., is called her (overall) **doxastic state**.[19] So the reading of *think* that we are after is the one that is used to describe subjects' doxastic states.

The key idea behind Hintikka semantics is that doxastic states (and analogous ones, to be considered later) may be characterized in terms of Logical Space. Take Mary again. In the scenario at hand, there are two kinds of possible worlds (or situations) as far as she is concerned: the ones that are *truly possible* for her, and the rest, which are *excluded* by her (current) doxastic state. The worlds she considers possible are those that she cannot distinguish from the real world in the sense that, for all she takes to be the case, any of these worlds may be the actual one she inhabits; and the ones she excludes are those that she does not take herself to be in because they do not conform to what she takes to be the case in that actual world she inhabits. For instance, any possible world in Logical Space in which John is in Los Angeles (at the time considered) is one that Mary excludes. In fact, one may say that she excludes such worlds *because* of John's location; however, there may be more reasons to exclude them from her point of view, e.g., if a world is also inhabited by living dinosaurs, or if Helmut Kohl is still the German chancellor in it. By the same token, there are also a lot of possible worlds that she excludes even though in them, John does happen to be in Rome; again there may be lots of other factors that count against them. However, to be sure, there are also loads of possible worlds that Mary does not exclude. One thing these worlds have in common is that in each of them, John is in Rome—otherwise Mary would have reason to exclude it. But there are many details of greater or lesser importance that these worlds disagree about and about which Mary is undecided: in some but not all of these worlds, the number of persons worldwide turning off a light within the next hour is a prime number; in some but not all of these worlds, her old schoolmate Jane whom Mary lost track of ages

---

19   From the ancient Greek word for belief, *doxa*.

ago is still alive, in others she died a year ago after suffering from a long disease, in a car accident, or whatever—but not, say, in an earthquake in Mary's hometown, because such an earthquake is a reason for Mary to exclude that world. All in all then, Mary's doxastic state may be characterized by a *cut* through Logical Space, separating those worlds she takes to be possible in the sense indicated from those she excludes. We will refer to the former ones as Mary's **doxastic alternatives**.

Obviously, Mary's doxastic alternatives are fully determined by her doxastic state. And it turns out that they in turn determine the truth value of attitude reports like (34). This is so because, according to (34), Mary takes herself to inhabit a world in which John is in Rome; as we have seen this means that in all her doxastic alternatives, John is in Rome: she excludes worlds in which he is not, and that they are excluded means they are not among her doxastic alternatives. So (34) is true if the set of Mary's doxastic alternatives is a *subset* of the set of those worlds in which John is in Rome. Since the latter form the proposition expressed by the embedded clause, we arrive at the following truth condition:

(35)   (34) is true of a world w iff $\text{Dox}_{Mary,w} \subseteq [\![\,\text{John is in Rome}\,]\!]$.

Two notational details in (35) may not be self-explanatory. First, the set "Dox" of doxastic alternatives has two subscripts, relating to the attitude subject and the world she is in. The second subscript is necessary because doxastic states (and hence alternatives) depend on, and change with, situations in Logical Space; in a scenario in which Mary thinks that John is in Los Angeles (at the time under consideration), her doxastic state differs accordingly. The second notational detail concerns the intension of the embedded clause, which we have identified here with the proposition it expresses (i.e., the set of worlds the intension characterizes, rather than the characteristic function itself as defined in (7) on p. 172). We will make use of this harmless sloppiness whenever convenient.

Given (35), it is now easy to adjust the compositional treatment of attitude reports given in Section 2 by adding a Hintikka-style lexical interpretation of *think*:

(36) $[\![\,\text{think}\,]\!]_w = \{\langle x, p \rangle : \text{Dox}_{x,w} \subseteq p\}$

We can now follow Hintikka's advice and generalize (36) to (more or less) arbitrary attitude verbs including *know* and *want*. All we need to assume for this is that these verbs, too, relate to corresponding kinds of mental states that can be characterized in terms of Logical Space, i.e., by sets of pertinent alternatives. In the case of knowledge and desire, these alternatives are known as **epistemic** and **bouletic**, respectively.[20] We thus have, in analogy with (36):

(37) $[\![\text{know}]\!]_w = \{\langle x, p \rangle : \text{Epi}_{x,w} \subseteq p\}$

(38) $[\![\text{want}]\!]_w = \{\langle x, p \rangle : \text{Bou}_{x,w} \subseteq p\}$

Of course, the exact nature of these types of alternatives still needs to be illuminated—a task which is ultimately left to psychology, since this is what these particular attitude verbs are about.

Whatever the precise specifications of the lexical meanings of attitude verbs, they need not rest on the assumption that they are independent of each other. As a case in point, there is an obvious connection between *think* and *know*, as the following inference illustrates:

(39)   Mary knows that Bill snores
⊨   Mary thinks that Bill snores

If the premise of (39) is true, it is hard to deny the conclusion.[21] However, the above analyses do not capture this inference—not until the pertinent alternatives, Dox and Epi, are suitably related to each other. Again this would have to be done by a thorough cognitive analysis of what it means to think and know, which is not at all easy.[22] However, the relation between doxastic and epistemic alternatives that is responsible for the validity of (39) is rather easily accounted for. The truth conditions of premise and conclusion are:

(40)   a. $\text{Epi}_{Mary,w} \subseteq [\![\text{Bill snores}]\!]$
        b. $\text{Dox}_{Mary,w} \subseteq [\![\text{Bill snores}]\!]$

Generalizing from the example, one would thus have to guarantee that, for any subjects x and propositions p, the following holds:

---

20   From the ancient Greek words for knowledge and wish, *episteme* and *boule*.

21   One may feel that the latter carries an implication to the effect that Mary does not exactly *know* that Bill snores; this, however, is best explained by pragmatic principles of communicative efficiency: speakers who use *think* thereby indicate (if defeasibly so) that they are not in a position to use the more informative verb *know*.

22   An ancient myth had it that knowledge can be characterized in terms of belief, truth, and justification alone. The myth was debunked in a famous (and famously short) article by the American philosopher Edmund Gettier, which is highly recommended to interested readers; cf. Gettier (1963).

(41) $\text{Dox}_{x,w} \subseteq p$ whenever $\text{Epi}_{x,w} \subseteq p$.

Surprisingly, the following relation between a person x's epistemic and doxastic alternatives guarantees just that:

(42) $\text{Dox}_{x,w} \subseteq \text{Epi}_{x,w}$

Assumption (42) does *not* say that x knows whatever x believes; this would be the reverse of (41). Instead, what (42) does say is that any world that is *not excluded* by what x thinks (or believes) is *not excluded* by what x knows. In other words, any world that *is* excluded by x's knowledge is also excluded by what x thinks. And in fact, (42) implies (41), as the reader is invited to verify in an exercise.

Another inference for which the above semantic clauses need to rely on further epistemic analysis is this:

(43)   Mary knows that Bill snores
⊨   Bill snores

In fact, it would be contradictory to say

(44)   #Mary knows that Bill snores, but Bill doesn't snore

Therefore (43) is a valid inference. This is specific to the verb *know*; the inference does not hold with a verb like *believe*:

(45)   Mary believes that Bill snores
⊭   Bill snores

For it is fully consistent to say:

(46)   Mary believes that Bill snores, but (in fact) Bill doesn't snore

We therefore seem to have missed something in our account of the meaning of *know*. Again the inference is captured by a simple and straightforward assumption about epistemic alternatives, viz., that they contain the worlds they are alternatives to:

(47) $w \in \text{Epi}_{x,w}$

Again we leave the verification to the reader and end this section on a gloomy note.

The power of Hintikka semantics lies in its specificity as to the nature of propositional attitudes, which is basically due to the exploitation of Logical Space as a model not only of linguistic meaning, but also of mental content. However, in this specificity lies its vulnerability. As the reader may care to verify in detail, the following so-called **monotonicity inference** is predicted to be valid by Hintikka semantics:

(48) Mary thinks that Bill has two or three children
$\vDash$ Mary thinks that the number of Bill's children is prime

Roughly, (48) comes out as valid because the premise says that Mary's doxastic alternatives A are part of one set of worlds p, and the conclusion says that the same alternatives form a subset of a certain superset q—which they would have to if the premise is true: $A \subseteq p$ and $p \subseteq q$ implies: $A \subseteq q$. However, this seems to sneak in mathematical expertise and deductive powers Mary does not necessarily have. And worse, it is readily seen that (48) generalizes to all sorts of complicated cases in which the clause embedded in the conclusion follows from that in the premise by some intricate reasoning impossible to comprehend by ordinary human beings. Hence the pattern behind (48) is quite unwelcome, but it seems part and parcel of Hintikka semantics. Whether it can ultimately be avoided by pragmatic maneuvers, or whether this shows that Hintikka semantics is but an approximation of propositional attitudes is an open question.

EXERCISE 33:

  Show that (42) implies (41).

EXERCISE 34:

  Use (47) to explain the validity of (43).

6. From Intension to Extension and Back Again

Before leaving this chapter we take a closer look at the distinction between extension and intension. At the beginning of the previous chapter we already mentioned an obvious reason why extensions cannot be, or adequately represent, meanings: as far as sentences are concerned, there are only two of them.

Intensions clearly fare better in this respect: after all, there are infinitely many of them.

Another reason why extensions cannot stand in for meanings was relevant to our discussion of lexical matters (cf. Section 4): someone who learns the meaning of an expression does not automatically know its extension. Again, sentences may illustrate this point. Even if your German (or English) is perfect, you will not know the truth value of all German (English) sentences. Our initial example (2) on p. 170 is a case in point: of course we all know its meaning, but its extension is known to only very few people (who have every reason to keep this a secret). However, do intensions fare any better in this respect too? In fact, doesn't anyone who knows the intension of (2) also have to know its extension? After all, given a table with truth values and possible worlds, we only have to pick out the actual world in order to arrive at the truth value. This is certainly the case, but then how do we know which of the worlds is our actual one? In Logical Space, the input column to our intensions, possible worlds, are given as maximally detailed and specific states of affairs. Yet even if we know that any case in which Barschel committed suicide is one in which he was not murdered, we do not know which of these cases corresponds to what actually happened. And, to be sure, even if we did know he committed suicide, this would still not put us in a position to pick out the actual world. If it did, we would be omniscient. For there remain infinitely many details in the world we inhabit that we do not know about and that distinguish it from other points in Logical Space.

Knowing the intension of a sentence therefore does not imply knowing its truth value. It only involves knowledge of which *hypothetical* states of affairs would make it true. And this may well be an adequate criterion for understanding a sentence: "*Einen Satz verstehen, heißt, wissen was der Fall ist, wenn er wahr ist*" (*To understand a proposition means to know what is the case if it is true*; Wittgenstein (1921), 4.024). Adopting this slogan we agree that the intension of a sentence exhausts its meaning, whose core thus turns out to be informativity.

The fact that intensions correspond to meanings does not leave extensions without interest or importance, though: the extension results from the intension as its value for the actual world; it is thus what the intension is all about. However, in order to find out what the extension of an expression is, one must know enough about reality to identify it. So there is a road from intensions to extensions, and those who know enough about the actual world can see where it leads. This observation on the relation between extension and intension is captured by a famous slogan usually attributed to Frege: *Sense determines reference*. In our notation and terminology,[23] it boils down to the following general principle holding for any expression A and possible world w:

(49)   *Frege's Assumption*
       The extension of A (at w) is determined by its intension $[\![A]\!]$, viz., as the value that $[\![A]\!]$ assigns to w.

Frege's Assumption thus paves the way from intension to extension. But is there also a way back? In a sense, there is. This is so because, by definition, the totality of possible extensions of an expression makes up its intension. We thus obtain a principle mirroring (49), which may be seen as one of Carnap's most fundamental (and most ingenious) contributions to semantic theory:

(50)   *Carnap's Assumption*
       The extensions of A varying across Logical Space uniquely determine the intension of A, viz., as the set of pairs $\langle w, [\![A]\!]_w \rangle$ matching each world w with the extension of A at w.

It should be noted that, while (49) has a unique intension determine a unique extension, (50) has the (unique) intension depend on the totality of extensions across Logical Space. The latter dependence is obviously much more involved than the former. In other words, the way from intension to extension is simpler than the way back. However, the former requires knowledge of all pertinent facts, the latter only purely conceptual knowledge of Logical Space.[24]

In terms of a corny metaphor, we have thus seen that the extension and the intension of an expression are two sides of the same coin—its meaning; somewhat more precisely, the upshot of the assumptions above is that they represent two different but interdependent functions of meaning—reference and information. However, there is more to be said about the relation between the two. They also interact in complex ways when more than one expression is at stake. This aspect of the theory of extension and intension reveals itself most clearly in the way compositionality works. In Section 1 of the previous chapter, we saw that the Principle of Extensional Compositionality fails when

---

23   Some terminological clarification will be given at the end of the current section.

24   Whereas the relation postulated in (49) is one of functional application (applying the intension to an input world), (50) employs an operation known as *functional abstraction*. Assumptions (49) and (50) are implemented in Montague's *Intensional Logic*, where the two routes are expressed by logical operators known as Cup and Cap.

it comes to so-called *intensional contexts*. However, this does not mean that we had to give up on compositionality altogether. In fact, in Section 2 if the current chapter we saw that intensions do behave compositionally. In effect, we thus argued for the

(51)   *Principle of Intensional Compositionality*
        The intension of a compound expression is a function of the intensions of its immediate parts and the way they are composed.

Now, given the near identification of intension and meaning suggested above, (51) turns out to be a variant of (52), and is thus hardly a surprise:

(52)   *Principle of Compositionality of Meaning*
        The meaning of a compound expression is a function of the meanings of its immediate parts and the way they are composed.

However, closer inspection of the way compositionality actually works in connection with intensional contexts reveals that matters are more complex than these last two slogans suggest. Let us reconsider the original case of propositional attitude reports. In order to escape the substitution predicament to which the Principle of Extensional Compositionality had led, we followed Frege's strategy of feeding the intension of the complement clause into the compositionality process where its extension (i.e., its truth value) failed. This was a strictly local repair in that we only replaced the extension of the embedded sentence by its intension, and left the rest of the compositional contributions untouched: it is the *extension* of the verb phrase that is determined by the *intension* of the embedded clause and the *extension* of the attitude verb. This local shift from extension to intension allowed us to integrate the analysis into the composition of extensions, which we assumed to work as before. It was only afterwards that we noted that this overall strategy of combining extensions and, if need be (i.e., in intensional contexts), intensions conforms to (51). However, it seems that the compositionality process itself is better described by the following principle, which brings out more clearly that intensional contexts are handled with a kind of repair strategy:

(53)   *Frege's Principle of Compositionality*
        The extension of a compound expression is a function of the (a) extensions or (b) intensions of its immediate parts and the way they are composed.

The principle, which is given in a rather imprecise form here (but could be made precise in an algebraic setting), is to be understood as allowing (a) and (b) to co-occur in the following sense: the extension of a compound expression may be determined by combining (a) the extension of one of its parts with (b) the intension of another one—just as we had it in the case of propositional attitude reports. It should be noted that (53) does not say that intensions are only invoked as a last resort, i.e., when extensions lead to substitution problems; this, however, is the way in which the principle is usually applied.[25]

As pointed out at the end of Section 2, the strategy of determining extensions of expressions from the extensions and/or intensions of their parts guarantees that intensions behave compositionally. In other words, (53) implies (51). One may wonder, though, whether (53) actually says anything over and above (51), or whether it only splits up intensional compositionality into two different cases, viz., (a) extensional vs. (b) intensional constructions.[26] There is, however, a slight difference between the very general principle (51) and Frege's more specific strategy (53). Although (51) looks more uniform than (53), the latter, but not the former, imposes a certain amount of homogeneity on the combinations of intensions: if the extension of an expression B remains stable across two worlds w and w', then according to (53), so does its contribution to the extension of a larger expression A at those worlds; however it would still be in line with (51) if the intension of A differed across w and w'. Although no natural combinations of intensions with this property are known to us, their very possibility and the fact that they are ruled out by (53) show that Frege's strategy does restrict the possible combinations of intensions.[27]

---

25 With notable exceptions, among them Montague (1973), where a default mechanism has expressions in argument positions always contribute their intension, whether or not extensional substitution fails.

26 Note that a construction is already intensional if one of the parts contributes its intension, whatever the contribution of other part(s). As a matter of fact, syntactic environments that are intensional with respect to *all* (immediate) parts appear to be extremely rare—if they exist at all.

27 Here is an artificially constructed example of a grammatical modifier Φ embedding sentences B (of a non-existent language, to be sure):

(*) $[\![\Phi B]\!]_w = 1$ if and only if $[\![B]\!](w) = [\![B]\!](w^*)$

where w^* is the actual world. Here Φ is not an expression on its own but indicates a particular kind of embedding (realized by some morpho-syntactic process like inversion, say). Hence the embedding is a unary construction, with B being the only immediate part

Some historical and terminological remarks on the origin of the distinction between extension and intension may be in order. Even though we have attributed some of the principal concepts and assumptions to Frege, his original writings do not conform to the terminology employed here. In particular, Frege used the German noun *Bedeutung* (in ordinary contexts translated as "meaning") as a technical term for reference and extension. According to this terminology, a sentence "means" (= *bedeutet*) its truth value—which is more than just a bit confusing; we thought this kind of a warning would be appropriate for those who want to read Frege (1892) in the original; the English translations make up for the confusion by philological inaccuracy, rendering *Bedeutung* as "reference" or "denotation". In any case, most of what we have said about extensions and how to find them goes back to Frege's work. However, and more importantly, while Frege's *Bedeutung* closely corresponds to our "extension", his *Sinn* ("sense") does not truly match what we have been calling the "intension" of an expression: a sense (in Frege's sense) is not a function whose values are extensions. It is not at all easy to explain (and understand) just what exactly Fregean sense is, and we will not even try to do so here, but refer the reader to the extensive literature on Frege's work.[28] We would still like to point out that our loose identification of Fregean senses with intensions is not completely arbitrary; they do have a lot in common. To begin

---

of ΦB. (This aspect of the example is merely to avoid unnecessary distractions.) It is easy to see that (*) conforms to the Principle of Intensional Compositionality: the intension of an expression ΦB is determined by the function F that assigns to any (characteristic function of a) proposition p the intension of (the characteristic function of) the set of worlds in which p has the same truth value as in the actual world; applying F to $[\![B]\!]$ then results in the intension described by (*).

On the other hand, (*) is not in line with (53), as can be seen by considering a particular sentence B_0 that expresses the proposition which is only true at the actual world. (Again, this assumption is made for convenience and dramatic effect; the reader is invited to find a more natural example.) Now, clearly, the truth value of ΦB_0 cannot be determined from the truth value of its only immediate part B_0: at any non-actual world w, B_0 has the same truth value as a contradictory sentence $\bot$, but according to (*), ΦB_0 comes out false whereas $\Phi \bot$ is true. However, the truth value of ΦB_0 cannot be determined by merely looking at the intension of B_0 either: ΦB_0 is true at w^* and false at any other world, but the intension of its sole immediate part B_0 is always the same.

28 The account in Stepanians (2001), Chapter 7, is particularly recommendable. We should also mention that there are more differences between Frege's and Carnap's distinction than we have mentioned here, mostly due to the fact that Frege's underlying notion of a function was not the set-theoretic one, which he explicitly rejected. Again, we have to refer the interested reader to the literature.

with, even though senses are not functions, they do determine extensions relative to facts, thereby justifying the attribution of (49) to Frege. Moreover, the way extension and intension interact compositionally is precisely as Frege described his *Bedeutungen* and *Sinne* at work—with the (somewhat confusing) twist that he also used the term *Bedeutung* for the compositional contribution a part makes to the extension of the whole (compound) expression. Keeping this in mind, it is certainly fair to attribute (53) to Frege, too.

Although the terms had some currency among philosophers of language and logicians before, the distinction between extension and intension as we have been using it ultimately goes back to Carnap (1947), who already pointed out the connection with, and differences from, Frege's distinction. Consequently, this approach to meaning has been dubbed "Frege-Carnap semantics". It has been popular among linguists ever since Montague (1973) showed how it can be generalized beyond the restricted phenomena analyzed by its founders. However, the approach is not without its rivals, even within the tradition of analytic philosophy. In particular, Bertrand Russell criticized Frege as needlessly complicating matters by splitting up meaning into two dimensions. Instead, he developed a framework for semantic analysis that is based on one kind of semantic value only. As it turns out, the two approaches are inter-translatable, preferences for one or the other being largely a matter of taste; cf. Kaplan (1975) for details.

7. Tense, Time, and Logic*

In this section we will briefly comment on an additional component of propositions that has hitherto been ignored. Suppose I utter

(54)   I have a beard

And twenty minutes later, I say

(55)   I don't have a beard

This sounds like a contradiction, but in fact it isn't. For suppose I shaved between the utterances. Then both sentences should be true. But of course they are true only at the time of utterance. This reveals that time is an important issue in our reasoning with sentences. In fact, even Frege, who was mostly concerned with mathematical, hence eternal truths, acknowledged that reference to time should be part of any proposition.[29]

Technically this is usually achieved by making interpretations time dependent. Previously, interpretations assigned an extension to every possible world; now interpretations assign extensions to every pair $\langle w, t \rangle$ consisting of a possible world w and a moment of time t (or sometimes a time interval). We thus assimilate moments of time (or time intervals) to possible worlds in that assignment functions (which determine the extensions) not only depend on a world w but also on a time t. This renders (54) and (55) perfectly consistent, if t and t' in (56) and (57) are different moments of time:

(56) $[\![\text{I have a beard}]\!]_{w,t} = 1$

(57) $[\![\text{I don't have a beard}]\!]_{w,t'} = 1$

Reference to different moments of time is also needed in order to express the tense operators in (58):

(58)   a. $[\![\text{It will be the case that S}]\!]_{w,t} = 1$
         iff there is a moment of time t' after t, such that $[\![S]\!]_{w,t'} = 1$.
         b. $[\![\text{It was the case that S}]\!]_{w,t} = 1$
         iff there is a moment of time t' before t, such that $[\![S]\!]_{w,t'} = 1$.

It is tempting, then, to analyze (59)

(59)   John will come

by reformulating it in such a way that the semantics defined in (58-a) can be applied to *John comes*:

(60)   It will be the case that John comes

Analyses along these lines have been proposed in philosophical logic, which employs **translations** of natural language sentences into logical notation, thereby presupposing that the meanings of the logical formulae (their semantic interpretations) and those of their natural language analogues coincide. The future tense, for example, would be represented by an operator $\mathcal{F}$ that

---

29   *"Alle Bestimmungen des Orts, der Zeit, u.s.w. gehören zu dem Gedanken, um dessen Wahrheit es sich handelt."* (Frege (1893), p. xvii) ["All determinations of the place, the time, and the like, belong to the thought whose truth is in point", translated by Montgomery Furth in Frege (1964), p. 16].

has the same semantics as "it will be the case that" in (58-a), and a sentence like (59) would be translated into a formula like $\mathscr{F}\varphi$, where φ is a logical formula too.

For the linguist, however, this is not quite satisfactory. For one thing, linguists would not be content to merely find *some* translation that seems to work on intuitive grounds alone. What they would like to see is an explicit translation *procedure* that starts off with natural language syntax, rigorously applies transformational processes, and finally ends up with the formulae proposed by the philosophers, logicians or mathematicians on intuitive grounds. Moreover, and more often than not, linguists detect inadequacies in intuitive formalizations, due to a mismatch between the proposed formal system and the rules of natural language. Let us briefly discuss two examples.

(61)   Everyone will win

According to the strategy sketched above we would expect that this sentence comes out as meaning that there is a future time at which (62) holds:

(62)   Everyone wins

This, however, is not the most natural reading of (61). If it were, it would have to be the case at some moment in the future that everyone wins *at that moment*. So there must be several simultaneous winners—a very implausible situation. Rather, the preferred reading is one that seems to be more in line with the syntax of natural language in that for every person there will be a (different) time t' after t so that that person is *the* winner at t'. In other words, in the preferred reading *everyone* has wider scope than *will*. This fact reveals that we have to analyze the internal structure of a sentence in order to capture the fact that *will* has wide scope over *win*, but not over *everyone*, as would be predicted by a formula like $\mathscr{F}\varphi$, where the scope of $\mathscr{F}$ is an entire sentence.

Likewise, a past tense sentence like

(63)   Everyone went to school

can be ambiguous, depending on the range of *everyone* in considering either a small situation, where all the pupils went to school simultaneously, or a large situation, where concurrency is implausible. In one reading the semantic operator corresponding to the past tense has wide scope over *everyone*, in the other the reverse must hold. The interesting thing with (63) is that either way we even have to analyze the morphology of a *single word* (*went*) in order to pick out the parts that are relevant for semantic interpretation.

As a second example, imagine a family going on a vacation; they are just leaving town in their car when Mary says:

(64)   I didn't turn off the stove

The information conveyed by the sentence should make Arthur turn around and drive back home again. Arthur, a famous logician, quickly paraphrases (64) as (65) and interprets it according to (58-b):

(65)   It is not the case that at some moment in the past it holds that Mary turns the stove off

But this amounts to saying that Mary *never* turned off the stove before now. This is obviously false and therefore cannot be the intended meaning of the sentence. Arthur then concludes that he might have misconstrued the scope of negation, so the next formula he tries is this:

(66)   At some moment in the past it does not hold that Mary turns the stove off

This looks much better: at some moment in the past it is not the case that Mary turns the stove off. However, thinking about the literal meaning of (66) it turns out that this is trivially true: it is obvious that there might be indefinitely many moments where Mary did other things than turning the stove off. So either the sentence is trivially false, or it is trivially true. In neither interpretation would the content of the sentence have the intended effect of making Arthur drive home.

This example taken from Partee (1973) reveals that natural language does not work the way a simple-minded logician would like to have it in the simplest of all possible worlds. This is an important insight. It tells us something about natural language that we might not have found out without any attempt at formalization. The example shows that something is going wrong in the way we conceive of tense, and that truth conditions like (58-b)—which are crucial in the formulation of formal languages of tense logic—are too simplistic.

However, it is not obvious which lesson is to be learned from the example. An educated guess at a better paraphrase is this:

(67)   At some relevant time interval before the utterance time (immediately
        before leaving the house) it's not the case at any moment within that
        interval that Mary turns the stove off.

The kind of relevant interval mentioned in (67) (the relatively short interval before leaving) has been called the **reference time** (*Betrachtzeit*) by the
German philosopher ☞ Hans Reichenbach [1891–1953]. He distinguished
between reference time, **utterance time** (*Äußerungszeit*), and **event time**
(*Ereigniszeit*). The reference time in the above example is partly determined
by pragmatics, so the basic insight here is that tensed sentences can only be
dealt with in a system that leaves some room for pragmatic considerations.
However, there is a restriction on which time intervals can be relevant, which
is expressed by the grammatical tenses: the future tense expresses that the
reference time is located anywhere on the time line after the utterance time,
and the past tense expresses that the reference time lies anywhere before the
utterance time. The event time then still has to be related to the reference
time; this is done by a grammatical system called **aspect**. Note also that the
paraphrase given in (67) involves two different quantifying expressions: an
existential quantifier relating to the reference time and a universal quantifier
relating to the event time. The paraphrase is thus much more involved than
one might have expected.

   According to Reichenbach, a sentence like

(68)   John had slept for three hours when Jill came in

then expresses that the event time of sleeping is an interval (of three hours)
that occurred *before* the reference time of Jill's entering. Hence the information contained in *had* is relevant for the location of the event time before the
reference time described by the *when*-clause. In (64), however, aspect plays
no role, so it follows that the event time must be located within the reference
time.

   Reichenbach's analysis suggests that any system that treats tense operators as simple operators on propositions (as we attempted with $\mathscr{F}$ and $\mathscr{P}$ in
the sketch of a formal language above) cannot account for tense and aspect
in natural language. He proposes that tense expresses a relation between moments of time and time intervals (rather than a relation between propositions,
as in our formal language). The reference time is often pragmatically determined, but can also be made explicit by the use of adverbials, as is done by
the adverbial *when*-sentence in (68), which also delineates the initial phase

of the sleeping interval. The semantics of adverbials when combined with the tenses also explains the awkwardness of (69):

(69)   #John slept tomorrow

The adverbial *tomorrow* says that the reference time is the day after the time of utterance; on the other hand, the past tense contained in *slept* says that the reference time is before the time of utterance. This is a plain contradiction, which explains the unacceptability of (69). See Reichenbach (1947) and Rathert (2004) for more on tense and aspect in logic and grammar.

Chapter 9
Presuppositions

1. The Definite Article

In Section 3.1 of Chapter 4 (p. 62ff.), we noted that referential expressions do not always have referents, Russell's classic description *the present king of France* being a case in point. However, when it came to composing extensions and to constructing intensions, we chose to ignore this complication. In the present chapter, we will revise this decision and scrutinize the very notion of a referential gap. In doing so, we will find that referential gaps are part of a more general phenomenon. But before we get to this, we will address the seemingly simple question of whether failure of reference implies lack of extension. As it turns out, this is not obvious.

To achieve clarity on this point, let us look at an empty description in the context of a sentence—the original example from Russell (1905):

(1)   The present king of France is bald

Given the political facts of our actual world at the time of writing, the subject of (1) has no referent. As a consequence, (1) cannot be true. It is thus tempting to conclude (as Russell did) that the sentence is *false*, with 0 as its extension. Interestingly, this conclusion has repercussions for the question of what the extension of the subject in (1) is: if the truth value of the sentence is to be derived by the Principle of Extensional Compositionality (= (18) from Chapter 5, repeated below for the readers' convenience), then the extension of the subject cannot be its referent—simply because it has no referent.

(2)   *Principle of Extensional Compositionality*
        The extension of a compound expression is a function of the extensions of its immediate parts and the way they are composed.

However, (1) may still obtain its truth value in a compositional way. For the fact that its subject has no referent does not mean that it has no extension either: as we have seen in Chapter 6, there are DPs that do not refer to anything but still have extensions, viz., quantifiers like *no king*. So what if the subject of (1) is one of them—contrary to what we have been assuming all along? As it turns out, in that case, its extension could be specified so that (1) comes out false. Given the interpretation of sentences with quantificational subjects, this means that it must not contain the extension of the predicate of (1). In fact, it should not contain the extension of *any* predicate, because *no* sentence with the same subject as (1) should come out as true. We thus venture the following **quantificational analysis** of the extension of the subject at our actual world w^*:

(3) $[\![\text{the present king of France}]\!]_{w^*} = \emptyset$

Equation (3) only captures the extension of the definite description under scrutiny at the actual world. In order to account for its *intension*, a more general equation must be found, covering its extensions across Logical Space. Given an arbitrary possible world w, two cases need to be distinguished according to whether *the present king of France* has a referent: if not, then (3) carries over from w^* to w:

(4) $[\![\text{the present king of France}]\!]_{w} = \emptyset$

If, on the other hand, the French do have some person k_w as their king in a given world w, the extension sought can be constructed following the strategy laid out in Chapter 6, Section 2, as the set of all sets (of individuals) that contain k_w as a member.

(5) $[\![\text{the present king of France}]\!]_{w}$
= $\{X : k_w \in X\}$

where k_w is the only member of $[\![\text{present king of France}]\!]_{w}$. Both cases, (4) and (5), may be captured at one fell swoop—and in a variety of ways:

(6) $[\![\text{the present king of France}]\!]_{w}$
= $\{Y : \text{for some } x, [\![\text{present king of France}]\!]_{w} = \{x\} \text{ and } x \in Y\}$
= $\{Y : \text{for some } x, [\![\text{present king of France}]\!]_{w} = \{x\} \text{ and } [\![\text{present king of France}]\!]_{w} \subseteq Y\}$
= $\{Y : \text{for some } x, [\![\text{present king of France}]\!]_{w} = \{x\} \text{ and } [\![\text{present king of France}]\!]_{w} \cap Y \neq \emptyset\}$

We leave it to the reader to verify that the above chain of equations is correct.

According to (6), then, a predicate extension Y is a member of the extension of Russell's famous description if it meets two conditions: (i) that the extension of the noun phrase *present king of France* be a singleton; and (ii) that it is a subset of Y. Obviously, (i) is a degenerate condition in that it is independent of Y: if one set meets it, any set does; and if some set does not meet it, none does. In this second case, condition (ii) does not play a role because (i) alone makes the extension of the description literally empty, ultimately leading to the falsity of sentences like (1). We already noted this effect in connection with (4), which is a special case of (6).

By treating the subject of (1) as quantificational, (6) manages to assign an extension to it in a uniform way and independently of whether it has a referent. Moreover, (6) can be extended to a fully compositional interpretation, combining the extension of *present king of France* with that of the definite article.[1] In fact, the latter still needs to be adapted to fit our quantificational analysis of definite descriptions. Recall that we already analyzed the extensions of determiners as relations between two sets (of individuals). In the case at hand, the sets related are the extensions X of *king of France* and Y of *[is] bald*. According to (6), the relation expressed by *the* holds if and only if Y meets the abovementioned conditions that X be (i) a singleton and (ii) a subset of Y. Generalizing from the particular predicate, we may thus characterize the extension of *the* (at any world w) as follows:

$$
\begin{aligned}
(7) \quad & [\![\, \text{the} \,]\!]_w = \{ \langle X, Y \rangle : \text{for some } x,\ X = \{x\} \text{ and } x \in Y \} \\
= \quad & \{ \langle X, Y \rangle : \text{for some } x,\ X = \{x\} \text{ and } X \cap Y \neq \varnothing \} \\
= \quad & \{ \langle X, Y \rangle : \text{for some } x,\ X = \{x\} \text{ and } X \subseteq Y \}
\end{aligned}
$$

Condition (i) can be formulated in a variety of ways, too. In particular, it is customary to split up this cardinality condition into two parts: (i-a) that the nominal extension X has at least one member; and (i-b) that X has at most one member. Moreover, (i) can be seen to express conditions on the **cardinality** $|X|$ of X, i.e., the number of X's elements, viz., $|X| = 1$; hence (i-a) and (i-b) come out as saying that $|X| \geq 1$ and $|X| \leq 1$, respectively. We will employ this reformulation and, from now on, adopt (8) as our "official" quantificational analysis of the definite article:

$$
(8) \quad [\![\, \text{the} \,]\!]_w = \{ \langle X, Y \rangle : |X| \geq 1 \text{ and } |X| \leq 1 \text{ and } X \subseteq Y \}
$$

Since condition (i-a) amounts to there being members of X, it is also known as the **existence condition**, and (i-b) is called the **uniqueness condition**.

---

1   The basic strategy of analyzing definite descriptions as quantifiers goes back to Russell's criticism of Frege's naive analysis (see below), against which Russell (1905) brought forward a number of arguments—some good, some debatable, some confused. The compositional formulation of Russell's theory of descriptions goes back to Montague (1970).

Using (8), (6) can be derived by the extensional combination of determiners D and noun phrases N from Chapter 6 (= (9) on p. 119), notationally
adapted in (9):

(9) $[\![D + N]\!]_w = \{ Y : \langle [\![N]\!]_w , Y \rangle \in [\![D]\!]_w \}$

Although (8) is adequate when applied to sentences like (1), problems
arise once we replace the noun phrase *present king of France* by something
more mundane:

(10)   The table is dirty

Sentences like (10) can be uttered truthfully, it seems, even if the extension
of *table* in the world (or situation) talked about contains more than one table.
For instance, a customer in a coffee bar may use (10) and thereby talk about
the table she and her friends are sitting at, notwithstanding all the other tables
in the place. However, the cardinality condition (i) seems to rule out such
a situation. More precisely, it is the uniqueness condition (i-b) $|X| \leq 1$ that
appears to be violated in this case, whereas the existence condition (i-a) $|X| \geq$
1 is obviously satisfied.

There are at least two plausible ways in which the quantificational analysis
of the definite article can be upheld to cover such cases; both shift part of the
burden of explanation to pragmatics:

— One may employ pragmatics to see to it that, in the situation described (10) is understood as relating to a small situation with respect
to which the uniqueness condition does hold (because there is only
one table in that situation, viz., the one closest to the speaker).

— One could add a further, contextually determined condition (of
salience or pertinence) to (8) which in the situation at hand, is only
satisfied by the table the speaker is talking about.

We will not decide between these options because the issue is largely or-
thogonal to the topic of the current chapter.[2] But then, however the issue is
resolved, the uniqueness condition will continue to be part of the quantifica-

---

2   A lot has been written about the subject. We only mention two sources corresponding to
the two options, viz., Reimer (1998) and Neale (1990). Moreover, definite descriptions
allow a number of usages that appear to escape the quantificational analysis for independent reasons. We cannot go into these matters here and recommend Heim (1991, 2011)
for a thorough survey.

tional analysis of the definite article, on a par with the existence condition and condition (ii).

Unfortunately, however, the parity is deceiving. To see this, it should first be noted that there are limits to the above maneuver of circumventing the uniqueness condition. Consider our coffee bar scenario again. Although a guest sitting at a table may use (10) to convey something true (or false) about the table she is sitting at, the manager of the establishment cannot do so—not if he is standing behind the counter, talking to one of the temps and there simply is no obvious candidate for the table he would be talking about. And, more to the point: if the manager did utter (10), his utterance would not be false but somewhat inappropriate, likely to provoke a reaction like *Hey, wait a minute—there are 15 tables out there, which one are you talking about?* rather than *No, sir, you're wrong: there is more than one table here.*[3]

A similar reaction may ensue if someone were to use our initial Russellian sentence (1): one would not judge the utterance as plain false but rather as misguided, based on wrong presumptions. On the other hand, if our coffee bar guest had said (10) even though her table was spick-and-span, her utterance may have been rejected as false. In other words, there is an asymmetry between condition (i)—existence and uniqueness—on the one hand, and condition (ii) on the other: if one of the former fails, the utterance is somewhat beside the point; if (ii) fails, it is merely false.

While this asymmetry may or may not be within reach of a pragmatically enriched quantificational analysis of definite descriptions, it is a direct consequence of the so-called **naive** analysis of definite descriptions.[4] According to this, an expression like *the table* has no extension if there is no table or more than one; otherwise, its extension is its referent (as we had it in the previous chapters). Therefore, the intension of the expression *the king of France* must be a partial function: it does not have a value for a world w if there is no (pertinent) table in w (**failure of existence**), or more than one (**failure of uniqueness**). In other words, the semantics of *the* introduces a gap in the intension of *the table* if the extension of the predicate *table* is not a singleton. But then, by the principle of extensional compositionality (see above), the whole sentence also lacks an extension, that is, it does not have a truth value in w. This way the gap in the intension—the missing extension—of a

---

3   In fact, in an influential paper, Kai von Fintel (2004) has proposed the appropriateness of *Hey, wait a minute*, as opposed to *No*, as a diagnostic of (denial of) presupposed content.

4   The naive analysis goes back to Frege (1892) and was one of the targets of criticism of Russell (1905).

certain expression propagates to or is inherited by the extension of the entire expression, which will not determine an extension (at some worlds).

An elementary pragmatic observation has it that truth-valueless sentences cannot be used to make (felicitous) assertions. Asserting a sentence like (1) therefore requires that the extension of *present king of France* be a singleton. Hence, according to the naive analysis, condition (i) is a prerequisite for the sentence (1) to have a truth value. And a violation of the prerequisite explains the oddness or infelicity of the utterance. Such prerequisites are called **pre-suppositions**.[5] Sentence (1) is thus said to have an **existence presupposition** and a **uniqueness presupposition** (*Einzigkeitspräsupposition*), both of which only concern the extension of the noun phrase *present king of France*. Taken together the uniqueness and the existential presuppositions are the combined presuppositions of (1), induced by the determiner *the*.

One difference between the naive and the quantificational analysis of descriptions reveals itself in sentences like:

(11)   The present king of France is not bald

The naive analysis would obviously attribute a truth value gap to (11), inherited from the referential gap of the subject. And indeed, at first blush, (11) seems just as odd as (1). However, the sentence can also be understood as saying something trivially true; after all the present king of France *cannot* be bald because France is no longer a monarchy. One way to arrive at this reading is by posing an ambiguity in the negation and assuming that, apart from reversing the truth value (if there is one), it may also turn a truth-valueless sentence into a true one ("**weak negation**"). We will not go into this possibility here but only mention that it has its limits when it comes to sentences containing more than one definite description.The following one, due to Hans Kamp (1980), is a case in point:

(12)   My dog did not bite your cat—I don't even have a dog

---

5   The term *presupposition* is a translation of Frege's notion *Voraussetzung*; the re-translation of *presupposition* into German as used in linguistics is not *Voraussetzung*, but *Präsupposition*. We will not attempt to give a precise definition of the term. From what we have said, it may refer to properties of:

(i)   a. sentences and/or their parts
       b. statements or utterances of sentences
       c. speakers when making statements or utterances
       d. propositions

Any of these except (d) can be found in Frege's original writing.

The problem is that the presupposition introduced by the object—that the hearer has one cat—does not seem to be affected by the negation. Neither the weak nor the strong (truth-value-reversing) construal of negation captures the fact that the above sentence still seems to presuppose that the addressee owns a cat: the former would propagate the truth value gap, while the latter would be consistent with the addressee's not having a cat.

The quantificational analysis predicts (12) to be true if construed as the negation of (1), i.e., if the negation outscopes the subject at the relevant level of syntactic analysis, Logical Form. On the other hand, if the subject may also take wide scope, its existence condition would be in force, whereupon (12) comes out as false. Hence, as indeed Russell already pointed out, the two different usages of (12) can be explained in terms of structural ambiguity. This analysis has not been accepted by all linguists though.

To summarize, the important properties of the definite article *the* and its analyses are the following:

Under the naive analysis, (1) and its negation (11) can be true or false only if condition (i), expressed in (13), is true.

(13)   There is (exactly) one King of France

That is, (13) is an entailment of (1) and it is also entailed by (11). Under the quantificational analysis, (13) is also an entailment of (1), and there is an analysis of (11) which still entails (13). However, there is a difference between the two analyses: On the naive analysis, the existence and uniqueness presuppositions follow from a sentence S containing a definite description and from its negation. On the quantificational analysis, the presuppositions also follow from S, but they do not follow from the logical negation of S (this would be inconsistent with two-valued logic); they only follow if negation is applied to the predicate of S, not to its subject. In a technical sense, then, the Fregean notion of a presupposition has no counterpart in Russell's two-valued analysis.

2.   More on Entailments and Truth Value Gaps

Even if the two-valued, quantificational analysis of the definite article turns out to be superior to the naive, Fregean approach, the latter is of some principled interest to semantics. For it seems that something like a Fregean presuppositional analysis may be applicable to a variety of other phenomena which are distinct from the definite article. In this section, we will look at some of them.

As a point of departure, recall our analysis of the verb *know* in Section 5 of Chapter 8. One important fact to be accounted for there was the entailment shown in (14):

(14)   John knows that Berta is sick
⊨   Berta is sick

The validity of the inference was guaranteed by a condition on subjects' epistemic alternatives, viz., that the actual world be among them; cf. (42) on p. 192. Alternatively, the effect described in (14) could have been accounted for more directly as a trait of the lexical item *know*, to wit by a meaning postulate like (15):

(15)   If $\langle x, p \rangle \in [\![\,\text{know}\,]\!]_w$, then $w \in p$ (i.e., $p(w) = 1$).

In prose: if x knows that p in w, then p is true of w. Given that the inference in (16) is invalid, there cannot be an analogous postulate for verbs like *believe*, of course.

(16)   John believes that Berta is sick
⊭   Berta is sick

Still, there are more verbs that behave like *know* in this respect, among them *remember* and *manage*:

(17)   John remembers that Berta is sick
⊨   Berta is sick

(18)   Berta managed to become sick
⊨   Berta became sick

On the other hand, many other verbs, including *try* and *seem*, pattern with *believe*:

(19)   Berta tried to become sick
⊭   Berta became sick

(20)   It seems that Berta is sick
⊭   Berta is sick

Verbs which, like *know, remember, manage, regret,* ... , entail (the truth of) their complements are called **veridical**. Veridical verbs are thus unlike verbs like *believe*, *seem*, and *try*, which leave the truth of their complements open. We say that, in the case of veridical verbs, the inference to the truth of the complement is licensed by the lexical item *know, remember, manage,* ... (but not by *believe, try, seem* ...)—and is thus **lexically triggered** because it is the meaning of the (lexical) verb that licenses the inference.[6]

Now, the relevant observation that will motivate the remainder of this section is the following:

(21)   John didn't know that Berta was sick

⊨   Berta was sick

Like (14), (21) seems to be a valid inference. If I truthfully utter that John didn't know S, I must believe that the sentence S is true. Even when I say:

(22)   I didn't know that Berta is sick

I express that now I take it to be true that Berta is sick. Veridical verbs like *know*, which entail the truth of their complement even if they are negated, are called **factive**. It appears that veridical verbs tend to be factive in general, but there are a few notable exceptions, among them *prove* and *show*. In order to capture factivity, we can try a new meaning postulate similar to the one stated in (15):

(23)   If $\langle x, p \rangle \notin [\![\text{know}]\!]_s$, then $w \in p$ (i.e., $p(w) = 1$).

Again, in prose: if x does not know that S in w, then S is true of w. But now, taking (23) and (15) together, it follows that S must be true of any world in which x knows S, and that S must also be true of any world in which S does not know that S. If knowing and not knowing were the only possibilities, it

---

6   Curiously, in some cases the meaning of the verb interacts with the kind of complement it takes. Compare the following inferences:

(i)   John forgot that Berta wanted to come

⊨   Berta wanted to come

(ii)   Berta forgot to come

⊭   Berta came

The verb *forget* is only veridical when it takes a *that*-complement, not when it takes an infinitival complement; on the contrary, it then implies that the complement is false:

(iii)   Berta forgot to come

⊨   Berta didn't come

would now follow that S must be a *tautology*, i.e., true throughout Logical Space. But surely the sentence *Berta is sick* is not. So what went wrong?

Of course, one of the premises above must give way, and it seems that the most plausible way out is to permit **truth value gaps**: if S is false, then it is neither true nor false to say of someone that (s)he knows that S. If in fact Berta is not sick, then neither the sentence *John knows that Berta is sick*, nor the sentence *John doesn't know that Berta is sick* can be uttered truthfully. Of course, this is quite analogous to, and in the spirit of, Frege's presuppositional analysis: as the use of a definite description presupposes the existence and uniqueness of its referent, so does the use of a factive verb presuppose the truth of its complement.

As another illustration, consider the following inferences:

(24)   a.   Berta managed to make a phone call
        ⊨   Berta made a phone call
        b.   Berta didn't manage to make a phone call
        ⊨   Berta didn't make a phone call

Since these inferences seem to be valid, we now get into a similar predicament as before. If there are only two truth values and if S_1 implies S_2, and 'not S_1' implies 'not S_2', then S_1 and S_2 would have to be synonymous: according to (24-b), the (doubly negated) conclusion of (24-a)—i.e., Berta's making a phone call—would have to imply the (doubly negated) premise of (24-a). Again, this is clearly wrong for the sentences above: *Berta managed to make a phone call* reports some effort on Berta's side to make the call— perhaps due to recovery from illness, or general stress. And she would also have made this effort if she didn't manage to make the call. So both premises have truth value gaps if Berta did not make any effort to make a call.

EXERCISE 35:

The verb *regret* has the same presupposition as *know*. Explain why it is weird to say (25-d) while this kind of awkwardness does not show up in (25-c):

(25) a.   John regrets that Berta is sick
     b.   John doesn't regret that Berta is sick
     c.   I don't regret that Berta is sick
     d. #I don't know that Berta is sick

The admittance of truth value gaps thus allows us to solve our problem: the presupposition is not a tautology, because it can be false if and only if its trigger sentence lacks a truth value. Furthermore, the premises and the conclusions in (24) are not equivalent, because the premises might lack a truth value while the conclusions do not, other truth values being equal. Moreover, truth value gaps allow us to *define* the notion of presupposition:

(26)   *Definition:*
       If a sentence S_1 entails a sentence S_2, and if the negated sentence 'not S_1' also entails S_2, and if S_2 is not a tautology, then S_2 is called a **presupposition** of S_1.

According to this definition, *Berta took some effort to make a phone call* is a presupposition of *Berta managed to make a phone call*. Likewise, *that Berta is sick* is a presupposition of *John knows/doesn't know that Berta is sick*.

EXERCISE 36*:

   Prove the following theorems:

   Theorem 1: If S_2 is a presupposition of S_1, then $[\![S_1]\!] \subset [\![S_2]\!]$ and
             $[\![\text{not } S_1]\!] \subset [\![S_2]\!]$.

   Theorem 2: If S_2 is a presupposition of S_1, and if $[\![S_2]\!]_w \neq 1$, then S_1 is
             neither true nor false of w.

   Theorem 3: If S_1 and S_2 have the same presuppositions, then S_1 lacks a
             truth value if and only if S_2 does.

Truth value gaps create an additional complication in our semantics. Recall that above we defined the intension of a sentence as a function from possible worlds to truth values characterizing the proposition it expresses, i.e., the set of possible worlds of which it is true. This simplification is no longer possible once presuppositions have entered the scene. In order to describe that S_2 is a presupposition of S_1 in the way we did a minute ago, we have to say (a) that S_2 is true of all S_1-worlds, (b) that S_2 is true of all '*not*-S_1' worlds, and that (c) S_2 is false of all worlds where S_1 has no truth value. By this last step the intension of S_1 divides Logical Space into three (disjoint) parts: the **positive intension**, where S_1 is true, the **negative intension**, where S_1 is false, and a remaining set of worlds where S_1 has no truth value. This tripartition would get lost if we identified the intension of a sentence with the set of possible worlds of which it is true. We therefore have to be stricter about the fact that intensions are *functions* from worlds to truth values, with the additional twist that these functions may be partial, i.e., undefined for some worlds. Being undefined of course means that the sentence has no truth value in that world, which in turn should imply that some of its presuppositions are *violated* in that world. Violation of presuppositions therefore leads to undefinedness, or partiality. As the phenomenon of presupposition is ubiquitous in semantics, partiality is not restricted to the meanings (intensions) of sentences. For example, whether I say *I like him* or *I don't like him*, whatever the pronoun *him* refers to will, under normal circumstances, be an animate male being; similarly, the pronoun *her* is confined to females. This seems to be part of the meaning of these pronouns, and, in fact, that part of the meaning is a presupposition. When saying *I don't like him*, I cannot thereby deny that the referent of *him* is male.

Arguably, something similar happens if someone tells you:

(27)   #The table knows me

Presumably, you find it difficult to tell (let alone find out) whether or not (27) is true. The sentence just does not make sense, because *knowing* requires a conscious subject. In philosophy, violations of presuppositions of this kind have been called **category mistakes**; in the case at hand, the speaker using (27) may be accused of erroneously putting a piece of furniture in the category of conscious beings. In Chapter 2, Section 3, we already encountered the terms linguists use to describe this phenomenon, viz., that a **selectional restriction** of the verb *know* has been violated. Indeed it would seem that the factivity of *know*, too, could be construed as the result of a selectional restriction to the effect that the object clause must describe a fact in the actual world of utterance.

By the same reasoning, suppose we want to describe the meaning of

(28)   John is hungry

where I happened to give my TV set the name *John*. Then sentence (28) does not make much sense, unless we try to understand *hungry* in a metaphorical sense. Confining ourselves to literal meaning, we would certainly say that *hungry* requires that the subject be animate. If it is not, the literal extension should be undefined. But if we were to stick to the old truth conditions, this would not come out correctly, as the sentence would merely count as false.

Now recall how Russell derived the presupposition of the definite article. This was basically achieved by tampering with the scope of negation. But in the case of *know* discussed above, it is not so clear how the presupposition could escape the scope of negation; after all, the complement of *know* is in the syntactic domain of the negation. And what is worse, the presupposition induced by *manage* is not even the complement of *manage*. Rather, it must be described semantically as a property of the lexical item *manage*. There is no way to apply Russell's method to this kind of presupposition. Nor could this work for any of the selectional restrictions discussed above.

Summarizing, selectional restrictions may be analyzed in terms of presuppositions; conversely many presuppositions triggered by lexical items and in relation to their arguments may be due to selectional restrictions. If this is so, our system of semantic rules faces a major complication, since almost any predicate comes with selectional restrictions and therefore leaves room for undefinedness. For instance, a predicate like *glatzköpfig* (= *bald*) should divide the universe of entities into three domains: the set of people who can be meaningfully asserted to be *glatzköpfig*, those who can meaningfully be denied to be *glatzköpfig*, and the remainder who do not have a head at all. This means that, like propositions, predicate extensions cannot be sets. Rather, the extension of a predicate P at a world w splits the domain of individuals into three disjoint subsections: the positive extension, consisting of those individuals the predicate is true of; the negative extension, containing the individuals of which the predicate is false; and the rest—i.e., the individuals for which the predicate does not make sense.

As a result of these complications, truth conditions need to be split up into conditions for truth and for falsity, with respect to a positive and a negative extension. Thus, (28) receives the truth value 1 iff John is an element of the positive extension of the VP; its truth value is 0 iff John is an element of the negative extension of the VP; and it is undefined in all other cases. As interpretation functions are partial functions, and VP-denotations can themselves be complex, being composed from smaller building blocks, truth conditions become more complicated in intriguing ways, as evidenced by some of the examples that will be discussed below.

3. Presupposition and Assertion

It is common to explain the notion of presupposition by appealing to a contrast between what is asserted and what is presupposed. Here are some representative examples:

(29)   Susan will be late again

    a. *Presupposition:* Susan has been late in the past
    b. *Assertion:* Susan will be late

(30)   Susan won't be late again

    a. *Presupposition:* Susan has been late in the past
    b. *Assertion:* Susan won't be late

(31)   Susan stopped drinking

    a. *Presupposition:* Susan drank (for an indefinite period of time)
    b. *Assertion:* At a certain point in time and for a while, Susan didn't drink

(32)   Susan didn't stop drinking

    a. *Presupposition:* Susan drank (for an indefinite period of time)
    b. *Assertion:* At a certain point in time and for a while afterwards, Susan drank

By definition, then, the presupposition is neither asserted nor negated, but is "*communicated*" in both an affirmative assertion and the respective negative assertion. Given this **pragmatic** distinction between assertion and presupposition, semantic theory would have to characterize (and calculate formally) two propositions: the proposition stated by an utterance and the one presupposed by it. However, attractive though it may be, this idea runs into serious problems. In the above examples one may be able to tease apart what is *asserted* from what is *presupposed*. But, in general, it is not possible to spell out the asserted part without also mentioning the presupposed part of the "communicated" message. To see this, consider one of Frege's examples:

(33)   He who discovered the elliptic   *Der die elliptische Gestalt der*
       form of the planetary orbits died   *Planetenbahnen entdeckte,*
       in misery   *starb im Elend*

There are several presuppositions involved here, among others that planetary orbits are elliptic. Let us concentrate on the propositions expressed by the following two sentences:

(34)   a.   Someone discovered the elliptic form of the planetary orbits

          b.   Someone died in misery

Clearly, (34-a) is a presupposition of (33), presumably triggered by the free relative construction (*he who = whoever*), while (34-b) is the assertion made by (33). This seems straightforward. However, without anything else being said, the above account of the assertion vs. presupposition distinction is unable to express that the predicates of the two sentences in (34) must be instantiated by the same person. That is, whoever died in misery must be the one who discovered the elliptic form of the planetary orbits. At first blush this may look like a simple requirement on the subjects of (34-a) and (34-b), viz., that they be co-referential. However, the common subject is a quantifier, and as such does not even have a referent![7]

The problem was discovered by Lauri Karttunen and Stanley Peters; in a number of papers during the 1970s they developed a highly technical and sophisticated theory of presuppositions, but at the end of the day had to admit that they were unable to solve this particular problem. Before quoting from their original work (Karttunen and Peters (1979), p. 53), it must be pointed out that in the literature at that time, presuppositions were often treated as a special case of so-called *conventional implicatures*, a notion that goes back to the work of Paul Grice (cf. Grice (1967, 1975, 1981)). With this in mind, the following citation states the point clearly:

> NOTE: One problem with these rules is that they do not assign the correct conventional implicatures to sentences such as *Someone managed to succeed George V on the throne of England.* What the rules given here predict is (correctly) that this sentence is true iff someone succeeded George V

---

7   An additional problem can be identified in (i):

    (i)   Someone stopped drinking

          a.   *Presupposition:* Someone drank (for an indefinite period of time)

          b.   *Assertion:* At a certain point in time and for a while, someone didn't drink

Here again it is absolutely crucial to identify both "someones" as the same person, but in addition, the temporal relation between assertion and presupposition is crucial too: the time at which the presupposition holds must be immediately before the time the assertion is about, but this relation cannot be expressed by considering presupposition and assertion in isolation.

to the throne and (incorrectly) that it conventionally implicates that it was difficult for someone to do that. This is unsatisfactory because the implicature just stated is true (you or I would have found it extremely difficult), but the sentence is in fact an odd thing to say precisely because it conventionally implicates a falsehood—namely that George V's successor had difficulty ascending to the throne. What our rules as stated lack is any way of linking the choice of a person who is implicated to have difficulty to the choice of a person who is asserted to have succeeded. We expect that this deficiency will be remedied through further research, but we note here that the task is not a trivial one. [...] the problem arises directly from the decision to separate what is communicated in uttering a sentence into two propositions. In particular, it exists in connection with the notion of conversational implicature and also with any theory of presupposition that separates these from truth conditions (i.e., does not treat them simply as conditions for having a determinate truth value).

Arguably, this interdependence of assertion and presupposition may also be found in examples like Russell's king. If the presupposition is that there is a unique king, how can we formulate the assertion (i.e., the truth conditions) in isolation? *This* king is bald? So, who does *this* refer to? Perhaps the simplest way of framing the assertion is (35):

(35)   He is bald

In our above treatment we followed Russell and carefully avoided this complication by formulating the predication condition (ii) as a quantified statement. However, the anaphoric formulation (35) (which, incidentally, is very common in the semantic literature) seems straightforward and intuitive. More recent theories of presupposition rely heavily on this anaphoric relation without attempting to treat presupposition and assertion *as always separable* (cf. in particular van der Sandt (1992)). We cannot do justice to these developments in this introductory text.

4.   Presupposition and Discourse

We have seen that presuppositions are part and parcel of semantics in that they are triggered by semantic properties of lexical items or syntactic constructions. Nonetheless there is a pragmatic side to presuppositions: if a sentence S_1 presupposes S_2, then, in general, both the speaker when uttering S_1

and the hearer when understanding S_2 take the truth of S_2 for granted. For example, if someone utters

(36)   It was (not) Martha who died

he assumes that the hearer somehow takes the truth of *Someone died* **for granted**. In general, the participants in a conversation share quite a few assumptions; and some expressions (like *regret*) require that certain propositions be part of this conversational background. In pragmatics, the background assumptions of an ongoing conversation are known as the **common ground** (Stalnaker (1973, 1978)). If what a sentence presupposes is not part of the common ground, the utterance is more often than not felt weird or misleading. This is particularly obvious when the utterance is in conflict with what one of the participants believes or knows, provoking a reaction that goes beyond simply negating its content. For example, if I am convinced that Paul is alive and well, and then Mary tells me that he died years ago, I won't put her right before contradicting her: "That's wrong: I saw him only yesterday...", etc. However, if Mary had chosen to presuppose, rather than assert, the same piece of information, e.g. by saying:

(37)   Ringo doesn't know that Paul died years ago

it does not suffice to object *that's wrong* (or '(37)   *is false*'), because that would be understood by Mary as claiming that Ringo *knows* that Paul died, thereby still implying that we all know him to be dead. Since this is not what I want to say, I must utter something that makes it clear that Mary and I— as the participants in the conversation—do not share a common ground—for example, *Hey, wait a minute: Paul's not dead, I saw him only yesterday.*[8] What has to be denied, then, is precisely a presupposition.

This means that presuppositions must be part of the common ground. In other words, if an utterance of a sentence S can only be successful if a proposition p is part of the common ground, then p is expressed by a presupposition of S. And conversely, if I assert a sentence S successfully (without provoking weird consequences) and p is not part of the common ground both before and after the utterance of S, then p cannot be expressed by a presupposition of S.

This account of presupposition elaborates on a model of discourse semantics that has already been addressed in our motivation for intensions. Recall that we arrived at our characterization of propositions as sets of possible

---

8   Cf. footnote 3 above.

worlds by accounting for *information* in terms of permitting and excluding states of affairs. We will now define the notion of *new* information relative to a given common ground of a conversation. If p is part of the common ground, it cannot be new information relative to that common ground.

Let us, from now on, identify the common ground CG with the set of possible worlds that are compatible with the discourse participants' shared assumptions at a certain point in a conversation.[9] This means that if the truth of a proposition p is taken for granted, then p is entailed by CG (i.e., CG is a subset of p). As this holds for any such p, it follows that CG is the intersection of all propositions that are shared assumptions made by all of the participants of the conversation. Given CG, we may now describe the effect of uttering a sentence S in that context. If the assertion is successful and not objected to by the participants of the conversation, the effect will be that the proposition expressed by S is added to the common ground. This effect is a gain of information and will therefore result in a smaller set of possibilities, excluding states of affairs incompatible with S. That is, the common ground is modified or **updated** by removing the worlds of which S is false and by keeping the worlds of which S is true. Formally, we can describe the effect of uttering S as resulting in a modified conversational background CG' such that

(38) $CG' = CG \cap [\![\,S\,]\!]$

where $[\![\,S\,]\!]$ is the positive intension of S, i.e., the set of worlds of which S is true. We may now relativize informativity to a given context with a conversational background CG. A proposition p is **informative** with respect to CG iff $CG \cap p \neq CG$; otherwise, i.e., if $CG \subseteq p$, p is **uninformative** in CG.

What does all this imply for the notion of a presupposition? In general, if a speaker asserts a sentence containing an element that triggers a presupposition, and if the assertion is accepted by updating a common ground, then this may proceed successfully only if the common ground CG to be updated already contains the presupposition. In other words, the presupposed content of an utterance must be *uninformative* with respect to CG, i.e., already entailed by CG. If we now define the **context change potential** of a sentence S as the difference between CG and CG' in (38) (for any CG), then it follows that the potential assertion made by S is this difference, whereas the presupposition

---

9   Simplifying slightly, *shared* assumptions are not only shared, but also assumed to be shared by all participants.

is already entailed by *CG*. The presupposition must be part of the common ground; the assertion (the proposition that properly adds to this) must be new.

Let us visualize the situation in a Venn diagram.

(39)

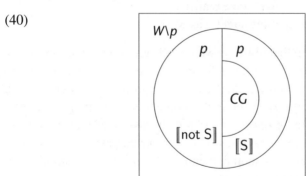

The presupposition *p*, represented by the outer circle in (39), contains all the worlds of which S can be true or false. Moreover, the presupposition follows from the common ground, represented by the inner circle: $CG \subseteq p$.[10] The proposition $[\![S]\!]$ is represented by the right semicircle, which overlaps with the common ground, as does the left semicircle representing $[\![\text{not } S]\!]_s$. The effect of uttering S is to eliminate all worlds incompatible with *CG*. The resulting common ground is shown in (40):

(40)

---

10   We have simplified a bit in assuming that the presupposition and its negation span Logical Space. This would not be the case, however, if the presupposition itself had presuppositions, as exemplified by *John knows that the king of France is bald*, where *p* is expressed by the complement of *know*. We abstract away from this additional complication.

The transition from (39) to (40) visualizes the context change potential of a sentence S, which may be characterized as the function that maps CG on CG', for any CG.[11]

Let us now address the problem discussed at the end of the previous section: there we observed that the presupposition and the assertion cannot be teased apart so easily. Nonetheless it is possible to describe that part of an assertion not being presupposed in a simple fashion while at the same time avoiding the pitfalls described above. As a concrete example, consider

(41)　Pete realized that the street was wet

Now, the communicated proposition **minus** the presupposition can be characterized as

(42)　If the street was wet, Pete realized that the street was wet

Or alternatively,

(43)　If the street was wet, Pete realized it

This is so because we can take the presupposed part for granted as (44-a) and adding (44-b) it follows by *modus ponens* that (44-c):

(44)　a.　The street was wet
　　　 b.　If the street was wet, Pete realized it
　　　 c.　Pete realized that the street was wet

Note that we do not claim that (44-b) is what has been said by uttering (44-c). Premise (44-b) only adds the truth conditions that must be added in order to get (44-c) given the presupposition, i.e., a common ground containing (44-a). It seems to us that the term *assertion* in this context is misleading, or at least rather vague: which of the propositions in (44) is "asserted"? This seems to be a matter of mere terminology to us. If the "asserted part" is the one that makes up the context change potential, then it suffices to take the implication (44-b) represented by (45) as "asserted":

11　The term goes back to Heim (1983), where what corresponds to our (i.e., Stalnaker's) common ground is called the "context". Since context change potentials correspond to meanings of (presupposing) sentences, they have also been called "propositions", a terminology which we prefer to avoid here—for obvious reasons.

(45)

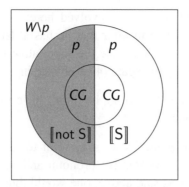

As the representation shows, the not-S-part of the CG is now shaded which is to be interpreted as a change in the CG as shown in (40). The assertion of a sentence S together with the proposition p expressed by its presupposition and the modified *CG* can thus be represented as (46):

(46)

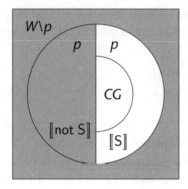

5. Accommodation

The model of conversation sketched above characterizes presuppositions as being part of the common ground. Unfortunately, there are some obvious exceptions to this. Suppose Peter arrives late at a party and his excuse is one of the following:

(47) a. Sorry, I had to find a parking space for my car
     b. Sorry, I had to find a baby sitter for my youngest daughter

There are a number of inferences involved here: (47-a) implies that Peter has a car; (47-b) allows one to infer that he has a daughter and in addition that he has more than one, otherwise the superlative *youngest* would not be appropriate. We might try to negate (47-b) by saying:

(48)   Peter wasn't late. This time, he didn't have to find a baby sitter for his youngest daughter

But the inferences still hold. So we may want to say that they are presuppositions triggered by the possessive pronoun and by the superlative of the adjective. Given what was said above, one would thus expect that these presuppositions need to be part of the common ground. However, it is clear that (47) can be uttered appropriately and successfully even if the host of the party does not know that the speaker has a daughter. This seems to be a problem, or a lacuna, in the theory sketched so far; some amendment is called for.

The point to be made is that the presuppositions of a sentence indeed often convey new information. A case in point is cited by Karttunen (1974), who found the following example in an official MIT bulletin about the spring 1973 commencement:

(49)   We regret that children cannot accompany their parents to commencement exercises

The point of (49) is not to remind one of a well-known fact; it is intended to convey new information (namely that, regrettably, children are not admitted) to anyone who didn't know already.

How can we reconcile this with the model of conversation developed above? The point is that the presupposition is not part of the common ground, but yet the utterance of (49) is successful. How can this come about?

The answer is that the hearer tacitly adjusts his version of the *CG* so as to make it compatible with the speaker's. This process has been dubbed **accommodation** (cf. Lewis (1979)). The point is that compatibility with the *CG* is necessary to interpret S correctly, but that our theory does not require this compatibility to exist before the utterance S has been made. In other words, an utterance may change the CG in a number of different ways, one of them being that, as a prerequisite of accepting (or rejecting) S in the current discourse, one also has to accommodate the *CG*.

The point has been emphasized in an unpublished paper by Kai von Fintel (2000), from which we quote the central paragraph (p. 5):

Our examples are clearly cases where the presupposed proposition is not in the common ground *prior to the utterance*. But note that this in fact is not what the common ground theory of presupposition says, at least not once we look very closely at what it tries to do. We saw that sentence presuppositions are requirements that the common ground needs to be a certain way for the sentence to do its intended job, namely updating the common ground. Thus, the common ground must satisfy the presuppositional requirements *before the update can be performed*, not actually *before the utterance occurs*.

Graphically, this can be illustrated as a transition from (50) to (51):

(50)

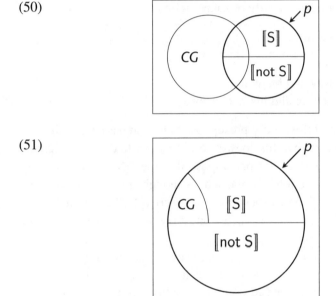

(51)

As a result of uttering S the common ground is adjusted so as to be compatible with both S and its presupposition.

In many cases this kind of adjustment is performed routinely, as in the above cases of accommodation. There are other cases where presuppositions cannot be accommodated so easily, e.g. in uttering (52) out of the blue:

(52)   Paul will come to the party as well

The *as well*-part presupposes that someone else who is relevant in the context will come to the party, but it does so without giving a clue as to who that other person may be. But this is crucial for *as well* to function properly: it requires that this person has already been identified in the *CG*. There is no way to fix the *CG* without further information, so that (52) will lead to a breakdown of communication, at least temporarily.

6.   Presupposition Projection*

Suppose that John has no wife. Now consider:

(53)   a.   Either John is away or John's wife is away
       b.   Either John has no wife or John's wife is away

(54)   a.   If John is away, his wife also is
       b.   If John has a wife, his wife is away

(55)   a.   John is away and his wife also is
       b.   John has a wife and his wife is away

The (a)-sentences straightforwardly presuppose that John has a wife; they are weird in the context given, but this doesn't seem to apply to the (b)-sentences. Uttering these sentences does not presuppose that the *CG* already contains as an established fact that John is married. Although this fact nonetheless follows from the truth of (55-b) (because it is asserted in the first conjunct), this does not hold for (53) and (54). So one may well ask what the truth conditions for these sentences are.

Frege held that failure to satisfy a presupposition leads to truth value gaps so that the fact that John has no wife should lead to a gap for the sentence *John's wife is away*, which, due to compositionality, affects the entire sentence, which also should lack a truth value (by extensional compositionality of *either or*, *if ... then*, and *and*). Intuitively this is correct for the (a)-sentences, but a wrong prediction for (53-b) and (54-b), which may still be true or false, whereas (55-b) is presumably judged false because the first conjunct is.

This compositionality problem is known as the **projection problem** for presuppositions. The question is: under which conditions can presupposition survive and "project" to the entire sentence, and which conditions determine that such a projection is "blocked"? Of course, one of the defining characteristics of presuppositions is that they are not blocked in negated sentences. But negation is just one context—what about conjunction, disjunction and implication, as illustrated in the above examples? It seems that it can't be the truth values, i.e., the extensions themselves, that determine the presuppositional behavior, but that it is rather some intensional relation between the sentences that makes the difference.

The data above exemplify that in certain syntactic environments, a certain presupposition does not project. It is readily seen that this holds for all sorts of presuppositions in these contexts; the phenomenon is quite general:

(56)   a.   John came and Mary came too
       b.   Either John didn't come, or Mary came too
       c.   If John came, then Mary came too

(57)   a.   John insulted Mary and regretted it
       b.   Either John didn't insult Mary, or he regretted it
       c.   If John insulted Mary, he regretted it

Many different explanations for the observed failure of presupposition projection have been proposed in the literature; cf. the brief survey in section 4.3.2 of Levinson (1983). In this introduction we will sketch a treatment that has been put forth in a paper by Irene Heim (1983). Her point of departure is discourse semantics as discussed above.

Recall that an utterance of S in the context of a common ground CG is well-formed iff CG implies S's presuppositions. One may therefore define:

(58) $CG + [\![S]\!]$ is well-formed iff CG is a subset of S's presupposition(s) and if so, $CG + S = CG \cap [\![S]\!]$.

This works fine as long as the presuppositions can be defined in an unproblematic and local way, i.e., as triggered within their minimal clause. However, as we have seen above, it does not work for complex clauses because we have not yet determined the presuppositions of any of the complex sentences. But in the framework of discourse semantics this can be done in a straightforward way, based on the presupposition(s) of the constituent sentences.

Let us first consider the simple case of a conjunction 'S_1 *and* S_2'. The basic intuition is simply that we first add $[\![S_1]\!]$ to a common ground CG, which yields a modified context CG', and we then add $[\![S_2]\!]$ to CG', which yields a doubly modified CG''. More formally:

(59) $CG + (S_1 \text{ *and* } S_2) := (CG + S_1) + S_2$

This already explains the difference between (55-a) and (55-b). In (55-b) we add as S_1 a sentence without presupposition. The result is a common ground CG' that is a subset of $[\![S_1]\!]$. But then, S_1 is a presupposition of S_2. At the point of adding S_2 it is indeed the case that the presupposition of S_2 is part of the modified common ground CG'. But then, $CG' + S_2$ is defined, so that we always get a well-defined common ground CG''. As there is no way of being undefined, this means that the complex sentence has no presupposition.

Example (55-a) is different. Adding S_1 to any CG is unproblematic. However, S_1 does not imply the presupposition of S_2. Hence, adding S_2 to CG' may indeed fail if John has no wife in CG. So the entire sentence has the presupposition that John is married.

Having defined conjunction, we still need to account for negation. This again is straightforward:

(60) $CG + \text{not } S = CG \setminus (CG + [\![S]\!])$

We first add S to the common ground, which by definition guarantees that the presupposition is satisfied. Then we subtract the result from CG, which accounts for the negation.

Having defined negation and conjunction, it turns out that, as far as implication and disjunction are concerned, certain paraphrases familiar from propositional logic not only work for their truth tables but generalize to their effects on context change potentials. In particular, as pointed out in Chapter 7 (p. 158), a material implication $p \rightarrow q$ is equivalent to $\neg(p \wedge \neg q)$, which suggests:

(61) $CG + (if\ S_1\ then\ S_2)$
= $CG + (not\ (S_1\ and\ not\ S_2))$
= $CG \setminus (CG + (S_1\ and\ not\ S_2))$
= $CG \setminus ((CG + S_1 + not\ S_2)$
= $CG \setminus ((CG + S_1 \setminus ((CG + S_1) + S_2))$

As in the case of conjunction, the stepwise addition of S_1 and S_2 guarantees that S_1 can introduce and satisfy the presupposition of S_2 so that the entire clause does not require its presupposition to already be implied by CG. The remaining calculations involving negation guarantee that the truth conditions come out correctly.

Finally, let us get back to (53-b), repeated as (62-a). Again a logical equivalence from propositional logic carries over, resulting in the paraphrase (62-b), and the same mechanism as before applies.

(62) a. Either John has no wife or John's wife is away
  b. If John has a wife, his wife is away

We cannot do justice here to the vast amount of literature on presuppositions, cf., e.g., wikis on ☞ **presupposition triggers**; influential papers that reflect on the semantic vs. pragmatic status of presuppositions include Donnellan (1966), Stalnaker (1974), and Kripke (1977). The formally most sophisticated analysis of semantic presupposition as context change potential is Beaver (2001). We should stress at this point, however, that due to Strawson's influence presuppositions in the literature are predominantly described as a pragmatic phenomenon, whereas we have tried to make it clear that presuppositions are lexically triggered and therefore belong to the lexical meaning of expressions, that is, their semantics.

EXERCISE 37:

Determine, and try to explicitly account for, the presuppositions in (63).

(63) a. John too is smoking again
  b. If I were rich, I would retire

Chapter 10
Compositional Variable Binding*

1. The Problem

In Section 4.1 of Chapter 6, we saw how sentences like (1) can be given a systematic interpretation if the object undergoes Quantifier Raising as in (2), and the remainder of the sentence is interpreted like the corresponding passive predicate, as in (3):

(1)   Paul loves every girl

(2) $\boxed{\;\boxed{\text{every girl}_y}\;\boxed{\text{Paul loves } y}\;}$

(3) $[\![\,\text{Paul loves } y\,]\!]_s = \{\,y: \text{Paul loves } y \text{ in } s\}$

Given (3), we may use the ordinary extension of *every girl* and derive the truth value of (1) as if it were in subject position, with the rest of the sentence forming the predicate. However, this procedure is not quite as systematic as it looks. The set term to the right of the equality sign in (3) contains a bound variable (viz., 'y'), i.e., a variable that does not refer to anything in particular. It is a typical feature of such bound variables that their particular form and appearance is immaterial to their content. As a consequence, the said set term may be rewritten with any other (bound) variable in lieu of y, without changing the set it stands for:[1]

(4) $\{\,y: \text{Paul loves } y \text{ in } s\} = \{\,z: \text{Paul loves } z \text{ in } s\}$

If we now use (4) to replace the set term in (3), the seeming systematicity of (3) turns out to be an illusion:

(5) $[\![\,\text{Paul loves } y\,]\!]_s = \{\,z: \text{Paul loves } z \text{ in } s\}$

---

[1]   Equation (4) is an instance of the law of *alphabetic variation* (or *bound renaming*) in formal logic. As a matter of fact, there are general logical principles (known as the *Laws of Freedom and Bondage*) that restrict the substitution of bound variables in 'nested' constellations. In particular, a specific renaming of one variable may only be available at the price of simultaneously renaming others. For the technical details, the reader may consult pertinent logic texts, e.g., van Dalen (2004), ch. 2, or Oberschelp (1992), § 25.

Equation (5) shows that equation (3) rests on an equivocation: the variable indicating the gap in the LF of (1) must not be confused with the meta-linguistic (bound) variable used to define its extension. To mark the difference, we will, from now on, use quotation marks whenever we refer to object-language variables.

In fact, since the only way to make sense out of (3) has it come out as equivalent to (5), the LF-variable 'y' should be treated as bound, too. However, unlike the bound variables in the meta-linguistic set terms, which we take to be sufficiently understood, we do not yet know the function of bound variables in LFs and their extensions.

2. Assignments

What we need, then, is a semantics of bound variables in syntax. To prepare the ground and to ensure compositionality (in a special sense to be elucidated),[2] we need to make sure that the variable 'y' in (2) ultimately could be replaced by any other variable without affecting the meaning of the sentence; again, this is what makes it a bound variable. However, 'y' occurs in both parts of (2). Hence when it comes to determining the extension of (2) from those of its immediate parts, one must take the contribution made by this very variable 'y' into account.

One way of doing so is to treat the variable as a third immediate part of (2)—contrary to appearances.[3] We may thus determine the truth value of (2) on the basis of the following three ingredients:

(6) a. $[\![\text{every girl}]\!]_s$
      b. $[\![\text{Paul loves } y]\!]_s$
      c. $[\![y]\!]_s$

---

2   If it were not for the sake of compositionality, simpler systematic approaches to variable binding than the one presented below would be available. However, we prefer to stick to semantic orthodoxy in this respect. We will briefly return to the matter at the end of Section 4 (p. 244).

3   If you think this is odd, you may rewrite (2) in a more suggestive way, for example:

(i) | every girl | y | Paul loves y |

In any case, it is up to the semanticist to define the part–whole structure of LFs.

The third component may look unfamiliar, but then defining it is a price we have to pay for having variables in our object language. As it turns out, only on the basis of a more involved understanding of what extensions are can the above three extensions be combined in a compositional way. In particular, it is easy to see that (6-b) cannot be a truth value, even though it is the extension of a sentence; but then again it is a rather special kind of sentence, one that contains a variable. In any case, what could (6-b) be if not a truth value (which we trust that the reader sees)? And what could (6-c) be? There are various, largely equivalent ways of going about answering these questions, and the strategy we pick is part of semantic and logical folklore. To this end, we introduce a new kind of semantic value which, for lack of a better (standard) term, we dub the 'local' extension.

Intuitively, a local extension of an expression is an extension it would have if the variables it contains were names. For instance, the local extension of *Paul loves y* would be 1 (in a given situation *s*) if Paul loved Mary (in *s*) and Mary were named '*y*'; and it would be 0 if Paul were named '*y*' and hated himself, etc. In order to define local extensions, we thus need to know what the variables stand for. Since any variable may stand for any individual whatsoever, any dubbing of individuals will have to be taken into account. In logic, and in what follows, such dubbings are called **(variable) assignments**. More precisely, a variable assignment is a function from the set of variables to the set of individuals; note that this includes the most degenerate and implausible dubbings according to which all variables stand for the same individual. Given an assignment *g*, we may determine the local extensions of arbitrary expressions. As for variables, their local extension is what the variable stands for according to the 'local dubbing'. Lexical items like *girl* retain their ordinary extension, the local extension of *girl* does not depend on *g* and therefore coincides with its ordinary extension. As for complex expressions, we apply the same rules of meaning composition as before, assuming that variables behave like names:

(7)   a. $[\![\, y \,]\!]_s^g = g(\text{'}y\text{'})$

  b. $[\![\, \text{Paul loves } y \,]\!]_s^g = 1$ iff Paul loves $g(\text{'}y\text{'})$ in s

  c. $[\![\, \text{every girl} \,]\!]_s^g = \{ Y : [\![\, \text{girl} \,]\!]_s^g \subseteq Y \}$

In (7) we superscript the local extensions with their locus, i.e., the variable assignments on which they depend. Given this convention, (7-a) is straightforward: the local extension of a variable is the value that *g* assigns to that variable. And on the assumption that variables in object position behave like names, (7-b) can be derived from (7-a) and the rest of our semantic clauses. Finally, (7-c) shows that local extensions coincide with ordinary extensions when there are no variables around. Again, this is a direct consequence of our rules of composition and the extension we assigned to the determiner *every*, which we now regard as its local extension.

Local extensions seem to be of no avail when it comes to determining the extensions of LFs like (2); after all, the local extension (7-b) of the gappy sentence is still a truth value and thus does not suffice to determine the extension (5) to be combined with the extension (7-c) of the object. However, (5) may be constructed from the local extensions as a whole—as the set of individuals for which *Paul loves y* has 1 as its local extension, where the variable 'y' stands for one of those individuals:

(8) $\{z: \text{Paul loves } z \text{ in } s\}$
= $\{z: \text{for some } g, g(\text{'}y\text{'}) = z \text{ and } [\![\text{Paul loves } y]\!]^{g}_{s} = 1\}$

Note that in (8) 'g' no longer stands for a particular given local dubbing but rather ranges over arbitrary variable assignments. Hence (8) has the set that the extension (7-c) of the quantifying object of (1) combines with depend on the truth values of *Paul loves y* under all assignments, not just on its local extension.

Generalizing the idea behind (8), it would seem that the rule in (10) gives the correct truth condition for arbitrary QR-constellations, i.e., any (part of an) LF of the form:

(9) $\boxed{\boxed{Q_y}\ \ldots\ y\ \ldots}$

So in order to determine the local extension of (9) under a given assignment g, one needs to look at the extensions of 'y' under arbitrary assignments h that make '$\ldots y \ldots$' true and collect them in a set to be fed to the quantifier Q:

(10)   *Interpretation of QR* (to be revised!)

$$\left[\!\!\left[\boxed{\boxed{Q_y}\ \ldots y\ldots}\right]\!\!\right]^{g}_{s} = 1 \text{ iff}$$

$$\{u: \text{for some } h, h(\text{'}y\text{'}) = u \text{ and } [\![\ldots y\ldots]\!]^{h}_{s} = 1\} \in [\![Q]\!]^{g}_{s}$$

Though the strategy behind (10) is on the right track, it is misleadingly simple in that it does not directly generalize to more complex constellations. To see this, let us look at (11), one LF of which we take to be (12):

(11)   A student read every book

(12) | a student$_x$ | | every book$_y$ | x read y |

In order to determine the local extension of (12) in a compositional way, we start from the innermost box:

(13) $[\![x \text{ read } y]\!]_s^{g^*} = 1$ iff in s, $g^*('x')$ read $g^*('y')$

Equation (13) gives the local truth condition of 'x read y' relative to a situation s and a particular local dubbing, which for later reference we have called 'g^*'; though g^* may be any assignment whatsoever, the reader should think of it as fixed throughout this section. Given our assumption that as far as compositionality is concerned, variables behave like names, (13) is straightforward. Note, however, that (13) is more involved than (7-b) in that the same assignment has to take care of two distinct variables. As we shall see shortly, it is this complication that stands in the way of a straightforward adaptation of (8) as a general recipe for interpreting Quantifier Raising.

Let us now take the next step in the compositional interpretation of (12) and see how (13) can be used to determine the local extension of (14):

(14) | every book$_y$ | x read y |

The ingredients are quite parallel to (7) above, the main difference lying in the lexical material (and the tense, which we are ignoring[4]). In particular, the fact that the subject position is occupied by a variable rather than a proper name should not make a difference, because we are assuming that variables behave like names in the compositional process. So we have:

(15)   a. $[\![\text{every book}]\!]_s^{g^*} = \{Y : [\![\text{book}]\!]_s^{g^*} \subseteq Y\}$

      b. $[\![x \text{ read } y]\!]_s^{g^*} = 1$ iff in s, $g^*('x')$ read $g^*('y')$

      c. $[\![x]\!]_s^{g^*} = g^*('x')$; $[\![y]\!]_s^{g^*} = g^*('y')$

---

4   For simplicity, we are sticking to the the the meta-linguistic relativization 'in s', which ought to be replaced by something like 'before s' to reflect the semantic contribution of the past tense morphology.

The set that needs to be combined with the (local) extension (15-a) of *every book* is:

(16) $\{u : g^*(\text{'}x\text{'}) \text{ read } u \text{ in } s\}$

If we combine (16) with the quantifier extension in (15-a), the result is the truth value 1 (given the situation s and the assignment g^*) iff (17) holds— which is what we want; for with (17) we may derive the truth condition of the entire structure (12) as in (18), using the same reasoning as in the simpler case (2) above (as well as the interpretation of the indefinite determiner from Section 1):

(17) $[\![\text{book}]\!]_s^{g^*} \subseteq \{u : g^*(\text{'}x\text{'}) \text{ read } u \text{ in } s\}$

(18) $[\![\text{student}]\!]_s^{g^*} \cap \{z : \text{for some } g, g(\text{'}x\text{'}) = z \text{ and}$
$[\![x \text{ read every book}]\!]_s^{g} = 1\} \neq \emptyset$

iff $[\![\text{student}]\!]_s^{g^*} \cap \{z : \text{for some } g, g(\text{'}x\text{'}) = z \text{ and}$
$\{u : g(\text{'}x\text{'}) \text{ read } u \text{ in } s\} \in [\![\text{every book}]\!]_s^{g}\} \neq \emptyset$

iff $[\![\text{student}]\!]_s^{g^*} \cap \{z : \text{for some } g, g(\text{'}x\text{'}) = z \text{ and}$
$[\![\text{book}]\!]_s^{g} \subseteq \{u : g(\text{'}x\text{'}) \text{ read } u \text{ in } s\}\} \neq \emptyset$

iff $[\![\text{student}]\!]_s^{g^*} \cap \{z : [\![\text{book}]\!]_s^{g^*} \subseteq \{u : z \text{ read } u \text{ in } s\}\} \neq \emptyset$

In the first line of (18) the argument of the denotation of *some student* is constructed as in (8), generalizing from the local extension under g^* to arbitrary assignments g. In the next step, we have applied (17) as the truth condition of (14) under (arbitrary) g. The next two steps only employ basic semantic and set-theoretic reasoning, the details of which are left to the reader. We merely note that the last line in (18) is indeed the adequate truth condition for the quantifier constellation in (12), for it says that there is at least one student in s who has read every book.

Before we go on, it is worth stopping to ponder on (16) a little bit more. Clearly, the precise nature of that set depends on the 'local dubbing' g^*: if g^* happens to assign Paul to 'x', the set in (16) contains whatever Paul has read (in s); if g^* happens to assign Mary to 'x', the set in (16) contains whatever Mary has read (in s); etc. In that sense, what (16) says depends on a given assignment g^*. In particular, if we consider a different assignment h^*, the corresponding set (19) need not be the same as (16):

(19) $\{u : h^*(\text{'}x\text{'}) \text{ read } u \text{ in } s\}$

The terms (16) and (19) denote the same set if h^* and g^* happen to assign the same value to 'x', i.e., if $h^*($'x'$) = g^*($'x'$)$, or if the individual that h^* assigns to 'x' happens to have read the same books, letters, pamphlets, etc. (in s) as the individual assigned to 'x' by g^*, even though $h^*($'x'$)$ and $g^*($'x'$)$ are not the same person. In all other cases though, (16) and (19) will be different sets. Trivial though this observation may seem, it will turn out to be of some importance in our very next step.

In order to complete the compositional picture, a definition of the set (16) in terms of the local extensions in (15) needs to be given. As before, the local truth value (15-b) does not suffice; and as before, we will invoke more local extensions of the form than just the special case where $g = g^*$. However, the simple recipe (10) above does not lead to the desired result, for the following set is not (16):

(20) $\{u : \text{for some } g, g($'$y$'$) = u \text{ and } [\![x \text{ read } y]\!]^g_s = 1\}$

We already saw that (16) depends on a given 'local' assignment g^*, but the set (20) obviously does not. The difference between (16) and (20) is that the latter collects all books, letters, pamphlets, etc. read by anyone whatsoever (in s). If, say, Jones read *The Lake of Darkness* (in s), then Ruth Rendell's novel will end up in (20), because there will be some assignment h assigning Jones to 'x' and *The Lake of Darkness* to 'y'; and for any such assignment h we have it that $[\![x \text{ read } y]\!]^g_s = 1$ and $h($'y'$) = $ *The Lake of Darkness*, which means that the latter is an element of (20). On the other hand, (16) only collects those books, letters, pamphlets, etc. read by $g^*(x)$. So if we want to capture (16) along the lines of (20), we must stop the variation in the readers. This can be done by restricting attention to those assignments g that leave the value of 'x' untouched:

(21) $\{u : \text{for some } g, g($'$y$'$) = u \text{ and } [\![x \text{ read } y]\!]^g_s = 1 \text{ and } g($'$x$'$) = g^*($'$x$'$)\}$

It is readily seen that in (21), only those books, letters, pamphlets, etc. are collected that have been read by $g^*($'x'$)$. In other words, (21) is the same set as (16). Moreover, (21) is defined in terms of the local extensions of the (sketchy) LF 'x read y'. Yet although 'x' and 'y' both appear in that LF, they play different roles in (21): 'y' contributes its (local) extensions under certain alternative assignments and the set (21) collects them; and while these alternative assignments vary as to the value of 'y', they do not tamper with the local extension of 'x' at g^*. In formal logic, variables that retain their local extension are called free, and are distinguished from bound variables, the interpretation of which requires taking (certain) alternative assignments into account.[5] This distinction is crucial for a general and principled interpretation of LFs involving Quantifier Raising (and, indeed, variable binding in general).

3. Interpreting Variable Binding

To finally arrive at this general interpretation, we need to get clear about two questions:

— How does the distinction between free and bound variables bear on QR constellations in general?
— What alternative assignments need to be taken into account to interpret the bound variables in QR constellations in general?

Turning to the first question, we should recall that QR constellations (9) come in three immediate parts: a quantifying expression Q, a variable 'y', and a (sentential) sub-LF '$\dots y \dots$' that contains 'y' (possibly more than once). In order to determine the local extension of (9) given a situation s and an assignment g^*, a set must be formed from the local extensions of '$\dots y \dots$', taking into account alternative (local) extensions of 'y'. Hence 'y' is the only variable that gets bound.[6] This answers the first question.

As to the second question, we saw in (21) that the alternative assignments divert from the given local dubbing g^* in the value they assign to the variable bound by the quantifier Q_y in (9). All other variables that occur in '$\dots y \dots$' retain their (local) extension at g^*. In fact, those that do not occur in '$\dots y \dots$' may do so too, for their extensions won't have an effect on the interpretation of (9) anyway. Hence the alternative assignments taken into account are precisely the so-called 'y'-**alternatives** to g^*, i.e., those assignments that differ from g^* only in the value they assign to 'y' (if at all). This answers the second question.

---

5 Actually, the logical distinction between free and bound variables is a syntactic one. Its semantic correlate in terms of local extensions and alternative assignments is due to Alfred Tarski [1901–1983].

6 'y' need not be the only bound variable in (9), though—as can be seen from (12), where both 'x' and 'y' are bound. However, as it turns out (and as we have already mentioned), bound variables within '$\dots y \dots$' do not depend on the local assignment anyway.

We are now in a position to define the local extension of a QR-constellation (9) given a variable assignment g^* and a situation s:

(22)   *Interpretation of QR:* (final version)

$$\left[\!\!\left[\,\boxed{\boxed{Q_y}\,\ldots y\ldots}\,\right]\!\!\right]^{g^*}_s = 1$$

iff $\{u : \text{for some '}y\text{'-alternative } g \text{ to } g^*, g(\text{'}y\text{'}) = u \text{ and } [\![\ldots y \ldots]\!]^g_s = 1\} \in [\![Q]\!]^{g^*}_s$.

As expected, the way the argument of the quantifier is defined in (22) generalizes (21). In particular, the condition that $g(\text{'}x\text{'}) = g^*(\text{'}x\text{'})$ is no longer necessary because it is part of g's being a 'y'-alternative to g^* (and 'x' $\neq$ 'y', which we are taking for granted). In fact, it can be shown that, since no other variables occur in the LF 'x read y', the condition that it be true under all 'y'-alternatives to g^* boils down to its being true under all assignments satisfying $g(\text{'}x\text{'}) = g^*(\text{'}x\text{'})$. For similar reasons the set construction in (22) can also be shown to generalize our original approach (10).[7] We may thus adopt (22) as our official clause for the interpretation of Quantifier Raising. Indeed, something along the lines of (22) is what most texts in logic and semantics offer by way of interpreting variable binding.

4.   Compositionality

There is no doubt that (22) accounts for the (local) extensions of QR-constellations in a systematic way—but is it compositional? This is actually a tricky question. On the one hand, (22) is not compositional on the level of local extensions: two LFs '$\ldots x \ldots$' and '$\ldots z \ldots$' may have the same truth value under a given assignment g^*, but they are likely to have different effects on the truth value of constellations of the form (9). On the other hand, there is a notion of *global* extensions with respect to which (22) turns out to be compositional after all; in fact, the approach to variable binding in terms of assignments has been developed, and is favored in current mainstream semantics, in view of its compositionality. As already indicated, the global ex-

---

7   In formal logic, the general fact behind this reasoning is known as the *Coincidence Lemma*, which states that only free variables depend on assignments, i.e., the latter have no effect on variables that are (only) bound or do not even occur in the formula (or LF) to be interpreted.

tension of an LF (given a situation s) is the entire landscape made up by its local extensions (to extend the metaphor). Formally, it is defined as the function that assigns to every variable assignment the local extension (at s) under that assignment:

(23) *Definition of global extensions* [8]

Let s and Ψ be a (possible) situation and an LF, respectively. Then the **global extension** of Ψ at s is that function $\overrightarrow{[\![\Psi]\!]}_s$ whose domain is the set Γ of all variable assignments and which assigns to any $g \in \Gamma$ the local extension of Ψ at s under g:

$$\overrightarrow{[\![\Psi]\!]}_s(g) = [\![\Psi]\!]_s^g$$

In order to ascertain that (22) is compositional with respect to global extensions, one needs to show that the global extension of any LF of the form (22) can be determined from the global extensions of its three immediate parts. In other words, what we need is a function Φ assigning to each triple of global extensions (of quantifying expressions, variables, and sentential LFs) the corresponding global extension of (22):

(24) $$\Phi(\overrightarrow{[\![Q]\!]}_s, \overrightarrow{[\![z]\!]}_s, \overrightarrow{[\![\ldots z \ldots]\!]}_s) = \overrightarrow{\left[\!\!\left[\; \boxed{Q_z} \; \ldots z \ldots \right]\!\!\right]}_s$$

Since global extensions are functions defined on variable assignments, we may describe the outcome of applying Φ pointwise for any $g^* \in \Gamma$, and then make sure that the following equation is always met:

(25) $$\Phi(\overrightarrow{[\![Q]\!]}_s, \overrightarrow{[\![z]\!]}_s, \overrightarrow{[\![\ldots z \ldots]\!]}_s)(g^*) = 1 \text{ iff } \left[\!\!\left[\; \boxed{Q_z} \; \ldots z \ldots \right]\!\!\right]_s^{g^*} = 1$$

Equation (25) makes use of the above definition and the fact that QR-constellations are sentential, with truth values as local extensions. Using (22), the right-hand side of (25) can be rewritten as:

---

8   In formal logic, global extensions are sometimes defined as sets of assignments rather than functions defined on them. As long as globalization is only applied to sentential expressions, this is equivalent to the definition to be given, due to the correspondence between sets and characteristic functions. However, when it comes to compositionality, global assignments must be generalized to arbitrary expressions and can then no longer be identified with subsets of Γ.

(26) $\{u : \text{for some 'z'-alternative } g \text{ to } g^*, g(\text{'z'}) = u \text{ and } [\![...z...]\!]_s^g = 1\} \in$
$[\![Q]\!]_s^{g^*}$

Now, $[\![...z...]\!]_s^g = \overrightarrow{[\![...z...]\!]}_s(g)$; moreover, $[\![Q]\!]_s^{g^*}$ can be rewritten as $\overrightarrow{[\![Q]\!]}_s(g^*)$. So (26) combines the global extensions of the raised quantifier and the remaining sentence. But it still refers to the variable 'z', rather than its global extension $\overrightarrow{[\![z]\!]}_s$. In order to get rid of this last trace of non-compositionality, we may define a function $\downarrow$ that maps global extensions of variables to the corresponding variables themselves so that the variable 'z' in (26) can be rewritten as $\downarrow(\overrightarrow{[\![z]\!]}_s)$. The following pointwise definition of $\downarrow$ does the job:

(27) $\downarrow(\chi) = $ that variable 'x' such that $\chi(g) = g(\text{'x'})$, for any assignment g

In (27) the (meta-linguistic) variable 'χ' ranges over global extensions of (object-linguistic) variables. In order for (27) to make sense, we need to make sure that no two variables have the same global extension:[9]

(28) $\overrightarrow{[\![x]\!]}_s \neq \overrightarrow{[\![y]\!]}_s$, whenever 'x' ≠ 'y'

Observation (28) is easily established by picking two distinct individuals u and v and considering the assignment h that maps 'x' to u and all other variables (including 'y') to v. We then obviously have:

(29) $\overrightarrow{[\![x]\!]}_s(h) = [\![x]\!]_s^h = h(\text{'x'}) = u \neq v = h(\text{'y'}) = [\![y]\!]_s^h = \overrightarrow{[\![y]\!]}_s(h)$

... and thus (28). Wrapping up, we may now give the following reformulation of (22), which combines the global extensions of the immediate parts of QR-constellations of the form (9) and is thus compositional:

---

9   For the same reason we could not just define $\downarrow$ by the simple (pointwise) equation (i), even though it does turn out to be true:

(i) $\overrightarrow{[\![x]\!]}_s = \text{'x'}$

In mathematical parlance, what needs to be shown in order for (27) and (i) to be correct is their independence of the (class) representative 'x'—which is what (28) expresses.

(30) $\quad \left\lVert \boxed{\boxed{Q_z}\ldots z\ldots} \right\rVert_s^{g^*} = 1$

iff $\quad \Phi(\overrightarrow{[\![Q]\!]_s}, \overrightarrow{[\![z]\!]_s}, \overrightarrow{[\![\ldots z\ldots]\!]_s})(g^*) = 1$

iff $\quad \{u : \text{for some } \downarrow(\overrightarrow{[\![z]\!]_s})\text{-alternative } g \text{ to } g^*, g(\downarrow(\overrightarrow{[\![z]\!]_s})) = u \text{ and}$

$\quad \overrightarrow{[\![\ldots z\ldots]\!]_s}(g) = 1\} \in \overrightarrow{[\![Q]\!]_s}(g^*)$

A few words on the astounding complexity of (22) and its compositional re-formulation (30) are in order. To begin with, it should be realized that this complexity is mostly due to moving from ordinary extensions to global extensions. This move was motivated by compositionality, for we have seen that, when it comes to variable binding, ordinary extensions do not behave compositionally. And although we could have employed somewhat different constructions instead, there is no way to escape the inherent complexity of the meanings needed to give a fully compositional account of variable binding.[10] As it turns out, the culprit is the inequality (28), which makes sure that denotations of LFs are fine-grained enough to distinguish any two variables; without this assumption no compositional account of variable binding can be given.

Apart from the fact that global extensions—or any of their substitutes—are rather unwieldy, they are also somewhat of a cheat. For other than ordinary extensions, which correspond to the objects referred to in the non-linguistic world, global extensions are language dependent in that they are functions whose domain is the set of variable assignments, which in turn are functions defined on variables, i.e., elementary building blocks of LFs, and hence linguistic expressions. And again, any attempt at avoiding this language-dependence of denotations either merely obscures the connection, or else fails on compositionality.[11] As a consequence, unless languages overlap in some of their basic means of expression (to wit, variables), no two expressions of two distinct languages could have the same global extension. This so-called *representationalism*, i.e., the fact that global extensions are language-dependent (aspects of) meaning, may be seen as a nuisance and too high a price to pay for the compositionality of variable binding. As an al-

---

10   The interested reader may consult Hodges (2001), where the minimal complexity of these denotations is characterized in terms of the granularity of synonymy classes of predicate logic formulae.

11   This dilemma is closely related to what has been called *the antinomy of the variable*; cf. Fine (2003).

ternative, some logicians and semanticists have therefore (and for different reasons too) proposed giving up on either compositionality or, indeed, variables in Logical Form. For reasons of space we cannot go into these options here but refer the reader to the relevant literature.[12]

Let us finally point out that the construction developed in this section only covers the extensional part of language. Once intensional constructions like clausal embedding are taken into consideration, global extensions would have to be replaced by their intensional analogues. So intensionality still adds complexity to compositional denotations if only in a less dramatic form than variable binding.

5.   Predicate Logic

The formal concepts and techniques introduced above originate in predicate logic, a formal system which—originally developed for the analysis of mathematical proofs— has become the standard tool of logical analysis in analytic philosophy and mathematics.[13] In this section, we briefly introduce predicate logic notation and its interpretation. The reader should be warned that this section is somewhat more dense and technical than the rest of the book; for a smoother introduction we recommend Hodges (1977).

5.1.   Basic Definitions

The formulae of predicate logic can be used to make statements about any given (non-empty) set of objects, the *universe*. The members of the universe are referred to (and quantified over) by means of variables, which are taken from a fixed infinite set *Var*. The basic (lexical) expressions of predicate logic come in two categories: individual constants, which are like names and stand

---

12   As to the first option, an alternative approach to variable binding employs substitution of variables by 'standard names' of objects quantified over. This so-called *substitutional quantification* has been popular in some of the philosophical literature for reasons entirely independent of compositionality; cf. Parsons (1971). *Variable-free semantics*, in contrast, is technically quite involved but does have some advocates among linguistic semanticists; see, for example, Jacobson (1999).

13   The first formulation of predicate logic can be found in Frege (1879); a similar system was developed independently in Peirce (1885). Modern versions radically differ from these ancestors in notation but not in their expressive means. Two pertinent textbooks for the philosophical and mathematical use of predicate logic are Forbes (1994) and Ebbinghaus et al. (1994), respectively.

for individuals; and predicates, which stand for sets of individuals or relations among them. More precisely, a *lexicon* of predicate logic is a function assigning to any natural number $n \geq 0$ a set $PRED_{n,L}$ of (primitive) symbols such that, whenever $n \neq m$, $PRED_{n,L}$ and $PRED_{m,L}$ are disjoint, i.e., $PRED_{n,L} \cap PRED_{m,L} = \emptyset$.[14] For $n = 0$, $PRED_n$ contains the individual constants of L; and if $n \geq 1$, the members of $PRED_n$ are called n-place predicates (of L). Moreover, the elements of $Var \cup PRED_{0,L}$ are called the *terms* (of L). Typically, in practical applications, all but finitely many sets $PRED_{n,L}$ will be empty.

Given a lexicon L, the set of formulae Fml_L is defined by the following recursion:

(31)   *Syntax of predicate logic:*

    a.   '$\perp$' $\in Fml_L$;

    b.   if a and b are terms of L, then '$(a = b)$' $\in Fml_L$;

    c.   if $R \in PRED_{n,L}$ (for some $n \geq 1$), and $a_1,\ldots,a_n$ are (not necessarily distinct) terms of L, then '$R(a_1,\ldots,a_n)$' $\in Fml_L$;

    d.   if $\{\varphi,\psi\} \subseteq Fml_L$, then '$[\varphi \rightarrow \psi]$' $\in Fml_L$;

    e.   if $\varphi \in Fml_L$ and $x \in Var$, then '$(\exists x)\varphi$' $\in Fml_L$.

The symbol '$\perp$' is called *falsum* and stands for an absurd (necessarily false) proposition. '$=$' is the identity symbol used to create equations; '$\rightarrow$' is a binary connective standing for the truth table of material implication; '$\exists$' is the existential quantifier used to express non-emptiness of a set. The precise meanings of the symbols and formulae will be given below, in the semantic clauses. Note that neither the symbols '$\perp$', '$=$', '$\rightarrow$', and '$\exists$' nor the variables occuring in the formulae Fml_L are part of any lexicon L; in this respect they are like the brackets that merely keep the formulae unambiguous by indicating the syntactic constellation. This rather common way of introducing symbols "on the fly"—i.e., as indicators of syntactic operations—is known as a **syncategorematic** treatment; however, there are alternatives, to be addressed in due course.

The interpretation of the formulae in Fml_L proceeds by assigning truth values relative to interpretations of the lexicon and variable assignments. As already indicated, an interpretation of a lexicon L assigns individuals and relations to members of $PRED_{n,L}$.[15] More precisely, an interpretation of a

---

14   In logic, lexicons are called *signatures* or *languages*.

15   In logic, interpretations are also called *models* or *structures*.

lexicon L is a pair $\langle U, F \rangle$, where $U \neq \emptyset$ is a (finite or infinite) set and F is a function defined on all members of all $PRED_{n,L}$ such that $F(a) \in U$ if a is an individual constant, and $F(P)$ is a set of n-tuples of members of U whenever P is an n-place predicate. (For the case $n = 1$, we assume that $\langle u \rangle = u$, so that $F(P) \subseteq U$ if $P \in PRED_{1,L}$.) As above, a variable assignment (for a given non-empty universe U) is a function from Var to U. Given an interpretation $M = \langle U, F \rangle$ and an assignment g, each term is assigned a (local) denotation by the union $F \cup g$, which will be a function (given that the variables do not overlap the individual constants and predicates). Defining the truth values of formulae requires a recursion on the structure of Fml_L:

(32)   *Semantics of predicate logic:*
    If $M = \langle U, F \rangle$ is an interpretation of a lexicon L, then for any formula $\varphi \in Fml_L$, $[\![\varphi]\!]^{M,g}$ is a uniquely determined truth value ($\in \{0,1\}$) satisfying the following equations for any variable assignment g for U:

    a. $[\![\bot]\!]^{M,g} = 0$;
    b. $[\![(a = b)]\!]^{M,g} = 1$ iff $F \cup g(a) = F \cup g(b)$;
    c. $[\![R(a_1, \ldots, a_n)]\!]^{M,g} = 1$ iff $(F \cup g(a_1), \ldots, F \cup g(a_n)) \in F(R)$;
    d. $[\![(\varphi \to \psi)]\!]^{M,g} = 1$ iff $[\![\varphi]\!]^{M,g} \leq [\![\psi]\!]^{M,g}$;
    e. $[\![(\exists x)\varphi]\!]^{M,g} = 1$ iff $\{ u \in U : $ for some x-alternative h to g, $h(x) = u$ and $[\![\varphi]\!]^{M,h} = 1 \} \neq \emptyset$.

The members of the set that the existential quantifier characterizes are called the **x-satisfiers** of the formula φ; obviously, the construction of this set is as in the interpretation (22) of QR-constellations; we will return to this observation.

    The following "formalization" of the (true) English sentence *Every prime that is at least as large as two distinct primes is odd* may give an idea of the remarkable expressive power of predicate logic:

(33) $(\forall x)[P(x) \wedge (\exists y)(\exists z)[[[[[P(y) \wedge P(z)] \wedge \neg y = z] \wedge R(x, y)] \wedge R(x, z)]] \to \neg E(x)]$

Formula (33) makes use of a lexicon containing the one-place predicates P and E, representing (the extensions of) *prime* and *even*, respectively, as well as the two-place predicate R, which expresses the relation $\geq$ among (natural) numbers. Of course, the correspondence between the predicates and the English words is a matter of choosing a suitable interpretation for the lexicon, and so is the prior choice of a suitable universe that includes numbers.

5.2.   Some Variants and Alternatives

Apart from material implication, other truth-functional connectives may be used in predicate logic; these can be defined in terms of '$\perp$' and '$\rightarrow$'. More specifically, if φ and ψ are formulae (i.e., elements of Fml_L, for some lexicon L), then the following conventions hold:

(34)   *Common abbreviations:*

    a.   '$\neg\varphi$' abbreviates '$[\varphi \rightarrow \perp]$';

    b.   '$[\varphi \vee \psi]$' abbreviates '$[\neg\varphi \rightarrow \psi]$';

    c.   '$[\varphi \wedge \psi]$' abbreviates '$\neg[\neg\varphi \vee \neg\psi]$';

    d.   '$[\varphi \leftrightarrow \psi]$' abbreviates '$[[\varphi \wedge \psi] \vee [\neg\varphi \wedge \neg\psi]]$';

    e.   '$(\forall x)\varphi$' abbreviates '$\neg(\exists x)\neg\varphi$'.

The final abbreviation introduces the universal quantifier, which says that the set of x-satisfiers coincides with the universe. It is easy to verify that (32) induces the following truth conditions for the abbreviated formulae:

(35)   *Interpreting abbreviations:*

    a. $[\![\neg\varphi]\!]^{M,g} = 1$ iff $[\![\varphi]\!]^{M,g} = 0$;

    b. $[\![[\varphi \vee \psi]]\!]^{M,g} = 1$ iff $[\![\varphi]\!]^{M,g} + [\![\psi]\!]^{M,g} \neq 0$;

    c. $[\![[\varphi \wedge \psi]]\!]^{M,g} = 1$ iff $[\![\varphi]\!]^{M,g} = [\![\psi]\!]^{M,g} = 1$;

    d. $[\![[\varphi \leftrightarrow \psi]]\!]^{M,g} = 1$ iff $[\![\varphi]\!]^{M,g} = [\![\psi]\!]^{M,g}$;

    e. $[\![(\forall x)\varphi]\!]^{M,g} = 1$ iff

        $\{u \in U$: for some x-alternative h to g, $[\![\varphi]\!]^{M,h} = 1\} = U$.

As pointed out above, the so-called **logical constants**, i.e., the symbols '$\perp$', '$=$', '$\rightarrow$', and '$\exists$', are treated syncategorematically. As a consequence, they receive their meaning only in the recursive evaluation (32) of the formulae in which they occur. However, they could be promoted to full-fledged symbols by some largely cosmetic syntactic measures plus concomitant changes in the definition of interpretations and the recursive truth value assignment (32). More specifically, one could include the logical constants (or some of them) in the lexicon, putting them in suitable categories, in addition to the families $PRED_{n,L}$. For instance, we may have (for any lexicon L):

$PROP_L = \{`\bot'\}$, $CONN_L = \{`\to'\}$, and $QUANT_L = \{`\exists'\}$; moreover, '=' could be be included in $PRED_{2,L}$, regarding equations '$(a = b)$' as notational variants of formulae '$= (a, b)$'. In fact, once the new categories have been added, one could also make them more inclusive by treating (some of) the connectives and quantifiers defined in (34) as basic lexical expressions instead.

Of course, with the new status of logical constants, the syntactic rules of predicate logic would have to be adapted accordingly. For instance, the last clause in (31) would have to read:

(36)   if $\varphi \in Fml_L$, $x \in Var$, and 'Q' $\in QUANT_L$, then '$(Qx)\varphi$' $\in Fml_L$.

Interpretations $\langle U, F \rangle$, too, would have to be adapted so as to assign suitable denotations to the logical constants:

(37)   a. $F(`\bot') = 0$
        b. $F(`\to') = \to$ (i.e., the truth table by the same name)
        c. $F(`=') = \{(x, x) : x \in U\}$
        d. $F(`\exists') = \{X : X \neq \emptyset \text{ and } X \subseteq U\}$

In other words, the *falsum* denotes the truth value 0; the arrow denotes the truth table of material implication; the identity sign denotes the (binary) relation of identity between members of the *U*niverse; and the existential quantifier denotes the set of non-empty subsets of U. Finally, the new recursive clauses need to be interpreted, which is rather straightforward. We only mention (36), for future reference:

(38) $[\![(Qx)\varphi]\!]^{M,g} = 1$ iff $\{u \in U :$ for some x-alternative h to g, $h(x) = u$
       and $[\![\varphi]\!]^{M,h} = 1\} \in F(Q)$.

5.3.   *Predicate Logic and Compositionality*

It is often overlooked that the standard semantics of predicate logic as given in (32) is not strictly compositional. Rather, it is a systematic specification of "local" extensions of formulae. In particular, the truth value of an existentially quantified formula, determined in the final clause, is *not* defined in terms of the extensions of its (immediate) parts. However, it is easy to convert the local values of (32) into global ones by applying the technique developed in Section 4. In fact, the reformulation (38) is strongly reminiscent of the 'pre-compositional' formulation (22) of the interpretation of QR. And it can be reformulated accordingly, in close analogy to (30):

(39) $\quad [\![(Qx)\varphi]\!]^{M,g} = 1$ iff $\{u : \text{for some } \downarrow(\overrightarrow{[\![z]\!]^{M}})\text{-alternative } h \text{ to } g,$

$\quad h(\downarrow(\overrightarrow{[\![z]\!]^{M}})) = u \text{ and } \overrightarrow{[\![\varphi]\!]^{M}}(h) = 1\} \in \overrightarrow{[\![Q]\!]^{M}}(g)$

(39) relies on predicate logic formulae with global extensions, which, however, have only been defined for LFs so far. In order to make sense of (39), then, the definition (23) (p. 241) needs to be adapted, which in turn requires a definition of local extensions of all **atomic *L*-expressions**, i.e., the elements of a lexicon *L* together with the variables in *Var* and the formulae in Fml_L:

(40) $\quad$ Let *L* be a lexicon, α an atomic L-expression, and $M = \langle U, F \rangle$ an interpretation of *L*.

$\quad\quad$ a. $\quad$ For any any variable assignment *g* for *U*, the *local extension of* α *at M under g*—in symbols: $[\![\alpha]\!]^{M,g}$—is the truth value of α (relative to *M* and *g*) if $\alpha \in Fml_L$; otherwise it is $F \cup g(\alpha)$.

$\quad\quad$ b. $\quad$ The *global extension of* α *at M* is that function $\overrightarrow{[\![\alpha]\!]^{M}}$ whose domain is the set Γ of all variable assignments and which assigns to any $g \in \Gamma$ the local extension of α at *M* under *g*:

$$\overrightarrow{[\![\alpha]\!]^{M}}(g) = [\![\alpha]\!]^{M,g}.$$

While (39) depends on the treatment (36) of quantifiers as atomic expression as sketched in the previous subsection, the essence of this clause can be preserved under the syncategorematic treatment of quantification. Again we only illustrate the procedure by reformulating the critical final clause of (32), leaving the rest of the definition to the patient reader:

(41) $\quad [\![(\exists x)\varphi]\!]^{M,g} = 1$ iff $\{u : \text{for some } \downarrow(\overrightarrow{[\![z]\!]^{M}})\text{-alternative } h \text{ to } g,$

$\quad h(\downarrow(\overrightarrow{[\![z]\!]^{M}})) = u \text{ and } \overrightarrow{[\![\varphi]\!]^{M}}(h) = 1\} \neq \emptyset$

5.4. *Validity, Logical Equivalence, and Entailment*

The semantic definition in (32) only concerns the truth values, which depend on specific interpretations (and assignments). In order to get at the content of predicate logic formulae, one needs to abstract aways from these 'local extensions', by generalizing over interpretations (and assignments). We illustrate this 'global' perspective by a couple of standard definitions:[16]

(42)   Let L be a lexicon and $\Sigma \cup \{\varphi, \psi\} \subseteq Fml_L$.

    a. φ is valid (in symbols: $\models \varphi$) iff $[\![\varphi]\!]^{M,g} = 1$, for all interpretations M of L and assignments g (for the universe of U).

    b. φ is equivalent to ψ (in symbols: $\varphi \equiv \psi$) iff $[\![\varphi]\!]^{M,g} = [\![\psi]\!]^{M,g}$, for all interpretations M of L and (suitable) assignments g.

The following immediate consequences of these definitions should help the reader to get acquainted with these concepts:

(43)   Let L, Σ, φ, and ψ be as in (35). Then the following hold:

    a. $\models \varphi$ iff $\varphi \equiv \neg \bot$

    b. $\varphi \equiv \psi$ iff $\models [\varphi \leftrightarrow \psi]$

    c. $\varphi \equiv \varphi$; if $\varphi \equiv \psi$, then $\psi \equiv \varphi$; and if both $\varphi \equiv \psi$ and $\psi \equiv \chi$ (for some χ), then $\varphi \equiv \chi$

    d. $[\varphi \vee \psi] \equiv [\psi \vee \varphi]$; $[\varphi \wedge \psi] \equiv [\psi \wedge \varphi]$; $[\varphi \leftrightarrow \psi] \equiv [\psi \leftrightarrow \varphi]$

                                              (commutativity laws)

    e. $[\varphi \wedge \psi] \equiv \neg[\neg\varphi \vee \neg\psi]$; $[\varphi \vee \psi] \equiv \neg[\neg\varphi \wedge \neg\psi]$

                                              (de Morgan's laws[17])

    f. $\varphi \equiv \neg\neg\varphi$ *(law of double negation)*

    g. $\models [\varphi \vee \neg\varphi]$ *(law of excluded middle)*

    h. $\models \neg[\varphi \wedge \neg\varphi]$ *(law of excluded contradiction)*

    i. $\models [[[\varphi \rightarrow \psi] \rightarrow \varphi] \rightarrow \varphi]$ *(Peirce's formula[18])*

    j. $(\forall x)\varphi \equiv \neg(\exists x)\neg\varphi$; $(\exists x)\varphi \equiv \neg(\forall x)\neg\varphi$ *(duality laws)*

The reader is heartily invited to verify the above observations! Most of them can be shown by way of truth tables as we have used them in Section 4.1 of Chapter 7.

---

16   Our use of the opposition 'local' vs. 'global' here is analogous to, but not identical with, the distinction above, where the loci were variable assignments; now we are speaking of *pairs* of interpretations and assignments.

17   De Morgan's laws (or "rules") are named in honor of one of the founding fathers of modern logic, the English mathematician Augustus de Morgan [1808–1871]; the laws themselves had already been known to medieval logicians though.

18   Peirce's formula (or "law") is so-called because Charles Sanders Peirce (cf. footnote 1 on p. 12) used it in his axiomatization of propositional logic, where it guarantees the bivalence of the system (i.e., that propositions must be either true or false).

One of the most fundamental semantic notions of predicate logic is that of logical entailment; before we can define it, we will give a syntactic characterization of free variables. This is done by the following recursion that associates with each formula $\varphi \in Fml_L$ (for given L) the set $Fr(\varphi)$ of all variables that 'have free occurrences in φ':

(44)   *Free variables:*

    a. $Fr(\bot) = \emptyset$;

    b. $Fr(a = b) = \{a, b\} \cap Var$;

    c. $Fr(R(a_1, \ldots, a_n)) = \{a_1, \ldots, a_n\} \cap Var$;

    d. $Fr([\varphi \rightarrow \psi]) = Fr(\varphi) \cup Fr(\psi)$;

    e. $Fr((\exists x)\varphi) = \{y \in Fr(\varphi) : y \neq x\}$.

The only interesting clause in (44) is the last one; in all other cases the variables occurring in the formula φ are just collected in the set $Fr(\varphi)$. But in the case of a quantified formula, the variable bound by the quantifier—i.e., the one occurring in the prefix —'$(\exists x)$' gets kicked out, which means that the quantifier binds the variables that have free occurrences in the *matrix*, i.e., the part φ that comes after the prefix $(\exists x)$. As a quick exercise, the reader may verify that

(45) $Fr([P(x) \wedge (\exists x)Q(x)]) = \{x\}$

whereas:

(46) $Fr((\exists x)[P(x) \wedge Q(x)]) = \emptyset$

where, of course, P and Q are unary predicates, i.e., members of $PRED_{1,L}$. Formulae φ for which $Fr(\varphi) = \emptyset$ are called *closed*.[19] They have an important property already mentioned above:

(47)   If $\varphi \in Fml_L$ is closed, then for any interpretation M of L and assignments g and h for M's universe the following equation holds:
$$\llbracket \varphi \rrbracket^{M,g} = \llbracket \varphi \rrbracket^{M,h}.$$

Theorem (47) follows from a more general observation known as the *Coincidence Lemma*, which says that the truth value of a formula φ under an assignment g is independent of the value g assigns to variables outside $Fr(\varphi)$; its (surprisingly complex) proof goes beyond this little survey.

---

19   In logic, closed formulae are also called *sentences*.

According to (47), the truth value of a closed formula does not depend on the variable assignment; note that the opposite is not true: '$x = x$' is *open* (= not closed), but its truth value is 1 under any interpretation and assignment. Given an interpretation M and a closed formula φ, we may therefore suppress reference to the assignment and define $[\![\varphi]\!]^M$ as the truth value of φ according to M. If $[\![\varphi]\!]^M = 1$, then M is also called a *model of* φ; and a model of a set of closed formulae is an interpretation that happens to be a model of all members of that set.

The impact of (47) derives from the fact that applications of predicate logic exclusively rely on formalizations of natural language statements by closed formulae, as illustrated in (33) above. Open fomulae only figure as parts of closed formulae. As such they are but necessary syntactic artefacts— and so are variable assignments. Now, according to (47), we may safely ignore these artefacts when it comes to interpreting closed formulae without getting into the details of compositionality.

We are now in a position to define the most central semantic concept of predicate logic:

(48)   *Definition:*
        Let L be a lexicon and $\Sigma \cup \{\varphi\} \subseteq Fml_L$ a (finite or infinite) set of closed formulae. Then Σ *(logically) entails* φ (in symbols: $\Sigma \models \varphi$) iff every model of Σ is a model of φ.

The following observations follow more or less immediately from (48):

(49)   For any lexicon L and any set $\Sigma \cup \Delta \cup \{\varphi\}$ of closed formulae, the following hold:
        a.   If $\varphi \in \Sigma$, then $\Sigma \models \varphi$.
        b.   If $\Sigma \models \varphi$ and $\Sigma \subseteq \Delta$, then $\Delta \models \varphi$.
        c.   If $\Sigma \models \varphi$ and $\varphi \equiv \psi$, then $\Sigma \models \psi$.
        d. $\Sigma \models \varphi$ iff there is no model of $\Sigma \cup \{\neg\varphi\}$.
        e. $\Sigma \models (\varphi \rightarrow \psi)$ iff $\Sigma \cup \{\varphi\} \models \psi$.
        f.   If $\{\varphi, \psi\} \subseteq \Sigma$, then $\Sigma \models [\varphi \wedge \psi]$.

The attentive reader will have noticed that the interpretations in predicate logic play a role similar to the possible worlds in semantics. In particular, global notions like validity and entailment are defined by generalizing over all interpretations, just like intensional concepts are defined by generalizing over all possible worlds. Despite these obvious similarities, the two approaches should be kept apart though. If two interpretations assign different truth values to a closed formula, this means that they disagree about what the formula means; but if a sentence is true of one world and false of another, it expresses one single meaning that accounts for one constellation of facts but not for the other.[20]

6. The Lambda Operator

6.1. Predicate Logic with Lambda Terms

Due to its expressive power, predicate logic has proved to be useful in a variety of fields far beyond the analysis of mathematical reasoning. Indeed, the tradition of **analytic philosophy**, which for a large part of the 20th century dominated the discipline in the English-speaking world, was centered around the practice of scrutinizing philosophical arguments by logical formalization. Here predicate logic played the role of an ideal *lingua franca*, devoid of the imprecision and ambiguity of ordinary language, and thus less likely to delude or confound the philosopher.[21] Nevertheless, a number of systematic observations on the semantics of natural language were made even during these skeptical days. Among these were the fundamental distinction between reference and quantification, the discovery of scope ambiguities, and the vagaries of intensional constructions. The central chapters of Quine's 1960 classic *Word and Object* summarize some of the main findings from this tradition of logical analysis.

However, it was not until the late 1960s that logical techniques were applied to a compositional analysis of natural language, an achievement ascribable mostly to Richard Montague. As it turns out, predicate logic is not well suited for this task, one reason being that its expressive power resides exclusively in the sentence-like category of formulae: only formulae are recursively combinable, all other expressions are lexical. As long as only the meanings of full sentences are at stake, this does not matter; but when it comes to representing their parts, the resources of predicate logic do not suffice. As a case in point, while the adjective *green* and the noun *cactus* can be

---

20   See Zimmermann (2011) and the literature cited there for more on the difference between worlds and models.

21   Rudolf Carnap's highly readable programmatic essay *Die Überwindung der Metaphysik durch logische Analyse der Sprache* is an explicit, if polemic, statement of the ideology underlying (early) analytic philosophy.

represented by the one-place predicates G and C, respectively, predicate logic offers no way of combining these predicates into a predicate corresponding to the complex noun phrase *green cactus*. Predicate logic makes up for this deficit by allowing combinations of formulae $G(x)$ and $C(x)$, which can be used to translate sentences containing that noun phrase; but the latter cannot itself be expressed in terms of the predicates G and C. Similarly, although sentences with the verb phrase *owns a cactus* can be expressed in predicate logic, the verb phrase itself cannot; and the same is true of sentences containing the (restrictive) relative clause *that nobody owns*. Finally, and even more disturbingly, quantifying DPs like *every cactus* and *nobody* do not have any analogues in predicate logic although, again, sentences containing them may be translated, and quite systematically so. So to adapt logical analysis to the compositional needs of natural language, predicate logic does not suffice.

But it can be extended. One of the most powerful technical tools for doing so is the addition of **functional abstraction**, expressed by the so-called **lambda operator**.[22] This little device allows the formation of arbitrarily complex predicates and even quantifiers. In fact, it is extremely helpful in settling almost all compositionality issues arising in the translation of natural language into logical notation. Moreover, it can also be used to shed some light on the very role of variable binding in natural language semantics.

To understand how lambda abstraction (= functional abstraction expressed by a lambda operator) works, let us take a closer look at the case of the green cactus. Given the one-place predicates G and C, it is easy to come up with a predicate logic formula that expresses the condition of being a green cactus, viz.,:

(50) $[G(x) \land C(x)]$

Obviously, the set of green cacti is the set of x-satisfiers of (50), which, as we have just seen, can be defined compositionally in terms of the (global) extensions of the variable 'x' and the formula (50):

---

22   Functional abstraction was already introduced by Frege (1891), who expressed it by accented Greek letters. Its importance for compositional semantic analysis was first realized by Richard Montague, who used lambdas—a notation that goes back to Alonzo Church's [1903–1995] work on the theory of computation (☞ Lambda Calculus); cf. Church (1932).

(51) $\{u : u$ is a green cactus$\}$

= $\{u :$ for some '*y*'-alternative g to g^*, $[\![G(x) \land C(x)]\!]^g_s = 1$ and
      $g(`y`) = u\}$

So what is missing is a way to turn formulae into predicates denoting their satisfaction sets. This lack of expressive power is an essential weakness of predicate logic—which is overcome by the lambda operator, with the help of which (51) can be reformulated as:

(52) $[\lambda x[G(x) \land C(x)]]$

The example suggests a syntactic rule for forming complex predicates by prefixing formulae with 'λx'. However, the rule of **lambda abstraction** is much more general than, and at the same time slightly different from, such a principle of predicate formation. We will get to the generality in a moment; for the time being let us adopt a restricted version of this rule:

(53)   If $x \in Var$ and $\varphi \in Fml$, then '$[\lambda x \varphi]$' is a lambda term of degree 1.

Rule (53) is meant as an extension of the syntactic rules (31) of predicate logic (cf. p. 245), which will be further extended as we go along. However, before doing so, we need to address a small but important semantic difference between predicates and lambda terms, exploiting an idea we already encountered in various circumstances (cf. pp. 126 & 170): given a non-empty 'universe' U (e.g. the set of all individuals), one may represent each subset X of U by its *characteristic function*, whose domain is U and which assigns to each $x \in U$ a truth value—viz., 1 if $x \in X$ and 0 if not. Now, instead of denoting the set of x-satisfiers of the formula φ, a *lambda term* '$[\lambda x \varphi]$' (of degree 1) stands for the characteristic function of that satisfaction set:

(54) $[\![[\lambda x \varphi]]\!]^{M,g}$ is that function f from U into the truth values $\{0,1\}$ such that for any $u \in U$, $f(u) = 1$ iff there is an x-alternative h to g such that $h(x) = u$ and $[\![\varphi]\!]^{M,h} = 1$.

Readers should convince themselves that (54) is equivalent to (55), where the qualification "minimal function" makes it explicit that f is defined only for elements in U and the reference to any x-alternative h expresses that all elements in U are in the domain of f:

(55) $[\![[\lambda x\varphi]]\!]^{M,g}$ is the minimal function f such that for any x-alternative h to g $f(h(x)) = [\![\varphi]\!]^{M,h}$.

So lambda terms (of degree 1) do not stand for sets of individuals but for their characteristic functions. This is the abovementioned difference between ordinary (unary) predicates of predicate logic and lambda terms. Actually, this difference is merely a matter of convention; after all, we could have (unary) predicates stand for characteristic functions too. However, in our treatment of predicate logic, we have preferred to keep close to the tradition of mainstream logic.

Lambda abstraction can also be iterated to form predicates of more than one place. This is done by stacking lambda operators on top of each other. So if $O \in PRED_{2,L}$ stands for the ownership relation, then the following lambda term denotes the (binary) relation of owning a cactus:[23]

(56) $[\lambda y[\lambda x[C(x) \wedge O(x, y)]]]$

Formula (56) is an example of a lambda term of degree 2. In a similar fashion, one may construct lambda terms of higher degrees n corresponding to n-place predicates. The general pattern is this:

(57)   If $x \in Var$ and φ is a lambda term of some degree n, then '$[\lambda x\varphi]$' is a lambda term of degree $n + 1$.

Interestingly, the above interpretation rule (55) carries over to lambda terms of arbitrary degrees. As a case in point, the one in (56) denotes a function that assigns to any individual u (the characteristic function of) the set of cacti owned by u. We leave this to the reader to verify and only add that this denotation can be construed as 'coding' the relation (56) is supposed to stand for, in a way similar to the coding of sets by their characteristic functions.[24] The advantage of this stepwise coding of relations will become apparent once we take the next step in our extension of predicate logic and allow lambda terms to be combined with ordinary terms, i.e., variables and individual constants:

---

23   Alternatively, the lambda term (56) can also be construed as standing for the relation of being owned as a cactus, i.e., the result of swapping the components of the pairs in the original relation. Which lambda terms stand for which relations (sets of n-tuples) is a question of convention and convenience.

24   This coding is known as **Currying**; cf. p. 128 above.

(58)   a.   If *a* is a term (i.e., a member of $Var \cup PRED_{0,L}$) and φ is a lambda
term of degree 1, then: '$\varphi(a)$' $\in Fml$;

  b.   if *a* is a term and φ is a lambda term of some degree $n+1$ (where
$n \geq 1$), then '$\varphi(a)$' is a lambda term of degree n.

The two cases need to be distinguished because there are no lambda terms of
degree 0; rather in case (58-a) the result ought to denote a truth value. In fact,
for both cases the interpretation is straightforward:

(59) $[\ ]\!]^{M,g} = [\![[\lambda x \varphi]]\!]^{M,g} ([\![a]\!]^{M,g})$

The rule (58) and its interpretation (59) are called **functional application**,
because the function denoted by the lambda term gets applied to the argument
denoted by the term. In the case (58-a), functional application corresponds to
combining a one-place predicate *P* with a term *a* to produce the formula
P(a). But (58-b) is more general. For instance, if *L* is a two-place predicate
(corresponding to the transitive verb *love*), and *j* a constant (corresponding to
the name *John*), '$[\lambda x L(j,x)]$' denotes the function that assigns 1 exclusively
to John's loved ones. So if *a* is any individual constant, then by (59),

(60) $[\lambda x \, L(j,x)](a)$

is true if and only if the individual denoted by *a* is in that set—i.e., if John
loves that individual, which again means that the following is true:

(61) $L(j,a)$

In other words, (60) and (61) are equivalent. Note that the latter derives from
the former by plugging in the 'argument' term *a* for the lambda-bound variable *x* and eliminating the prefix 'λx'. The reason for this equivalence is
obvious: the lambda-bound variable stands for an arbitrary argument, and the
term *a* in (60) provides a special case. Hence it should not come as a surprise
that this connection is quite systematic. In fact it is one feature of the lambda
notation that makes it extremely useful for linguistic applications, as we will
see below. So let us record that in general:[25]

(62) $[\lambda x(\ldots x \ldots)](a) \equiv (\ldots a \ldots)$

---

25   This equivalence does not hold, however, if *a* is short for a variable *y* and *x* is in the
scope of a binder of *y*. Although this restriction is technically very important, it can be
ignored for the purposes of this introduction.

In operational syntactic terms this equivalence comes about by omitting the lambda prefix 'λx' and substituting every occurrence of x by a. The equivalence (62) is called **beta-conversion** in logic; among semanticists it also goes by the name of **lambda conversion**. It turns out to be particularly useful in making formulae more readable by eliminating lambdas. This 'left-to-right' application of (62) is called **beta-reduction**.

EXERCISE 38:

Show that omitting the square brackets in lambda terms would result in ambiguous constellations such as (63):

(63) $\lambda x \lambda y \, L(x, y)(a)(b)$

HINT: Perform beta-reductions on the two readings of (63) and compare the results.

6.2.   Beyond Predicate Logic

The usefulness of the lambda operator for semantics shows when it is generalized so as to also bind variables ranging over predicate extensions, i.e., sets of individuals and relations between them. Let us, without getting entangled in too much technicality, sketch the direction this generalization takes by looking at a few examples. In particular, we will shy away from giving a complete formal definition of 'higher-order' variables and only mention that assignment functions need to be generalized so as to assign appropriate values to them.[26]

In Chapter 6, pp. 122ff., we introduced the technique of type shifting as applied to proper names. When type-shifted, a name like *Bill* has a set of sets as its extension, to wit: $\{X : \text{Bill} \in X\}$. Given a suitable generalization of lambda terms, the type-shifted name can be represented as in (64), where the individual term b corresponds to the name *Bill* and the variable P ranges over (one-place) predicate extensions:

(64) $[\lambda P \, P(b)]$

Now the composition of (type-shifted) *Bill* with the one-place predicate S (for *snore*) is straightforward:

---

26   A more serious treatment of generalizing lambda terms replaces degrees by types in the sense discussed in Section 3 of Chapter 6.

(65) $[\lambda P\ P(b)](S) \equiv S(b)$

This equivalence can actually be calculated mechanically relying on (62), and without pondering its set-theoretical meaning.

Lambda operators binding predicate variables also come in handy when it comes to formalizing quantifying expressions, as in (66), where B, F, and H are one-place predicates:

(66)   a. $[\lambda P[(\forall x)B(x) \rightarrow P(x)]]$
       b. $[\lambda P\neg(\exists x)[F(x) \wedge P(x)]]$
       c. $[\lambda P(\exists x)[H(x) \wedge P(x)]]$

Given a suitable understanding of these predicates, the above three lambda terms denote the extensions of the DPs *every boy*, *no fly*, and *some house*. If these are the subjects of a clause, they combine with their predicate—*snore*, say—by functional application:

(67)   a. $[\lambda P(\forall x)[B(x) \rightarrow P(x)]](S)$
       $\equiv$ $(\forall x)[B(x) \rightarrow S(x)]$
       b. $[\lambda P\neg(\exists x)[F(x) \wedge P(x)]](S)$
       $\equiv$ $\neg(\exists x)[F(x) \wedge S(x)]$
       c. $[\lambda P(\exists x)[H(x) \wedge P(x)]](S)$
       $\equiv$ $(\exists x)[H(x) \wedge S(x)]$

In the case of the DPs being in object position, we may apply QR as in (68):

(68)   every boy$_y$/no fly$_y$/some house$_y$ [John watched y]

We then only need a formula corresponding to the QR-constellation in (68), which is readily provided by (69), where Φ corresponds to any of the quantifying DPs in (68):[27]

(69) $\Phi([\lambda y\ W(j, y)])$

For example, taking Φ to be the third lambda term in (66), we get:

(70) $[\lambda P(\exists x)[H(x) \wedge P(x)]]([\lambda y\ W(j, y)])$
       $\equiv$ $(\exists x)[H(x) \wedge [\lambda y\ W(j, y)](x)]$
       $\equiv$ $(\exists x)[H(x) \wedge W(j, x))$

---

27   Note that, strictly speaking, the denotations of the lambda terms (of degree 1) would have to be re-interpreted as sets of individuals; in type logic, this complication is avoided by replacing sets with their characteristic functions across the board.

The scheme easily generalizes to any configuration DP$_y$ S, where the DP is again rendered by a lambda term Φ, the sentence containing y as a formula φ, and the entire configuration as '$\Phi((\lambda y)\varphi)$'. Note that, in this constellation, it is not the quantifying expression Φ itself that binds the variable; the true binder is the lambda prefix! This, then, is the logic of QR.

Finally, let us review the semantics of quantifying determiners. From (66) we already know the result of applying the determiner to a noun; we now only have to determine the form of the determiner before this application. This can be achieved by replacing the noun with a set variable (one that does not already occur in the result), say Q, and then prefixing the expression with λQ. The determiners *every*, *no*, and *some* may thus be rendered by the following lambda terms:

(71) a. $[\lambda Q[\lambda P(\forall x)[Q(x) \rightarrow P(x)]]]$
      b. $[\lambda Q[\lambda P\neg(\exists x)[Q(x) \wedge P(x)]]]$
      c. $[\lambda Q[\lambda P\exists x)[Q(x) \wedge P(x)]]]$

As the reader is invited to verify, combining the above lambda terms with the relevant predicates B, F, and H will result in formulae that are equivalent to those in (66), again due to lambda conversion.

Though lambda terms make up for the lack of compositional flexibility of predicate logic, they do not escape its extensionality. However, there are strategies of extending predicate logic so as to accommodate intensional constructions. Again, we refrain from a thorough discussion here and only mention that there are two standard methods— modal and two-sorted logic. In two-sorted logic, every predicate in the formal language comes with an additional argument presenting the world that determines its extension. Thus, a transitive verb like *love* would have to be formalized by a three-place predicate L; and a sentence like

(72)   Mary loves Bill

comes out as:

(73) $L(w, m, b)$

where w is a variable ranging over possible worlds. In modal logic, however, reference to worlds remains implicit, as in natural language. So (72) comes out as in predicate logic (or type logic, for that matter), namely, as:

(74) $L(m, b)$

with a two-place predicate L, which however denotes an intension rather than an extension, i.e., a function from possible worlds to binary relations; and the formula (74) stands for a set of worlds rather than a truth value.

In the early days of logic-based compositional semantics modal logic clearly prevailed, mostly due to the tremendous influence of the work of Richard Montague, who happened to be one of the pioneers of higher-order modal logic and who subsumed natural language under it.[28] The more recent linguistic literature, however, has shown a preference for two-sorted logic, primarily for reasons of elegance and simplicity. Moreover, the two-sorted universe has been extended so as to include moments of time as a third "sort"; cf. the discussion in Chapter 8, Section 7, where we have shown that natural language has means to explicitly (and implicitly) refer to moments of time.[29]

---

28 The opening sentence of his 1970 *Universal Grammar* reads: "There is in my opinion no important theoretical difference between natural language and the artificial languages of logicians." The rest of the paper makes it clear that he is talking about higher-order modal logic.

29 The classic textbook of applying higher-order modal logic to natural language semantics is Dowty et al. (1981). A quick introduction to the two-sorted approach based on types can be found in the final chapter of Heim and Kratzer (1998).

Solutions to the Exercises

SOLUTION TO EXERCISE 1, page 7:

Here is one of the many definitions for metaphors that can be found on the web: "A figure of speech in which an implicit comparison is made between two unlike things that actually have something in common." This definition makes it particularly clear that there is a sharp difference from irony, which implies incompatibility between the literal and the intended meaning. Idioms sometimes develop historically from metaphors, but their meaning has become less transparent, it must be learned and should be listed in a dictionary.

Idioms in (12): (a), (f); in (13): (c), (d), (f).
Metaphors in (12): (c), (e); in (13): (b).
Irony in (12): (b), (d); in (13): (a), (e).

SOLUTION TO EXERCISE 2, page 21:

öffnen/open (transitive) → *wandeln/verändern/transform,change*: hyponymy

schließen/shut ↔ *zumachen/make closed*; *öffnen/open* (transitive) ↔ *aufmachen/make open*: synonymy

sich öffnen/open (intransitive) ↔ *aufmachen/go open*: synonymy if restricted to things like doors

aufmachen/make open → *aufstoßen/push open* etc.: hyperonymy
shut ↔ *open*: incomatibility

open (intransitive) → *open* (transitive): this relation has not been given a name above. If the arrow had gone in the opposite direction, this would have been a case of causation.

SOLUTION TO EXERCISE 3, page 32:

(1) a. Fred will realize that Mary left when the party started
     b. Fred will realize that Mary left when the party starts

In (1-a) the *when*-clause has past tense whereas the main clause is in the future tense. A sentence like *Fred will do X when the party started* is incongruent, therefore the *when*-clause must be attached to the embedded clause *Mary left*, which is also in the past tense and agrees with the tense of *started*.

In (1-b), however, it would be incongruent to say *Mary left when the party starts*. This remains true even when the sentence is embedded. Therefore the *when*-clause cannot belong to the embedded clause but must modify the main clause.

SOLUTION TO EXERCISE 4, page 32:

(2) a. John realized that | Mary left when the party started |

     b. John | | realized | that Mary left | | when the party started |

(3) a. John said | the man died yesterday |

     b. John | said | the man died | | yesterday

SOLUTION TO EXERCISE 5, page 32:

(4)   a table of wood that was from Galicia
     a. a table (made) of Galician wood
     b. a wooden table from Galicia

(5) a. a table of | wood that was from Galicia |

     b. | a table of wood | that was from Galicia

Remark: most standard semantic theories would have difficulties with (5-b). For reasons we cannot discuss here, semanticists would rather assume the following structure:

(6)   a | | table of wood | that was from Galicia |

We deliberately ignore the difficulty; both answers are correct.

Ad (25-b): the girl with the hat that looked funny

(7) a. the girl with | the hat that looked funny |

     b. | | the girl with the hat | | that looked funny |

Here again, many semanticists would prefer different structures:

(8) a. the | girl with the | hat that looked funny |

     b. the | | girl with the hat | that looked funny |

Again, we cannot discuss the difference, both answers are correct.

Ad (25-c): the girl and the boy in the park

(9)   a.   the girl and | the boy in the park |

     b. || the girl and the boy || in the park ||

Note that in (9-b) the boy and the girl both are in the park, so that a paraphrase would be (10):

(10)   the boy and the girl who *are* in the park

This means that the *who*-clause has to modify a plural entity formed by conjunction. It would therefore not always be possible, as suggested in the alternative analyses in (8), to attach the modifying expression only to a noun which does not display any plural morphology. The plural comes in when conjoining *the boy* and *the girl*, therefore attachment cannot be to a noun in this case, and perhaps more generally so.

SOLUTION TO EXERCISE 6, page 46:

Concerning (69-a), consider the following situation:

(11)   people   books

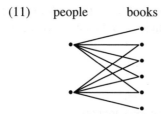

In one reading, saying that

(12)   there are exactly 5 books such that everyone read them

the sentence is false, since only 4 books were read by everyone. The other reading, saying that

(13)   everyone read exactly five books

is true in this situation. Next add one line to the above diagram:

(14)   people   books

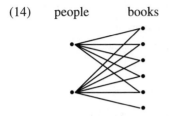

Then (12) is true of the situation depicted in (14) but (13) is false because one person read 6 books.

Now for (69-b). The two readings are:

(15) a. there are exactly 5 books such that no one read them
     b. no one read exactly five books

Suppose there are ten books and two persons, John and Mary. In the first scenario John and Mary both read the same book, but, unlike John, Mary read four books on top of that. Hence Mary read 5 books altogether, and thus (15-b) is false. On the other hand, (15-a) is true, given that five books still remain to be read. For the second scenario, suppose Mary reads one more book, and John does not. Then (15-b) becomes true, but now (15-a) is false, given that the book Mary read must be one of the five remaining ones.

SOLUTION TO EXERCISE 7, page 51:

In the more plausible reading there is a robbery every day and the victim is a student, but not necessarily the same one. This means that *every day* has wide scope with respect to *a student*. In the alternative reading, it's the other way around. There is a certain student who is robbed every day. Only in that reading is it possible to refer to that poor student with the pronoun *he*, as in *he is fed up with it*.

SOLUTION TO EXERCISE 8, page 53:

In one reading of *My brother wants to marry a Norwegian*, my brother might think as follows: "If I should marry, my wife should be a Norwegian." In the second reading I know that my brother wants to marry Linnea, a girl from Norway. In this situation the sentence is true even if my brother does not know that she is Norwegian. The different syntactic analyses result from optional QR. Structure (16) represents the transparent referential reading, and a structure without movement would correspond to the opaque analysis. The ambiguity is caused by the presence of the opaque verb *marry*, without which there is only one (specific) reading.

(16)

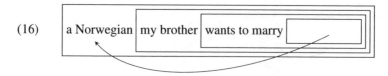

SOLUTION TO EXERCISE 9, page 56:

In one reading, the comparative has narrow scope with respect to the verb *thought*, in the other reading it has wide scope. The structural ambiguity can thus be captured by assuming that the comparative *than*-clause is either attached low or high. Low attachment to the comparative *longer* as in (17-a) represents the implausible reading where the object of thought is a contradiction; in this case the *than*-clause is in the scope of *thought*:

(17) a. I thought your yacht is longer than it is

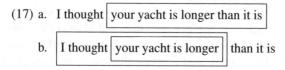

The high attachment reading in (17-b) can be paraphrased as (18) which makes clear that the *than*-clause is not in the scope of *think*:

(18)   I thought that your yacht is longer than its actual length is

SOLUTION TO EXERCISE 10, page 57:

Structurally, the ambiguity can only be accounted for if we assume that there is an unpronounced *than*-clause. The ambiguity would be the same as in the previous exercise, as far as structure is concerned. In one case, the *than*-clause would be in the scope of 20 years ago, and so would be "the professors are younger (than they are)", which is the inconsistent reading. The more plausible reading would have it that the *than*-clause is high in the structure, yielding a reading like:

(19)   the age of the professors twenty years ago is lower than their actual age

This sentence is non-trivial only if we interpret the age of the professors as meaning the average age. Note that (19) is still ambiguous: intuitively we want to refer to the set of persons who were professors twenty years ago. But (19) also allows a reading that talks about the present professors and their (average) age twenty years before now. This is an additional ambiguity involving the DP *the professors* and the PP *twenty years ago*.

SOLUTION TO EXERCISE 11, page 75:

The extension of *Frederick passed Berta the diary* is the empty set, because the sentence is false. To be true it must be the case that $\langle f,b,d \rangle \in \{\langle a,f,d\rangle, \langle f,d,d\rangle, \langle a,b,d\rangle\}$.

SOLUTION TO EXERCISE 12, page 81:

Ordinary extension of *kiss*: $\{\langle j,m\rangle, \langle m,j\rangle, \langle b,f\rangle, \langle p,m\rangle\}$
Ordinary extension of *kiss Mary*: $\{j,p\}$
Thematic extension of *kiss*: $\{\{\langle \text{agent}, j\rangle, \langle\text{theme}, m\rangle\}, \{\langle\text{agent}, m\rangle, \langle\text{theme}, j\rangle\},$
    $\{\langle\text{agent}, b\rangle, \langle\text{theme}, f\rangle\}, \{\langle\text{agent}, p\rangle, \langle\text{theme}, m\rangle\}\}$
Thematic extension of *kiss Mary*: $\{\{\langle\text{agent}, j\rangle\}, \{\langle\text{agent}, p\rangle\}\}$

Instead of "theme", it would be equally correct to use "experiencer" or even "patient".

SOLUTION TO EXERCISE 13, page 98:

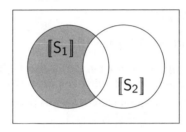

SOLUTION TO EXERCISE 14, page 103:

The only additional rule needed to account for clauses like (20)

(20)   *(dass) Paul Bernadette Geraldine vorstellt*
        (that) Paul Bernadette Geraldine introduces
        '(that) Paul introduces Bernadette to Geraldine'

is one that combines the three-place predicate *vorstellt* with its indirect object *Geraldine*:

(21) $[\![\text{PN} + \text{DTV}]\!]_s = \{\langle x,y\rangle : \langle x,y, [\![\text{PN}]\!]_s \rangle \in [\![\text{DTV}]\!]_s\}$

where PN abbreviates "proper name". The result is a two-place relation that behaves like a transitive verb TV.

SOLUTION TO EXERCISE 15, page 103:

Let PN abbreviate "proper name" again. Here is the proof:

$\llbracket$ the F of PN $\rrbracket_s$

$= \llbracket$ the $\rrbracket_s (\llbracket$ F of PN $\rrbracket_s)$ by (53)

$=$ that z such that: $\langle \llbracket$ F of PN $\rrbracket_s, z \rangle \in \llbracket$ the $\rrbracket_s$ def. functional value ("$f(x)$")

$=$ that z s.th.: $\langle \llbracket$ F of PN $\rrbracket_s, z \rangle \in \{ \langle X, y \rangle : X = \{y\}\}$ by (52)

$=$ that z s.th.: $\llbracket$ F of PN $\rrbracket_s = \{z\}$ def. set abstraction ("$\{x:...\}$")

$=$ that z s.th.: $\{y : \langle \llbracket$ PN $\rrbracket_s, y \rangle \in \llbracket$ F $\rrbracket_s \} = \{z\}$ by (49)

$=$ that z s.th.: $z \in \{y : \langle \llbracket$ PN $\rrbracket_s, y \rangle \in \llbracket$ F $\rrbracket_s \}$ set theory

$=$ that z s.th.: $\langle \llbracket$ PN $\rrbracket_s, z \rangle \in \llbracket$ F $\rrbracket_s$ def. set abstraction ("$\{x:...\}$")

$= \llbracket$ F $\rrbracket_s (\llbracket$ PN $\rrbracket_s)$ def. functional value ("$f(x)$")

SOLUTION TO EXERCISE 16, page 103:

$\llbracket$ the capital of Italy $\rrbracket_s = \llbracket$ the F of N $\rrbracket_s = \llbracket$ F $\rrbracket_s (\llbracket$ N $\rrbracket_s) = \llbracket$ capital $\rrbracket_s (\llbracket$ Italy $\rrbracket_s) =$ Rome

SOLUTION TO EXERCISE 17, page 103:

The extension of *surface* as used in (55) is the singleton containing the surface of the table x mentioned in the first conjunct: $\{\llbracket$ surface $\rrbracket_s (x)\}[= \{y : \langle x, y \rangle \in \llbracket$ surface $\rrbracket_s\}]$. So the general pattern for this reading N_1 of functional nouns N as count nouns is: $\llbracket N_1 \rrbracket_s = \{\llbracket N \rrbracket_s (x)\}$.

The extension of *mother* as used in (56) is the set of all persons that are someone's mother: $\{y$: for some $x, \llbracket$ mother $\rrbracket_s (x) = y\}$ $[= \{y$: for some $x, \langle x, y \rangle \in \llbracket$ mother $\rrbracket_s\}]$. So the general pattern for this reading N_2 of functional nouns N as count nouns is: $\llbracket N_2 \rrbracket_s = \{y$: for some $x, \llbracket N \rrbracket_s (x) = y\}$.

SOLUTION TO EXERCISE 18, page 111:

(22) $\llbracket$ noun phrase + prepositional phrase $\rrbracket_s :=$
        $\llbracket$ noun phrase $\rrbracket_s \cap \llbracket$ prepositional phrase $\rrbracket_s$

Using (22) and (68) on p. 109, it is readily seen that the two bracketings of *smart woman from Berlin* get the same extension in every situation s:

(23) $\llbracket$ smart [woman from Berlin] $\rrbracket_s$

$=$ $\llbracket$ smart $\rrbracket_s \cap \llbracket$ woman from Berlin $\rrbracket_s$

$=$ $\llbracket$ smart $\rrbracket_s \cap (\llbracket$ woman $\rrbracket_s \cap \llbracket$ from Berlin $\rrbracket_s)$

$=$ $(\llbracket$ smart $\rrbracket_s \cap \llbracket$ woman $\rrbracket_s) \cap \llbracket$ from Berlin $\rrbracket_s$

$=$ $(\llbracket$ smart woman $\rrbracket_s) \cap \llbracket$ from Berlin $\rrbracket_s$

$=$ $\llbracket$ [smart woman] from Berlin $\rrbracket_s$

The re-bracketing from line 3 to line 4 in (23) is motivated by a general set-theoretic fact:

(24) $(A \cap B) \cap C = A \cap (B \cap C)$

which is readily verified by the definition of intersection—and reduces to a corresponding fact about conjunction, to be addressed in Exercise 25 in Chapter 7:

(25) $x \in (A \cap B) \cap C$
iff $x \in A \cap B$ and $x \in C$
iff $x \in A$ and $x \in B$ and $x \in C$
iff $x \in A$ and $x \in B \cap C$
iff $x \in A \cap (B \cap C)$

SOLUTION TO EXERCISE 19, page 122:

(26) $[\![\text{something}]\!]_s =$
        $\{X : [\![\text{object}]\!]_s \cap X \neq \emptyset\} =$
        $\{X : X \neq \emptyset \text{ and } X \subseteq [\![\text{object}]\!]_s\}$

SOLUTION TO EXERCISE 20, page 136:

Type shifting of *Mary* yields $\{X : m \in X\}$. We then have to apply rule (49) on p. 134 to:

(27) $[\![\text{Paul loves Mary}]\!]_s = 1$
iff $[\![\text{Paul}]\!]_s \in [\![\text{loves Mary}]\!]_s$
iff $[\![\text{Paul}]\!]_s \in [\![\text{TV} + \text{DP}]\!]_s$
iff $p \in \{x : \{y : \langle x, y \rangle \in [\![\text{TV}]\!]_s\} \in [\![\text{DP}]\!]_s\}$
iff $\{y : \langle p, y \rangle \in \{\langle a, b \rangle, \langle p, p \rangle\}\} \in [\![\text{DP}]\!]_s$
iff $\{p\} \in [\![\text{Mary}]\!]_s$

Now, $m \notin \{p\}$ (because, we take it, $m \neq p$), and so $\{p\}$ is not an element of $\{X : m \in X\}$; consequently $[\![\text{Paul loves Mary}]\!]_s$ is not 1, hence the sentence is false.

SOLUTION TO EXERCISE 21, page 136:

If DTV is a ditransitive predicate, then:
$[\![\text{DTV} + \text{DP}]\!]_s := \{\langle x, z \rangle : \{y : \langle x, z, y \rangle \in [\![\text{DTV}]\!]_s\} \in [\![\text{DP}]\!]_s\}$.

SOLUTION TO EXERCISE 22, page 136:

Here is a pertinent scenario s. Suppose that, in s, Mary $(= m)$ has two dolls, Anna $(= a)$ and Bertie $(= b)$ and that she kisses both Anna and her mother Chloe $(= c)$, but no other kissings are going on. Then $[\![\text{kiss}]\!]_s = \{\langle m, a \rangle, \langle m, c \rangle\}$

and $[\![\text{doll}]\!]_s = \{a,b\}$. Then $\{y : \langle m,y \rangle \in [\![\text{TV}]\!]_s\} = \{a,c\}$. Is this an element of $[\![\text{every doll}]\!]_s$? Since this set contains all supersets of $\{a,b\}$ and b is not in $\{a,c\}$, the answer is 'no'. Thus, *Mary kisses every doll* is false. Now consider the extension of *a doll*. This is all sets with a non-empty intersection with *doll*. Is being kissed by Mary an element of that set? Since $\{a,c\}$ and $\{a,b\}$ have an element in common, the answer is 'yes', and the sentence is true.

SOLUTION TO EXERCISE 23, page 142:

(28) a. $\{8,12,14,15\}$
    b. $\{2,3,5,9\}$
    c. $\{3,4,7,8,11,12,15,16\}$
    d. $\{16\}$

SOLUTION TO EXERCISE 24, page 153:

In a truth value chart for '$((S_1$ *or* $S_2)$ *and* $S_3)$' we have to calculate the values for '$(S_1$ *or* $S_2)$' first. We do that by applying the rules for disjunction from Chapter 5, Section 1:

$[\![S_1]\!]_w$	$[\![S_2]\!]_w$	$[\![S_3]\!]_w$	$[\![S_1]\!]_w \vee [\![S_2]\!]_w$
1	1	1	1
1	1	0	1
1	0	1	1
1	0	0	1
0	1	1	1
0	1	0	1
0	0	1	0
0	0	0	0

Now we can calculate the chart for the entire formula using the conjunction truth table:

$[\![S_1]\!]_w$	$[\![S_2]\!]_w$	$[\![S_3]\!]_w$	$[\![S_1]\!]_w \vee [\![S_2]\!]_w$	$(([\![S_1]\!]_w \vee [\![S_2]\!]_w) \wedge [\![S_3]\!]_w)$
1	1	1	1	1
1	1	0	1	0
1	0	1	1	1
1	0	0	1	0
0	1	1	1	1
0	1	0	1	0
0	0	1	0	0
0	0	0	0	0

We now apply the same method to $(S_1$ *or* $(S_2$ *and* $S_3))$:

$[\![S_1]\!]_w$	$[\![S_2]\!]_w$	$[\![S_3]\!]_w$	$[\![S_2]\!]_w \wedge [\![S_3]\!]_w$	$(([\![S_1]\!]_w \vee [\![(S_2]\!]_w \wedge [\![S_3]\!]_w))$
1	1	1	1	1
1	1	0	0	1
1	0	1	0	1
1	0	0	0	1
0	1	1	1	1
0	1	0	0	0
0	0	1	0	0
0	0	0	0	0

Comparing the two results, we see the charts differ at two positions in the second and fourth rows. This corresponds to the already observed differences in the Venn diagrams.

SOLUTION TO EXERCISE 25, page 153:

No. The situation can be compared to $x + y + z$. There is no ambiguity because there is only one way of making a conjunction true, namely if both conjuncts are true. This generalizes to three conjuncts: all of them must be true for the entire expression to be true. This is confirmed by the truth tables, which coincide in their output shown in the rightmost columns:

$[\![S_1]\!]_w$	$[\![S_2]\!]_w$	$[\![S_3]\!]_w$	$[\![S_1]\!]_w \wedge [\![S_2]\!]_w$	$(([\![S_1]\!]_w \wedge [\![S_2]\!]_w) \wedge [\![S_3]\!]_w)$
1	1	1	1	1
1	1	0	1	0
1	0	1	0	0
1	0	0	0	0
0	1	1	0	0
0	1	0	0	0
0	0	1	0	0
0	0	0	0	0

$[\![S_1]\!]_w$	$[\![S_2]\!]_w$	$[\![S_3]\!]_w$	$[\![S_2]\!]_w \wedge [\![S_3]\!]_w$	$([\![S_1]\!]_w \wedge [\![(S_2]\!]_w \wedge [\![S_3]\!]_w))$
1	1	1	1	1
1	1	0	0	0
1	0	1	0	0
1	0	0	0	0
0	1	1	1	0
0	1	0	0	0
0	0	1	0	0
0	0	0	0	0

SOLUTION TO EXERCISE 26, page 153:

Truth table (with $p_i = [\![S_i]\!]_w$):

p_1	p_2	p_3	p_4	$(p_1 \wedge p_2)$	$(p_3 \wedge p_2)$	$((p_1 \wedge p_2) \vee (p_3 \wedge p_4))$
1	1	1	1	1	1	1
1	1	1	0	1	0	1
1	1	0	1	1	0	1
1	1	0	0	1	0	1
1	0	1	1	0	1	1
1	0	1	0	0	0	0
1	0	0	1	0	0	0
1	0	0	0	0	0	0
0	1	1	1	0	1	1
0	1	1	0	0	0	0
0	1	0	1	0	0	0
0	1	0	0	0	0	0
0	0	1	1	0	1	1
0	0	1	0	0	0	0
0	0	0	1	0	0	0
0	0	0	0	0	0	0

Venn diagram:

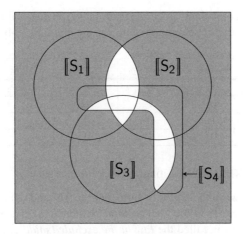

SOLUTION TO EXERCISE 27, page 155:

$(\neg \llbracket S_1 \rrbracket_w \wedge \llbracket S_2 \rrbracket_w)$:

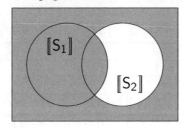

$\neg(\llbracket S_1 \rrbracket_w \wedge \llbracket S_2 \rrbracket_w)$:

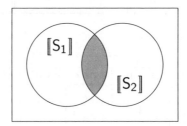

SOLUTION TO EXERCISE 28, page 164:

There is a causal relation involved: the reason for my leaving would be that I hadn't gotten a beer. Moreover, it is understood that I won't leave if I do indeed get my beer. But this is not guaranteed by the truth conditions of *or*. If I get my beer, one part of the disjunction will be true and so the other will be irrelevant for the truth of the whole. Analogous reasoning applies to (77-b).

SOLUTION TO EXERCISE 29, page 167:

Yes, they are equivalent, since the truth table for material implication (= (52) on p. 157) has the same output column as the one for (28-b):

$[S_1]_w$	$[S_2]_w$	$\neg[S_2]_w$	$\neg[S_1]_w$	$(\neg[S_2]_w \rightarrow \neg[S_1]_w)$
1	1	0	0	1
1	0	1	0	0
0	1	0	1	1
0	0	1	1	1

SOLUTION TO EXERCISE 30, page 167:

Again, by drawing the tables, it turns out that (b) and (d) are tautologies, that is they only have 1s in the final column. Sentence (a) is a contradiction (it has only 0s), and (b) is called the *law of the excluded middle*. Sentence (c) can be false, e.g., if S_1 is false and S_3 is true. Example (d) cannot be false, since 'S_1 *and X*' implies S_1, whatever X is:

$[S]_w$	$\neg[S]_w$	$([S]_w$ and $\neg[S]_w)$
1	0	0
0	1	0

$[S]_w$	$\neg[S]_w$	$([S]_w$ or $\neg[S]_w)$
1	0	1
0	1	1

And with $p_i = [S_i]_w$:

p_1	p_2	p_3	$(p_1 \wedge p_1)$	$((p_1 \wedge p_2) \vee p_3)$	$(((p_1 \wedge p_2) \vee p_3) \rightarrow p_1)$
1	1	1	1	1	1
1	1	0	1	1	1
1	0	1	0	1	1
1	0	0	0	0	1
0	1	1	0	1	**0**
0	1	0	0	0	1
0	0	1	0	1	**0**
0	0	0	0	0	1

p_1	p_2	p_3	$(p_2 \lor p_3)$	$(p_1 \land (p_2 \lor p_3))$	$((p_1 \land (p_2 \lor p_3)) \to p_1)$
1	1	1	1	1	1
1	1	0	1	1	1
1	0	1	1	1	1
1	0	0	0	0	1
0	1	1	1	0	1
0	1	0	1	0	1
0	0	1	1	0	1
0	0	0	0	0	1

SOLUTION TO EXERCISE 31, page 176:

(29) $[\![\text{try} + \text{to} + \text{VP}]\!]_w := \{x : \langle x, [\![\text{VP}]\!]\rangle \in [\![\text{try}]\!]_w\}$

The important observations to be captured are: 1) that it is the intension of the verb that contributes to the truth value, and 2) that the intensionality generalizes to all sorts of VPs. This implies, for instance, that

(30) a. John tries to employ a dancer
     b. John tries to employ a singer

can have different truth values even if coincidentally all singers are dancers. The rule even generalizes to all verbs that take an infinitival complement, like *want-to*, which was already discussed in Exercise 8.

SOLUTION TO EXERCISE 32, page 180:

By definition of a contradiction, $[\![S_1]\!] \cap [\![S_2]\!] = \emptyset$. It thus follows from set theory that an element of $[\![S_1]\!]$ cannot be an element of $[\![S_2]\!]$, and thus must be an element of the complement of $[\![S_2]\!]$ and vice versa, hence $[\![S_1]\!] \subseteq W \backslash [\![S_2]\!]$ and $[\![S_2]\!] \subseteq W \backslash [\![S_1]\!]$. By definition of negation, $W \backslash [\![S_1]\!] = [\![\text{not } S_1]\!]$ and $W \backslash [\![S_2]\!] = [\![\text{not } S_2]\!]$. Hence $[\![S_1]\!] \subseteq [\![\text{not } S_2]\!]$ and $[\![S_2]\!] \subseteq [\![\text{not } S_1]\!]$. By definition of entailment, S_1 entails '*not S_2*' and S_2 entails '*not S_1*'.

SOLUTION TO EXERCISE 33, page 193:

Suppose (42) holds and $\text{Epi}_{x,w} \subseteq p$. It must be shown that $\text{Dox}_{x,w} \subseteq p$. Now let w' be a member of $\text{Dox}_{x,w}$. Then, by (42), $w' \in \text{Epi}_{x,w}$, and thus $w' \in p$, by our assumption. Since this holds for arbitrary w', we may conclude that $\text{Dox}_{x,w} \subseteq p$.

SOLUTION TO EXERCISE 34, page 193:

Assume (47) and suppose the premise of (43) is true of some world w. By Hintikka semantics, this means that $\text{Epi}_{Mary,w} \subseteq [\![\text{Bill snores}]\!]$. Since, by (47),

$w \in \text{Epi}_{Mary,w}$, we may thus conclude $w \in [\![\text{Bill snores}]\!]$, which means that the conclusion of (43) is true of w.

SOLUTION TO EXERCISE 35, page 214:

Any sentence of the form:

(31)   I don't know p

is pragmatically ill formed because "x knows that p" as well as "x does not know that p" presuppose the truth of p. Therefore if a speaker utters (31) she also commits herself to the truth of p. Hence she should know that p holds, but this is denied by (31) and the use of "I", which refers to the speaker. The same argument does not apply to the remaining sentences. In particular, I may say and know that p without regretting p.

SOLUTION TO EXERCISE 36, page 215:

Proof of Theorem 1
By definition, S_1 must entail S_2, hence $[\![S_1]\!] \subseteq [\![S_2]\!]$ and 'not S_1' entails S_2, hence $[\![\text{not } S_1]\!] \subseteq [\![S_2]\!]$. Suppose the subset relation were not proper. If $[\![S_1]\!] = [\![S_2]\!]$, then $[\![\text{not } S_1]\!]$ must be the empty set. But then S_1 and S_2 must be tautologies, thus contradicting the definition of presuppositions. If $[\![S_1]\!] = [\![S_1]\!]$, then $[\![S_1]\!]$ must be the empty set. But then 'not S_1' and S_2 must be tautologies, contradicting again the definition of presuppositions.

Proof of Theorem 2
If S_1 were true of w, by $[\![S_1]\!] \subset [\![S_2]\!]$ it follows that S_2 must also be true of w, contrary to our assumption. And the same holds if S_1 s false, which means that 'not S_1' is true, hence $[\![\text{not } S_1]\!] \subset [\![S_2]\!]$ and S_2 must be true again.

Proof of Theorem 3
If S_1 lacks a truth value, there must be at least one presupposition S_3 of S_1 that is not true. But this must also be a presupposition of S_2, hence S_2 cannot have a truth value either.

SOLUTION TO EXERCISE 37, page 231:

The sentence *John too is smoking again* may be paraphrased as:

(32)   John and some x other than John have previously been smoking and x is smoking now

There are two presupposition triggers, *too* and *again*:

(33) a. NP too VP: someone other than NP does VP
    b. S again: it has previously been the case that S

By applying (33-b) we get:

(34)   It has previously been the case that John too has been smoking

By applying (33-a) to (34) we derive:

(35)   It has previously been the case that someone other than John has been smoking

This is so to speak the presupposition of the presupposition, a second-order presupposition. The first-order presupposition now reads:

(36)   It has previously been the case that John has been smoking and (35)

This is as far as we can get by the simple rules we formulated above. But observe that we have lost an additional presupposition, which would arise if we first evaluated *too*, namely that someone other than John is smoking (now). Now, trying to apply the rules in the opposite order, we get:

(37)   Someone other than John is smoking again (presupposition, first-order)

(38)   It has previously been the case that some x other than John is smoking, and x is smoking now

But now we have lost the implication that John himself has been smoking previously. This constitutes a challenge for compositionality. It shows that the presuppositions have to be calculated simultaneously in such a way that the triggers do not have scope with respect to each other. This requires advanced techniques we cannot discuss here.

Turning next to (63-b) (= *If I were rich, I would retire*) the presupposition of the subjunctive conditional is that I am not rich. In general:

(39)   '*If* S$_{subjunctive}$, *then X*' presupposes '*not* S'.

Note that the subjunctive as such does not always have this presupposition, cf. (40):

(40)   The new doctor advised that she get therapy, but she had already been getting treatment for years

Hence the rule must mention the conditional.

SOLUTION TO EXERCISE 38, page 258:

$\lambda x \lambda y\ L(x, y)(a)(b)$ corresponds to two properly bracketed lambda terms:

(41) $[\lambda x\ [\lambda y\ L(x, y)](a)](b)$

(42) $[\lambda x\ [\lambda y\ L(x, y)]](a)(b)$

(41) results from first forming $[\lambda y\ L(x, y)]$, then applying this to a, and prefixing the result with λx. To get (42), one needs to form the degree 2 lambda term $[\lambda x[\lambda y\ L(x, y)]]$ and successively apply it to a and b.

Applying beta reduction to (41) yields $[\lambda y\ L(b, y)](a)$, from which one can derive $L(b, a)$, by another beta reduction. In (42), beta reduction can only be applied to the left part, i.e., $[\lambda x\ [\lambda y\ L(x, y)]](a)$, reducing it to $[\lambda y\ L(a, y)]$. Inserting this result into the formula (42) yields: $[\lambda y\ L(a, y)](b)$, to which another beta reduction can be applied, with the outcome $L(a, b)$. But clearly $L(a, b) \neq L(b, a)$, and thus $\lambda x \lambda y\ L(x, y)(a)(b)$ turns out to be ambiguous indeed.

References

Baker, Mark (1988): *Incorporation. A Theory of Grammatical Function Changing*. The University of Chicago Press, Chicago.

Barwise, Jon and Robin Cooper (1981): 'Generalized Quantifiers and Natural Language', *Linguistics & Philosophy* **4**, 159–219.

Beaver, David (2001): *Presupposition and Assertion in Dynamic Semantics*. CSLI, Stanford, California.

Carnap, Rudolf (1931): 'Überwindung der Metaphysik durch logische Analyse der Sprache', *Erkenntnis* **2**, 149–241. Translated into English by Arthur Pap as Carnap (1959).

Carnap, Rudolf (1947): *Meaning and Necessity*. The University of Chicago Press, Chicago.

Carnap, Rudolf (1952): 'Meaning Postulates', *Philosophical Studies* **3**, 65–73.

Carnap, Rudolf (1959): The Elimination of Metaphysics through the Logical Analysis of Language. *In:* A. J. Ayer, ed., *Logical Positivism*. Free Press, New York, p. 60–81.

Cechetto, Carlo (2004): 'Explaining the Locality Conditions of QR: Consequences for the Theory of Phases', *Natural Language Semantics* **12**, 345–397.

Church, Alonzo (1932): 'A Set of Postulates for the Foundation of Logic', *Annals of Mathematics (Series 2)* **33**, 346–366.

Cresswell, Maxwell J. (1982): The Autonomy of Semantics. *In:* S. Peters and E. Saarinen, eds, *Processes, Beliefs, and Questions*. D. Reidel, Dordrecht, pp. 69–86.

Dalen, Dirk van (2004): *Logic and Structure*. Springer, Berlin.

Döhmer, Klaus (1978): *Leda & Variationen*. éditions trèves, Trier.

Donnellan, Keith (1966): 'Reference and Definite Descriptions', *The Philosophical Review* **75**, 281–304.

Dowty, David, Robert Wall and Stanley Peters (1981): *Introduction to Montague Semantics*. Reidel, Dordrecht.

Ebbinghaus, Heinz-Dieter, Jörg Flum and Wolfgang Thomas (1994): *Mathematical Logic*. Springer, Heidelberg & New York.

Fine, Kit (2003): 'The Role of Variables', *The Journal of Philosophy* **100**, 605–631.

Fintel, Kai von (2000): What Is Presupposition Accommodation?. Unpublished, cf. http://web.mit.edu/fintel/www/accomm.pdf.

Fintel, Kai von (2004): Would You Believe It? The King of France Is Back! (Presuppositions and Truth-Value Intuitions). *In:* M. Reimer and A. Bezuidenhout, eds, *Descriptions and Beyond*. Oxford University Press, Oxford, p. 315–341.

Forbes, Graeme (1994): *Modern Logic*. Oxford University Press, Oxford.

Frazier, Lyn and Charles Clifton (1996): *Construal*. The MIT Press, Cambridge, Mass.

Frege, Gottlob (1879): *Begriffsschrift. Eine der arithmetischen nachgebildete Formelsprache des reinen Denkens*. Louis Nebert, Halle. Translation into English in Frege (1972).

Frege, Gottlob (1891): *Function und Begriff*. H. Pohle, Jena. Reprinted in Frege (1962); translated into English as "Function and Concept" in P. Geach and M. Black (1960).

Frege, Gottlob (1892): 'Über Sinn und Bedeutung', *Zeitschrift für Philosophie und philosophische Kritik* **N.F. 100**, 25–50. Reprinted in Frege (1962); translated into English as "On Sense and Reference" in P. Geach and M. Black (1960).

Frege, Gottlob (1893): *Grundgesetze der Arithmetik. Begriffsschriftlich abgeleitet*. H. Pohle, Jena. Translated into English as Frege (1964).

Frege, Gottlob (1904): Was ist eine Funktion?. *In:* S. Meyer, ed., *Festschrift Ludwig Boltzmann gewidmet zum sechzigsten Geburtstage, 20. Februar 1904*. Barth, Leipzig, pp. 656–666. Reprinted in Frege (1962); translated into English as "What is a Function?" in P. Geach and M. Black (1960).

Frege, Gottlob (1962): *Funktion, Begriff, Bedeutung*. Herausgegeben von Günther Patzig. Vandenhoeck & Ruprecht, Göttingen.

Frege, Gottlob (1964): *The Basic Laws of Arithmetic*. Translated by Montgomery Furth. University of California Press, Berkeley.

Frege, Gottlob (1972): *Conceptual Notation and Related Articles*. Clarendon Press, Oxford.

Geach, Peter and Max Black (1960): *Translations from the Philosophical Writings of Gottlob Frege*. Blackwell, Oxford.

Gernhardt, Robert, F. W. Bernstein and F. K. Waechter (1979): *Welt im Spiegel. WimS 1964–1976*. Zweitausendeins, Frankfurt.

Gernhardt, Robert and Klaus Cäsar Zehrer (2007): *Bilden Sie mal einen Satz mit ... 555 Ergebnisse eines Dichterwettstreits*. S. Fischer Verlag, Frankfurt.

Gettier, Edmund (1963): 'Is Justified True Belief Knowledge?', *Analysis* **23**, 121–123.

Geurts, Bart (1997): 'Good News about the Description Theory of Names', *Journal of Semantics* **14**, 319–346.

Gibson, Edward (2000): The Dependency Locality Theory: A Distance-Based Theory of Linguistic Complexity. *In:* A. Marantz, Y. Miyashita and W. O'Neil, eds, *Image, Language, Brain. Papers from the First Mind Articulation Project Symposium*. The MIT Press, Cambridge, Mass., pp. 95–126.

Grice, H. Paul (1967): *Logic and Conversation. The William James Lectures*. Unpublished, Harvard. Published in Grice (1989).

Grice, H. Paul (1975): Logic and Conversation. *In:* P. Cole and J. L. Morgan, eds, *Syntax and Semantics 3: Speech Acts*. Academic Press, New York, pp. 41–58.

Grice, H. Paul (1981): Presupposition and Conventional Implicature. *In:* J. L. Morgan and P. Cole, eds, *Radical Pragmatics*. Academic Press, New York/San Francisco/London, pp. 183–198.

Grice, H. Paul (1989): *Studies in the Way of Words*. Harvard University Press, Cambridge, Mass.

Grimshaw, Jane (1990): *Argument Structure*. The MIT Press, Cambridge, Mass.

Heim, Irene (1983): On the Projection Problem for Presuppositions. *In:* M. Barlow, D. Flickinger and M. Wescoat, eds, *Proceedings of the 2nd West Coast Conference on Formal Linguistics*. Stanford, pp. 114–125.

Heim, Irene (1991): Artikel und Definitheit. *In:* A. v. Stechow and D. Wunderlich, eds, *Semantik: Ein internationales Handbuch der zeitgenössischen Forschung*. de Gruyter, Berlin, pp. 487–535.

Heim, Irene (2011): Definiteness and Indefiniteness. *In:* C. Maienborn, K. v. Heusinger and P. Portner, eds, *Semantics. An International Handbook of Natural Language Meaning, Vol. 2*. de Gruyter, Berlin, pp. 996–1025.

Heim, Irene and Angelika Kratzer (1998): *Semantics in Generative Grammar*. Blackwell, Oxford.

Hintikka, Jaakko (1962): *Knowledge and Belief*. Cornell University Press, Ithaca.

Hintikka, Jaakko (1969): Semantics for Propositional Attitudes. *In:* J. W. Davis, D. Hockney and W. Wilson, eds, *Philosophical Logic*. Reidel, Dordrecht, pp. 21–45.

Hodges, Wilfrid (1977): *Logic. An Introduction to Elementary Logic.* Penguin, London.

Hodges, Wilfrid (2001): 'Formal Features of Compositionality', *Journal of Logic, Language and Information* **10**, 7–28.

Jacobson, Pauline (1999): 'Towards a Variable Free Semantics', *Linguistics and Philosophy* **22**, 117–185.

Kamp, Hans (1980): Kommentar zu Seurens 'Dreiwertige Logik und die Semantik natürlicher Sprache'. *In:* J. Ballweg and H. Glinz, eds, *Grammatik und Logik*. Pädagogischer Verlag Schwann, Düsseldorf, pp. 104–113.

Kaplan, David (1975): 'How to Russell a Frege-Church', *The Journal of Philosophy* **71**, 716–729.

Karttunen, Lauri (1974): 'Presupposition and Linguistic Context', *Theoretical Linguistics* **1**, 181–193.

Karttunen, Lauri and Stanley Peters (1979): Conventional Implicature. *In:* C. Oh and D. Dinneen, eds, *Presuppositions*. Vol. 11 of *Syntax and Semantics*, Academic Press, New York, pp. 1–56.

Keenan, Edward and Dag Westerståhl (1997): Generalized Quantifiers in Linguistics and Logic. *In:* J. v. Bentham and A. ter Meulen, eds, *Handbook of Logic and Language*. Elsevier, Amsterdam, pp. 837–893.

Kluender, Robert (1998): On the Distinction between Strong and Weak Islands: A Processing Perspective. *In:* P. Culicover and L. McNally, eds, *Syntax and Semantics*. Academic Press, New York, NY, pp. 241–279.

Kratzer, Angelika (1977): 'What 'Must' and 'Can' Must and Can Mean', *Linguistics and Philosophy* **1**, 337–355.

Kratzer, Angelika (1981): The Notional Category of Modality. *In:* H. J. Eikmeyer and H. Rieser, eds, *Words, Worlds, and Contexts: New Approaches in Word Semantics*. de Gruyter, Berlin, pp. 39–76.

Kripke, Saul (1972): Naming and Necessity. *In:* D. Davidson and G. Harman, eds, *Semantics of Natural Language*. Reidel, Dordrecht, pp. 253–355 & 763–769.

Kripke, Saul (1977): 'Speaker's Reference and Semantic Reference', *Midwest Studies in Philosophy* **2**, 255–276.

Lang, Ewald and Claudia Maienborn (2011): Two-Level Semantics: Semantic Form and Conceptual Structure. *In:* K. v. Heusinger, C. Maienborn and P. Portner, eds, *Semantics. An International Handbook of Natural Language Meaning. Vol. 1.* de Gruyter, Berlin, pp. 709–739.

Larson, Richard (1988): 'On the Double Object Construction', *Linguistic Inquiry* **19**, 335–391.

Levinson, Stephen C. (1983): *Pragmatics*. Cambridge University Press, Cambridge.

Lewis, David (1972): 'General Semantics', *Synthese* **22**, 18–67.

Lewis, David (1973*a*): 'Causation', *The Journal of Philosophy* **70**, 556–567.

Lewis, David (1973*b*): *Counterfactuals*. Harvard University Press, Cambridge, Mass.

Lewis, David (1979): 'Attitudes *De Dicto* and *De Se*', *The Philosophical Review* **88**, 13–43.

Lewis, David (1986): *On the Plurality of Worlds*. Blackwell, Oxford.

May, Robert (1985): *Logical Form: Its Structure and Derivation*. The MIT Press, Cambridge, Mass.

Montague, Richard (1970): 'Universal Grammar', *Theoria* **36**, 373–398.

Montague, Richard (1973): The Proper Treatment of Quantification in Ordinary English. *In:* J. Hintikka and P. Suppes, eds, *Approaches to Natural Language*. Reidel, Dordrecht, pp. 221–242.

Musan, Renate (1997): *On the Temporal Interpretation of Noun Phrases*. Garland, New York.

Neale, Stephen (1990): *Descriptions*. The MIT Press, Cambridge, Mass.

Oberschelp, Arnold (1992): *Logik für Philosophen*. Bibliographisches Institut, Mannheim.

Parsons, Charles (1971): 'A Plea for Substitutional Quantification', *The Journal of Philosophy* **68**, 231–237.

Partee, Barbara (1973): 'Some Structural Analogies between Tenses and Pronouns in English', *The Journal of Philosophy* **70**, 601–609.

Pearl, Judea (2009): *Causality: Models, Reasoning and Inference*. Cambridge University Press, Cambridge.

Peirce, Charles S. (1885): 'On the Algebra of Logic: A Contribution to the Philosophy of Notation', *American Journal of Mathematics* **7**, 180–202. Reprinted in: Writings of Charles S. Peirce, 1884–1886: The Chronological Edition, The Peirce Edition Project, Bloomington: Indiana University Press, pp. 162-190.

Pullum, Geoffrey (1984): 'Topic ... Comment: Punctuation and Human Freedom', *Natural Language and Linguistic Theory* **2**, 419–425.

Putnam, Hilary (1975): The Meaning of 'Meaning'. *In:* H. Putnam, ed., *Mind, Language, and Reality. Philosophical Papers Vol. 2*. Cambridge University Press, Cambridge, Mass., pp. 215–271.

Quine, Willard Van Orman (1951): 'Two Dogmas of Empiricism', *The Philosophical Review* **60**, 20–43.

Quine, Willard Van Orman (1956): 'Quantifiers and Propositional Attitudes', *The Journal of Philosophy* **53**, 177–187.

Rathert, Monika (2004): *Textures of Time*. Akademie Verlag, Berlin.

Reichenbach, Hans (1947): *Elements of Symbolic Logic*. University of California Press, Berkeley.

Reimer, Marga (1998): 'Quantification and Context', *Linguistics & Philosophy* **21**, 95–115.

Reinhart, Tanya (1997): 'Quantifier Scope: How Labor Is Divided between QR and Choice Functions', *Linguistics & Philosophy* **20**, 335–397.

Reinhart, Tanya (2003): 'The Theta System', *Theoretical Linguistics* **28**, 229–291.

Russell, Bertrand (1905): 'On Denoting', *Mind* **14**, 479–493.

Sadock, Jerrold M. and Arnold M. Zwicky (1975): Ambiguity Tests and How to Fail Them. *In:* J. Kimball, ed., *Syntax and Semantics Vol. 4*. Academic Press, New York, pp. 1–36.

Sandt, Rob van der (1992): 'Presupposition Projection as Anaphora Resolution', *Journal of Semantics* **9**, 333–377.

Scheepers, Christoph et al. (2009): 'Structural Priming across Cognitive Domains: From Simple Algebra to Relative Clause Attachment', *Psychological Science* **22**, 1319–1326.

Schwarzschild, Roger (1996): *Pluralities*. Kluwer, Dordrecht.

Sharvy, Richard (1980): 'A More General Theory of General Descriptions', *The Philosophical Review* **89**, 607–624.

Stalnaker, Robert (1973): 'Presuppositions', *Journal of Philosophical Logic* **2**, 447–457.

Stalnaker, Robert (1974): Pragmatic Presuppositions. *In:* M. K. Munitz and P. Unger, eds, *Semantics and Philosophy*. New York University Press, New York, pp. 197–213.

Stalnaker, Robert (1978): Assertion. *In:* P. Cole, ed., *Syntax and Semantics 9: Pragmatics*. Academic Press, New York, pp. 315–332.

Stalnaker, Robert (1981): A Defense of Conditional Excluded Middle. *In:* W. L. Harper, R. C. Stalnaker and G. Pearce, eds, *Ifs*. D. Reidel, Dordrecht, pp. 87–104.

Stepanians, Markus (2001): *Gottlob Frege zur Einführung*. Junius, Hamburg.

Warmbrōd, Ken (1982): 'A Defense of the Limit Assumption', *Philosophical Studies* **42**, 53–66.

Wason, Peter C. and Shuli S. Reich (1979): 'A Verbal Illusion', *Quarterly Journal of Experimental Psychology* **31**, 591–597.

Winter, Yoad (1996): 'A Unfied Semantic Treatment of Singular NP Coordination', *Linguistics and Philosophy* **19**, 337–391.

Wittgenstein, Ludwig (1921): 'Logisch-philosophische Abhandlung', W. Ostwald's *Annalen der Naturphilosophie* **14**, 185–262. Revised version reprinted as Wittgenstein (1960); English version in Wittgenstein (1922).

Wittgenstein, Ludwig (1922): *Tractatus logico-philosophicus*. Routledge and Kegan Paul, London.

Wittgenstein, Ludwig (1960): Tractatus Logico-Philosophicus. In: *Schriften, Band 1*. Surkamp Verlag, Frankfurt, pp. 7–83.

Wunderlich, Dieter (2006): Argument Hierarchy and Other Factors of Argument Realization. *In:* I. Bornkessel, M. Schlesewsky, B. Comrie and A. Friederici, eds, *Semantic Role Universals: Perspectives from Linguistic Theory, Language Typology and Psycho-/Neurolinguistics*. Mouton de Gruyter, Berlin, pp. 15–52.

Zimmermann, Thomas Ede (2011): Model-Theoretic Semantics. *In:* K. v. Heusinger, C. Maienborn and P. Portner, eds, *Semantics. An International Handbook of Natural Language Meaning, Vol. 1*. de Gruyter, Berlin, pp. 762–802.

Index